Adolf Hitler

Adolf Hitler:
A Psychological Interpretation
of His Views on Architecture
Art and Music

Sherree Owens Zalampas

Bowling Green State University Popular Press
Bowling Green, Ohio 43403

Acknowledgements

The author gratefully acknowledges the inspiration of Jay Kloner, art historian with the University of Louisville, the support of Ron Horvath, President of Jefferson Community College, and the love of Michael Zalampas.

I wish to dedicate this study to the memory of my father, Edgar Otha Owens, a victim of Adolf Hitler's war, and to my loving mother.

Contents

Chapter 1
Statement of the Problem

It is customary and even obligatory for any new study of Adolf Hitler to provide a rationale for its appearance. Hitler was a mass murderer *sui generis*. Other political and military leaders, whether ancient or modern, killed due to the perceived demands of their objectives. Hitler, on the contrary, systematically killed millions although their deaths were inimical to his ultimate success. Hitler murdered even when the acts ran counter to Germany's national interest or to his own political and military agenda. The murders became an end in themselves and were not a means either to victory or escape from defeat.

At first glance there appears to be a surfeit of works on his life, the Third Reich, the disaster he created for Europeans in general, and the Jews in particular. In 1976, Stierlin estimated there were "more than 50,000 serious works" on the subject. In 1979, Carr noted "hardly a month goes by without some work" on Hitler and the Third Reich seeing publication. Harris noted in 1980, that there were over seventy serious biographies of Hitler already in existence—twice as many as there were of Churchill and three times as many as there were of Stalin and Roosevelt.[1] Indeed, more pages have been written on Hitler than the total pages of the original source documentation available to the student. Ayçoberry summed up the situation in 1981 by his insistence that "a single reader would be unable to glance through them all even if he were to devote his life to the task" and that such publications had reached the point where "one sees a growing number of histories of the history" of Hitler and the Third Reich.[2]

Yet, in spite of this plethora of works, there remain proper and even pressing reasons for further research into the life and mind of Adolf Hitler. Some works belong to what George Will had called the "I was Hitler's toothbrush" genre—their authors "saw much but understood nothing."[3] Others are suspect either because they are uncritical[4] or because they were clearly written to advance the writers' anti-Hitler[5] or pro-Hitler bias.[6] A number fail to advance our understanding because they dismiss Hitler as a "fanatic," a description that fails to advance our understanding although it may meet our emotional needs. Simply because these works fail to advance our understanding, there remains the need for new works based on interpretation of new materials.

1

There is ultimately the need for each new generation of scholars to reassess and grapple with the unique phenomenon of Adolf Hitler. As Friedlander insisted, Hitler "remains the key reference point of contemporary history."[7] Hitler not only dominated the first half of this century but has determined the historical course of the second half of the century by awakening Russia, creating the partition of Europe and the morass in the Middle East, and by accelerating the de-colonization of the Third World. George Will insisted Hitler will always compel attention because he was "not just a demon or madman; he is a dark mirror held up to mankind." Hitler challenged, as has no one else, our philosophical, political, and moral heritage, and called into question our most fundamental concepts of the nature of man.

Any understanding of the nature of the Third Reich certainly must place Hitler at the center of its existence. It is impossible to envision the Third Reich without Hitler, although Mosse made a valiant but futile effort to construct such a model.[9] It is also impossible to accept the standard Marxist interpretation of Hitler as merely the frontman for German monopoly capitalism.[10] All too clearly, Hitler stamped his own personality on the Third Reich and ultimately, when he killed himself, it immediately died. The understanding of his Reich and the understanding of his personality are indissoluble.

One area that cannot be neglected if Hitler is to be understood, for it goes to the heart of the matter, is the systematic study of Hitler's art and his aesthetic theories about the arts in general. Most biographers refer to these matters in passing, or on the basis of limited evidence. As Price noted, Hitler's "career as an artist has been considered insignificant" even though his "art undoubtedly reflected his philosophy and his life, in turn, derived considerable substance from his art."[11] Some works do direct their attention to Third Reich art, film, music, and architecture but neglect Hitler's centrality or fail to place his aesthetic theories in the context of his entire life. Above everything else, Hitler defined himself as an artist.[12] Even if his own watercolors, paintings, and architectural sketches were undistinguished, they still serve to illuminate one, if indeed not the major, formative influence on his life. An appreciation of this opens the possibility for an observation into the convolutions of his mind and, by extension, the nature of the Third Reich.

It is obvious Hitler was "a man of infinite evil, a moral monster."[13] However, to condemn him is not to explain him. The task of such explanation has produced much debate but little illumination, as it has consistently utilized a Freudian, psychoanalytic approach. While this approach has provided some insights, ultimately there are several objections to it. One lies at the very heart of the matter—the requisite psycho-sexual information is simply not available and must be invented, assumed, or accepted on the basis of analogy or third-hand gossip.[14] A second objection arises from the first—there is no agreement among the analysts and, at times, the same analyst has radically re-evaluated his assumptions and arrived at a substantually different interpretation.[15] Finally, these psycho-sexual approaches have neglected a prime source of material, namely the aesthetic theories, attitudes and artistic creations of Adolf Hitler taken as a whole in the context of his psychological life.

It may be argued that only a trained analyst is qualified to attempt a psychological interpretation of Hitler as artist and aesthetician. As Carr stressed, this would be "an insuperable obstacle" if these interpretations were based "on first-hand knowledge of the patient."[16] However, as such direct knowledge is not available, the analyst cannot plead a special case. Waite is only one of a number of historians who have refused to be deterred by the task.[17] Literary critics and art historians have long asserted the right to propose psychological explanations of persons and their creations. Are these researchers to be denied the right to apply the models developed by students of the human mind and so, by default, concede to analysts the status of an esoteric, gnostic priesthood?

The present study makes no claim to infallibility or irrefutable conclusions. It asks "what is known of the role of the arts in Hitler's mind and what does this tell us about his mind?" This information is available, and lends itself to interpretation by an Alderian model. The Adlerian model does not need to make assumptions where the evidence is unavailable. Its virtue arises from its very insistence that one begins with observable behavior that is available.

To accomplish this task, this study will review Hitler's early life and artistic consciousness, his use of the arts in his struggle to become chancellor, and the subsequent imposition of his aesthetic theories on the Third Reich in art, architecture, and music. At that point, it will argue that the Adlerian model most successfully explains his psychological character and life scheme. This study makes no claim to be the definitive psychological analysis of Hitler, but it does hope to contribute to a more viable explanation of his personality. By choice, it limits itself to his aesthetic theories about architecture, the plastic arts, and music. It is left to others to consider the possibility of applying the model to his strictly political and military behavior.

Chapter 2
The Formative Years

Adolf Hitler was born April 20, 1889, in Branau am Inn, a small town in an impoverished agricultural region of Austria. He was the legitimate son of Alois Hitler, a customs official, and Klara Hitler, née Poelzl. Two days after his birth on Easter Saturday he was christened a Catholic by Father Ignaz Probst, who entered Adolf's birth and baptism in the Parish registry. This Austrian would become the Chancellor of Germany's Third Reich.

Scholars have given considerable attention to an examination of Adolf Hitler's family and its antecedents. Hitler, however, made every effort to obscure and misrepresent his origins. He never complied with the requirement in the NSDAP directive which stipulated that all Germans must provide documentary evidence about their lineage. He regarded any interest in his private life as insulting. In 1939, Hitler became furious when the British press interviewed Patrick Hitler, the son of his half-brother Alois and an Irish woman. Hitler exclaimed:

I've always taken such care to keep my private affairs out of the press! These people are not to know who I am. They're not to know where I come from or what my family background is. Even in my book I never mention a word about these things, not a word! And now they've gone and let on my nephew. Inquiries are set on foot and people sent to pry into our past![1]

Fest interpreted this attitude as a sense of inferiority within Hitler arising out of his realization of the ambiguousness of his ancestry.[2] Maser believed he deliberately tried to detach himself from his immediate family background because Hitler sought to appear both as "the emissary of history and as the incarnation of what in his view was the 'commendable and legitimate' desire of the German people."[3]

It has also been suggested that Hitler was reticent to discuss his background because he knew or feared he had Jewish blood. This suspicion was due in large part to the failure of his paternal grandmother, Maria Anna Schicklgruber, to reveal the father of her illegitimate son, Alois, Adolf's father. Among the candidates for his paternity there was a Graz Jew named Frankenberger for whom his grandmother reputedly worked at the time of her pregnancy. It has also been suggested that Frankenberger's son was Alois' father.

4

At the Nuremberg trials, Hitler's lawyer, Hans Frank, reported that Frankenberger was part of an investigation precipitated by a letter to Hitler from his nephew in which he referred to "very odd circumstances in our family history."[4] But neither Frank's investigation in 1930, the investigation which Heinrich Himmler had the Gestapo conduct in 1942, nor any study since then has been able to verify the identity of Adolf Hitler's paternal grandfather.[5] Fest and Waite believed, however, that the significance of the question of a Jewish antecedent lies not so much in who he was but in the doubts it created in Adolf about his own descent.[6]

Maser has convincingly refuted not only the theory that Frankenberger was Hitler's grandfather but the entire question of a Jewish antecedent. Maser noted Frank admitted that after his investigation, Hitler still rejected the idea of a Jewish ancestor.[7]

Although illegitimacy was frowned upon by the authorities, especially by the Catholic Church, it is doubtful that the simple fact that his father was illegitimate would have caused Hitler any consternation. In Alois's day, it was a common occurrence in Valdviertel, and the birth of Alois Schicklgruber would have caused no particular surprise as no disgrace was attached to illegitimate births. In lower Austria, illegitimacy was common and in some areas reached as high as forty percent. As late as 1903, the figure was twenty-four percent.[8]

The Chancellor of the Third Reich could have borne his paternal grandmother's maiden name and been called Adolf Schicklgruber. His father was called Alois Schicklgruber until he was nearly forty years old. At that time, his foster father, Johann Nepomuk Huttler, convinced Father Zahnschirm of the Dollersheim parish, to legitimize Alois in the church registry. He gave his brother's name, Johann Georg Hiedler, as that of Alois's natural father. The priest recorded Hiedler's name as Hitler, and Alois Schicklgruber became Alois Hitler.[9]

Johann Georg Hiedler had married Alois's mother sometime after his birth, and it was assumed that he was Alois's father. Alois lived only a short time with his mother and Hiedler. He then went to live with Huttler, who was assumed to be his uncle. It is unclear exactly why no effort was made to legitimize Alois for three decades. Maser suggested that Johann Nepomuk Huttler was, in fact, Alois's natural father and postponed his legitimation until the death of Eva Maria, his domineering wife.[10] It was perhaps just such a lack of bravery which caused Huttler to declare that his brother, long since dead, was Alois's father. The family tradition was that Johann George Hiedler was Alois's father, and Smith argued that Adolf Hitler himself accepted this explanation.[11]

Adolf Hitler's mother, Klara Poelzl, was the third wife of Alois Hitler and the granddaughter of Johann Nepomuk Huttler. If Maser's conclusions regarding the paternity of Alois were correct, then Johann Nepomuk Huttler was Adolf Hitler's paternal grandfather, and, at the same time, his maternal great-grandfather. Adolf was then "the issue of a union between Alois Hitler and the woman who was both the latter's niece and the daughter of his half sister."[12] Alois and Klara were officially second cousins and within the degree of consanguinity prohibited by the Catholic Church. So, Alois applied for a marriage dispensation to the priest of Branau, Father Kostler. The request passed from the priest to the bishop, who had the diocesan scholars in Linz translate it into Latin, and it was dispatched to Rome. Johann Nepomuk Huttler attended the wedding of Alois and Klara on January 7, 1885. At the time of their marriage Klara was twenty-four and Alois was forty-seven. She continued to call him "uncle" for sometime.[13] The question of whether Klara and Alois were truly related by blood, however, remains as unanswerable as the question of who Alois Hitler's father was.

Klara bore Alois six children, four sons and two daughters. Three children died in infancy before Adolf's birth, but for nearly five years after his birth no other children were born. Hitler's mother believed he was a delicate child and watched over and protected him. There is general agreement that Hitler responded to his mother's solicitude with a deep and abiding love. No other woman could conceivably compare to her, and he kept her picture with him always.[14]

In 1893 and 1896, two more children were born to Klara. Of the six she bore, only two survived, Adolf and Paula. Lest one be tempted to suggest that Adolf Hitler came from weak stock, it should be noted this mortality rate was not abnormal at the time. In the early years of their marriage, Klara also cared for two children by Alois's second marriage, Alois Jr. and Angela.

In *Mein Kampf* Hitler represented himself as a child of poverty.[15] In Branau am Inn, however, his family lived in a relatively imposing home with an attractive playground.[16] Hitler wanted desperately to be German and not Austrian, so later he claimed little memory of his years in Branau.

Alois' work next took the family to Passau, where they lived from August, 1892, when Adolf was three years and four months old, to April 1895. These impressionable years were as close to paradise as Hitler ever came. It was in Passau that he learned the Austro-Bavarian dialect with which he would later hold millions spellbound. It was this dialect he called his mother tongue, and it was this old German imperial city which caused him later to say that he "always felt more German than Austrian."[17] In Passau he encountered wonderful Gothic and Baroque architecture and saw the Renaissance flowering around him.

In 1895, Alois Hitler decided to retire and purchased a home in Hafeld which had nine acres of land. Gardening and bee keeping had long been pleasurable avocations to him, and to them he dedicated his retirement years. From the time Alois Hitler went to Passau until his retirement, his salary was considerably higher than that of a headmaster of an elementary school.[18] During his retirement years, he received a guaranteed income which was paid in monthly installments. From birth to fourteen years of age, therefore, Adolf thus lived on a middle-class standard in which privation was unknown. In 1897, the imposing Hitler home in Hafeld was sold to the Viennese nobleman Ritter Conrad von Zdekauer.[19]

In 1895, Adolf Hitler began his formal education. He received top marks from his teachers in the primary school at Fischlam near Lambach and at the denominational school of the ancient Benedictine foundation in Lambach, where he attended classes from 1896 to 1898. In Lambach, Hitler was a choir boy in the Junior Choral Institute where he joined in the singing lessons in his spare time.[20] As a server and choir member, he knew of Abbot von Hagen, who ruled over the monastery in the middle of the nineteenth-century. Von Hagen wore a ring on his finger which contained a stylized swastika, and he also had one carved on the pulpit. In German, the swastika is termed *Hakenkreuz* and von Hagen may have regarded it as a pun on his own name. It has been suggested that von Hagen's swastikas were inspirations for the hooked-cross flag which Hitler later designed for the Nazi movement.[21]

In *Mein Kampf* Hitler stated that the abbot of Lambach seemed to him "the highest and most desirable ideal," and he thought of becoming a priest. Although he admitted he had only temporary aspirations for this profession, he insisted he was diverted from "such youthful ideals by a father who could not appreciate the oratorical talents of his pugnacious boy." Hitler was intoxicated with the church music, the oratory, and the "the solemn splendor of the brilliant church festivals."[22]

In 1899, Alois purchased a solidly middle-class home in Leonding. Adolf continued to be successful in school for the first year in Leonding, but a picture of him in 1900, when compared with one taken the year before, shows a decided change. Hitler then became a withdrawn, introspective and moody child. This change was evident in his grades. Never again was he a successful student.[23] It is possible that the reason for this dramatic change was the death of his younger brother, Edmond, who had succumbed to measles. It was also likely Adolf's emotional development was affected by the family's numerous moves. Adolf's environment fell far short of the "clear, continuous, dependable, and purposeful system of love and guidance," which psychologists regard as necessary for "the healthy development of a child."[24]

In *Mein Kampf* Hitler portrayed his father and himself as opponents in a battle of wills—his father wanted him to be a civil servant, and he wanted to be an artist. He confessed, however, that his father sent him to the *Realschule* rather than the *Gymnasium*, because the former was "more suitable to his aptitude for drawing, a subject which in his opinion was neglected in the Austrian *Gymnasium*."[25] The *Realschule* had no special course of study in art, but the students studied both geometrical and freehand drawing. The *Realschule* was intended to prepare boys for a technical or commercial career, though only one of Hitler's fellow students actually became a civil servant. In September, 1900, at the age of eleven, Adolf began the four-year course of practical studies at the Linz *Realschule*. The journey to school took one and one-half hours by foot, but he often traveled there by train through the beautiful Austrian countryside.

Hitler's desire to be an artist apparently paralleled his interest in a military career. In *Mein Kampf* he described his discovery of two periodicals on the Franco-Prussian War among his father's books. Their reading caused him to become fascinated with war and soldiering. This led to his enthusiasm for playing war games with his friends. He was always the ringleader and cajoled the boys into obedience with his oratorical skills. Payne believed Hitler's decisions to be an artist and to become a military figure of importance "were not necessarily incompatible; on the contrary, they reinforced each other, drawing him deeper into a dream world."[26] His fascination with the excitement of war and his view of the life of an artist were thoroughly romantic. Such romanticism was also reflected in his love of the imaginary Wild West adventures written by Karl May and his fascination with the heroic figures of Wagner's musical drams.

Hitler stated in *Mein Kampf* that he decided to fail in his studies in *Realschule* to show his father the seriousness of his dream of being an artist. Certainly Hitler did not lack intelligence. However, his obstinate nature and inability to do regular, sustained work combined with his romanticism to preclude even average grades. These work habits were to continue throughout his adult life.[27]

Alois Hitler died in 1903, while Adolf was in the second form at the Linz *Realschule*, but his mother persuaded him to continue his studies. Adolf's continuance in school was one indication of the family's financial stability after Alois' death. Such security made it possible for Adolf to stay at a boy's home in Linz during the weekdays, so he did not have to make the journey from Leonding each day to attend *Realschule*. Hitler, however, worked diligently to create a myth that his father's death left the family in poverty.

Since the publication of Hans Frank's book, it has been accepted that Alois was a drunkard who abused his son. Frank stated that:

Many a time the boy Adolf had to fetch his father from the inn at a late hour after the latter's evening indulgence...Hitler himself told me...Often I had to stand for a quarter of an hour or more, pleading and scolding before I could get him to his legs. Then I supported him home...[W]hat a daemon alcohol can be! Because of my father, it was the bane of my youth.[28]

Family members also accused Alois of physical abuse. Bridget Hitler, for example, testified that her husband, Alois Jr., told her his father beat the dog, the children, and on one occasion, beat his wife Klara. Angela, Adolf's half sister, allegedly once asked Adolf if he remembered that she and his mother would pull on his father's uniform coat tails when his father was trying to hit him.[29] Adolf himself once told his secretary, "I never loved my father. I therefore feared him all the more. He had a terrible temper and often whipped me."[30] Hitler admired the Indians in Karl May's stories, who would not cry out when tortured, and stressed his own silence when his father beat him for the last time. Patrick Hitler, Alois Jr.'s son, remembered his father's story about Adolf's attempt to run away from home. When his father found Adolf constructing a raft to float down the Danube on, he beat Adolf so badly he believed he had killed him.[31] There is conflicting evidence at this point. A friend of Alois in Leonding, Josef Mayerhofer, agreed that Alois was strict with his family and that Klara had nothing to smile about. Mayerhofer argued Alois had a rough exterior, that he often scolded and threatened to bash Adolf, but he refused to state that he beat Adolf.[32]

Two days after Alois Hitler's death, his obituary appeared in the *Linz Tagespost*. Included among the many words of praise was the comment that Alois was fond of singing. This is the only indication that music played any part in the life of Hitler's father or any other member of his family. There is no evidence that any of his forebearers were gifted or even interested in art. Adolf's obsession with art and music seems to have been stimulated by experiences outside the home—in schools, churches, and in his *Realschule* years, in the museums and performance halls of Linz.

In *Mein Kampf* Hitler stated that he saw his first opera, *Lohengrin*, at the age of twelve and was "captivated at once."[33] Herr W. Hagmüller, the son of a baker whose shop was near the Hitler home in Leonding, stated that he often took evening meals with the Hitlers, and responded to a 1938 Nazi Party inquiry about the Fuehrer's youth by stating Hitler was particularly fond of Wagner, and he had seen Hitler pacing up and down singing arias from Wagner's operas. Hagmüller was also able to recall Hitler spent a great deal of time making architectural sketches, drawing plans for a theater at Linz and painting both people and still-lifes.[34] Several drawings like those described by Hagmüller appear in a recently published book of Hitler's art works by Billy F. Price.

Price's work contains 723 works dating from 1899 to the late 1930s. Price drew from over a dozen collections to complete his book. As might be expected, the primary problem in such an effort is one of authentication of the paintings and drawings. In 1935, collection and authentication of Hitler's art works was part of the NSDAP's research of Hitler's past. Wilhelm Heinrich Dammann and Dr. August Priesack were directed to authenticate all Hitler art that could be traced, purchased, or borrowed. These researchers "used photos (including color photos), copies, or loaned originals which had been previously authenticated, as references and comparative controls." Hitler was often called upon to authenticate a found work. Artists named Mühlbrecht and Kraus were employed to make copies of selected genuine works to be used in the authentication process. To prevent the copies from passing as originals a one millimeter hole was punched in the right-hand corner of each copy, ten millimeters in from the top and side.[35] Forgeries were found by Dammann and Priesack, and Hitler's signature to that affect is affixed to the back of at least one work in Price's collection.[36] Price admitted that some of the other paintings may be doubtful.[37] However, he availed himself of the best possible advice of those who should know—namely, former art experts of the Third Reich, Heinrich Hoffmann, Jr., son of Hitler's official photographer, as well as August Priesack.[38] The Price collection should be accepted, with reservations about certain works, as representing authentic works

Price's collection includes several examples of the young Hitler's drawings from the Leonding period, which are similar to those mentioned by Hagmüller. They appear to be copies from schoolboy texts and other printed material. A number reveal a military interest, such as *Tilly*, a *Soldier of the Middle Ages*, an *Officer Before Caesar*, a *Bust with Warrior's Helmet*, and what appears to be the head of a Russian Cossack with bandoleers.[39] Others are of a *Kurd*, an *Old Castilian* in priestly attire, a *Russian*, and one entitled *Ben Ali Ba(ba)*, which has pseudo-Arabic words and letters.[40] Most were done in pencil or pen and ink. Only the *Bust with Warrior's Helmet* was done in a more sophisticated wax and opaque paint technique. There is little of psychological interest in these works except for the military theme. They are not interpretations of subject matter so much as a schoolboy's efforts at copying pictures that struck his fancy. It is noteworthy that they include not only profiles but also more technically difficult three-quarter views. An *Officer Before Caesar*, shows a Roman soldier lifting his arm in salute to a figure about to draw a sword. The two figures crowd the vertical edges of the picture and portions of both figures are missing. Strangely, the middle portion of the picture is empty. Hitler evidently had not reached the point in his artistic development where he could scale the figures to fit the size of the paper. Such a problem is also apparent in *Camel Driver*,[41] a watercolor of this early period. It shows a rather well-painted youth leading a camel. Only the head of the camel and its attenuated neck, which is stretched to reach the right edge of the picture, are included. The drawings of this early period exhibit an uneven attention to detail. Some of them obviously were hurriedly sketched and are quite crude. Others, such as *Tilly* and *Ben Ali Ba(ba)*, exhibit Hitler's considerable attention to modeling, highlights, and shading through the use of hatching.

While it must be assumed that none of the works discussed above were drawn or painted from life, Hitler attempted at least three portraits of people around him during this period. One of these is a *Caricature of a Teacher* with an anguished facial expression, who holds near his groin a paper cone on which is written the word "pepper." Waite, without other confirmation, believed the teacher was frightened because he was caught in the act of masturbation, and used Hitler's drawing of this subject in the creation of a sexual profile of the youthful Hitler.[42] In 1904, Hitler drew a portrait of a *Realschule* teacher named Dr. Leopold Poetsch. Although his technical skills were still unrefined, when this portrait is compared with a photograph of the teacher, it is apparent that at this time he was developing some facility in drawing from life.[43] Unfortunately, a portrait of his mother, drawn one year later, shows no improvement in drawing human forms from life.[44]

The earliest landscapes by Hitler included in Price's collection date from 1904. These works are entitled *Mill and Water Wheel with Fir Trees*, *Castle in the Mountain*, and *Chalk Burners in the Hills*.[45] From the colorplate of the castle scene much can be learned of Hitler's watercolor techniques of this period. The work looks much like it was drawn with a pen and tinted with watercolor washes. Evidently, in this work he used a very fine brush to paint details and create forms in a light brown hue. This same color was used for shading, while a gold wash was delicately applied to give some color interest. Although the colors are not true to nature, the work is quite effective and perhaps more expressive than many of his later landscapes. The two other landscapes of 1904 are not provided in color by Price, but it is quite obvious from the black and white plates that they have a dominance of tonal masses over line as a means of defining form. In all three, perspective is well handled.

From an examination of Hitler's youthful works it becomes apparent that quite early he developed the practice of copying from textbooks or other printed sources, that he occasionally attempted to draw or paint from nature, that from his early and natural dependence upon pencil and pen and ink he moved toward the medium of watercolors, that he had considerable difficulty in the development of skills in drawing human forms from life but that by 1904 he was quite accomplished in the execution of landscapes in watercolors. While these landscapes may not be considered prodigious, they demonstrate why Hitler believed he had a promising career in art.

Leonding was his home during critical years of his life, but he received his education at Linz. It was a provincial city of 50,000 inhabitants, while Leonding was a peasant village. In Leonding, Hitler had been the uncontested leader of his playmates and had enjoyed the aura of his father's social position. In Linz "he found himself a rough-hewn rustic, a despised outsider among the sons of academics, businessmen, and the persons of quality." The contrast between Leonding and Linz gave him his class consciousness.[46]

Adolf's father had been born of peasant stock, but, with the support of Johann Nepomuk Huttler and his own wit, Alois had raised himself to the position of a civil servant. Like countless other Austrian families, Adolf's "underwent the transition to lower middle-class status as European society gradually adjusted to an industrial rather than an agrarian economy.[47] It was a mobile society in which children who resisted parental authority and social status were considered rebellious. Leonding and Linz stood like two rungs on a social ladder for the young Adolf. While he would hold great affection for both places all his life, Linz offered opportunities for him to fulfill his own dreams and enjoy the arts.

After his father's death, Hitler's years at *Realschule* continued to be a succession of problems with grades, confrontations with teachers and practical jokes. Most of the latter were harmless pranks which paralleled those traditionally played by Austrian schoolboys. In 1904, he failed French. The school permitted him to repeat the exam, and he passed with the understanding that he would enroll in a different *Realschule*. In September, 1904, therefore, Klara enrolled Adolf in the *Realschule* in Steyr, where he lodged in a boarding house. At the end of this term, he was not permitted to graduate because he failed mathematics. He had to repeat this exam in the fall.

In *Mein Kampf*, Hitler stated that he was allowed to stop his studies in *Realschule* when a physician told his mother he had a lung ailment which would never permit him to work in an office. Klara took Adolf to Spital to recuperate. He passed his time there playing the zither, drawing, painting, and exploring the countryside.[48] From the accounts provided by those near the family during this time there can be little doubt that the illness was genuine and that Hitler probably suffered from consumption.[49] By the fall term, he was able to repeat the examination in mathematics, and he was successful. There is some confusion in the Hitler literature regarding Hitler's completion of *Realschule*. Smith initially suggested that this examination in mathematics completed his course of studies in *Realschule* and that Klara had permitted him to stop application to *Oberrealschule*, the next rung up the educational ladder. Later, like other scholars, he stated that Hitler did not complete *Realschule*.[50] In reality, Hitler had no desire to apply to the *Oberrealschule*, for he wanted to fulfill his dream of being an art student at the Vienna Academy of Art.

Hitler's lifelong views of education, educators, and intellectuals were much affected by his *Realschule* experiences. Some thirty-eight years later, during reminiscences about his Austrian school days, Hitler recalled he and his fellow students had little respect or mercy for their teachers for they regarded them as enemies. He insisted many were deranged and ended their days as lunatics.[51] Hitler measured their intelligence in relation to the ease with which they fell prey to student pranks. He believed they persecuted students who showed originality, and he was repelled by their failure to be clean and well dressed.

On June 15, 1905, Klara sold the home in Leonding and moved the family to Linz. Alois Jr. and Angela had left the family roof, so it was Klara, Adolf and Paula who shared an apartment in a newly built tenement house which was entirely respectable. Adolf had a small room of his own with books and painting materials. By the autumn of 1905, he was free of the *Realschule* studies he hated and could indulge in the many cultural opportunities Linz had to offer. He joined libraries and adopted a romantic, bohemian life. Hitler regularly attended the theater and Wagnerian productions. He devoted the remainder of his time to painting, the composition of poetry, music and grandiose architectural plans. He read until the small hours of the morning, pursued his artistic efforts in the afternoon and, at night, sauntered about the city or attended the theater. He prided himself on dress and deportment. Such enjoyment of his free time caused Jetzinger to refer to him in this period as "The Young Man of Leisure" and Payne to call him "The Young Dilettante."[52]

In the autumn of 1905, Hitler met a Czech youth named August Kubizek at the Linz Opera Theater. Kubizek, tired from working in his father's upholstery shop and unable to afford a seat at the opera, often dashed to the theater early enough to enjoy the selection of the left or right column to lean against in the standing room section. One night he arrived to find that another youth had already selected the right column. Kubizek's rival for the column was Adolf Hitler. In time, Kubizek and this youth with the glistening eyes became close friends.[53]

In 1953, Kubizek's book, called *Adolf Hitler—Mein Jugendfreund*, was published. Before that time, relatively little was known about Hitler's youth in Linz. Scholars vary widely in their acceptance of Kubizek's account of these years. Since the book was not published until forty-eight years after Kubizek met Hitler, it was suggested that his memories were inaccurate due to the passage of time. More caustic criticism accused Kubizek of deliberately manipulating his writing to enhance the image of Hitler as a youth. Also, subsequent interviews with Kubizek did not always support his writings.[54]

Smith and Jetzinger provided documentary evidence to support their criticism of Kubizek's inaccuracies.[55] Toland admitted that Kubizek had "a tendency toward exaggeration, over-emphasis and occasional flights of imagination," but he also warned his readers that Jetzinger, who was imprisoned in Vienna during the Hitler régime, had "a tendency to accent events that make Hitler look bad."[56] Payne also admitted that it is easy to find fault with Kubizek's inaccurately remembered dates and tendency to write as fact "things he only half remembered." Nevertheless, Payne believed Kubizek's possession of letters which Hitler wrote to him and several of Hitler's drawings and paintings demonstrate their friendship. Further, Payne appreciated the color and atmosphere which Kubizek's account provided of Linz.[57]

Kubizek, for example, described the level of musical life in Linz during those days as quite active. Auguste Gollerich, a disciple of Liszt and a collaborator with Wagner, was the director of the Linz Music Society. Each year the society gave a number of symphony concerts, performed a major choral work and one special concert of mixed works.[58] Kubizek's account supports Payne's assertion that opera goers in Vienna looked down on the performances in Linz, but the people of Linz were proud of their performers.

Kubizek and Hitler became close friends, but Kubizek confessed that they had extremely different personalities. Kubizek was somewhat dreamy, sensitive and subservient to Hitler's moods. Hitler, on the contrary, was "exceedingly violent and high-strung." Trivial events would produce tremendous outbursts of temper. While many things could upset Adolf, Kubizek recalled that Hitler always fell into a rage when he heard the words "civil servant," the occupation his father had expected him to follow. Hitler's tempestuous feelings also burst forth with theatrical, volcanic eruption on such topics as "the excise duty levied at the Danube bridge, or a collection in the streets for a charity lottery." Kubizek usually complied with Hitler's need for agreement with his views except when they disagreed on musical matters. Kubizek was a musician and naturally considered his own opinions valid in this area.[59]

In 1906, Kubizek and Hitler attended a performance of Wagner's *Rienzi* at the Linz Stadtheatre. The libretto showed the rise of Rienzi to be the Tribune of the people of Rome and his subsequent downfall.[60] After the performance, the friends ascended the Freinberg hill and there, Hitler emotionally "conjured up in grandiose, inspiring pictures his own future and that of his people." Hitler spoke of "a *mandate* which, one day, he would receive from the people, to lead them out of servitude to the heights of freedom."[61]

In 1939, when Hitler and Kubizek visited Wagner's widow in Bayreuth, Hitler told her that his political career had been miraculously laid open before him one night in Linz when, as a boy, he attended a performance of Wagner's *Rienzi*. That was the hour, it all began, he said. In tribute to the significance of that night, Hitler opened the enormous Third Reich party rallies in Nuremburg with the overture to Wagner's *Rienzi*.[62]

It was Kubizek who preserved the story of Hitler's great love for Stefanie, a beautiful, wealthy girl of Linz. Kubizek and Hitler spent endless hours discussing Stefanie, including the suitability of her voice for singing various Wagnerian roles. Kubizek was often sent on scouting expeditions by Hitler to find bits of information about Stefanie. Hitler was thrilled when Kubizek discovered she had a good soprano voice. He brooded, however, over the news that Stefanie had danced with "some 'blockhead' of a lieutenant." Hitler wrote countless love poems to Stefanie and decided to build a house for her in the Renaissance style. The shape and acoustics of the music room and the placement of Stefanie's piano particularly concerned him. Kubizek suggested the villa be built in Italy, but Hitler "insisted that it would only be built in Germany, in the neighborhood of a big city so that he and Stefanie could go to the opera and concerts."[63]

Stefanie's reciprocation of Hitler's affection was limited to some innocent glances and a flower thrown to him as she passed during a Flower Festival. Kubizek could not convince him to speak to her. The contact might have destroyed his picture of her as "the incarnation of all womanly virtues" and "the female counterpart of all his knowledge and interests." Hitler believed she would wait for him while he attended the Vienna Academy and toured abroad for a year. They would marry and live in their Renaissance style villa. Hitler was very concerned, however, that such a marriage might force him off his chosen path. Stefanie remained a real human being while at the same time she became a creature of Adolf's romantic dream world. Kubizek saw this mixing of dream and reality as a characteristic of the young Hitler.[64] His fantasies about Stefanie strongly paralleled his romantic view of himself as an artist, the excitement of war, the novels of Karl May and the relevance of Wagner's mythological subjects to real life. The story of Stefanie has been completely rejected by some scholars.[65] Others have used it as part of a more complete examination of Hitler's relationships with women, his psychological profile, and his sexuality.[66]

In 1906, Hitler made his first trip to Vienna. He stated he intended to study the pictures in the imperial museum but instead spent his time exploring the architectural details of the building itself. In *Mein Kampf* Hitler stated that this trip lasted only a fortnight, but Kubizek said Hitler stayed in Vienna about four weeks.[67] From a note written on a postcard which Hitler mailed to Kubizek from Vienna, it is evident Hitler was struck by the musical performances at the Opera House. During this first stay in Vienna, Hitler attended performances of Wagner's *The Flying Dutchman, Tristan and Isolde,* and *Lohengrin.* By comparison, "the performances in the Linz Theatre appeared provincial and inadequate."[68] As Chancellor of the Third Reich, Hitler worked to improve the quality of opera in small cities.[69]

In 1906, Adolf decided to take piano lessons with Josef Prevatsky-Wendt, a former military bandmaster and Kubizek's teacher.[70] The fact that his mother purchased a Heitzmann-Flügel grand piano for his new interest is further indication that the family was financially secure. Jetzinger stated that the lessons lasted for a year, but Maser and Smith believed they lasted for only a few months.[71] There is little indication of the degree of progress which Hitler achieved during this period of piano study, but Kubizek stated that Adolf was not psychologically suited to monotonous finger exercises.[72]

On January 18, 1907, Klara Hitler had surgery to remove a malignant growth in her breast. She was a patient of Dr. Edmund Bloch, an excellent and kind Jewish physician, who was known as the "doctor of the poor." The operation was performed, however, by a local surgeon named Dr. Karl Urban. It was assumed that the surgery was successful, and Klara did not see her physician for two months after her release from the hospital. The pattern of visits to the doctor for the next several months indicated there were periods of grave concern and times when she had temporary improvement.[73] Her illness took its toll on the family financially and psychologically. Her sister, Johanna, joined the family to care for her, and for some reason they moved to Urfahr, a suburb of Linz across the Danube, in May or June of that year.

In the fall of 1907, Adolf went to Vienna to sit for the October admission examination of the General School of Painting at the Academy of Fine Arts. For two days, applicants had to choose two subjects for compositions to be executed in two sessions of three hours each. The subjects included such academic themes as *Explusion from Paradise, Summer, Cain Killing Abel, The Magi,* and *The Hunt, Dance,* and *The Fisherman.*[74] Without providing the source of his information, Walter C. Langer states that Hitler was assigned to draw a picture of *The Expulsion from Paradise,* on the first day of the examination, and *An Episode of the Great Flood,* on the second day. In fact, there is no documentary evidence to show which of the themes Hitler chose or was assigned, but it is known that he passed this portion of the examination when thirty-three others failed. The second part of the examination involved presentation of previously prepared works to the examiners. Hitler and fifty-one other fellow candidates failed this portion of the examination. Of the 133 applicants, only twenty-eight passed both portions.[75]

Price's collection contains four pencil drawings and three watercolors which Hitler submitted to the Vienna Academy of Fine Arts in 1907. Hitler stated that the four drawings showed "nature in relation to buildings seen during a walk."[76] They are rural architectural studies with detailed attention to humble structures surrounded by water and vegetation. The architecture is of prime importance in these works. While there is evidence of a distant horizon in three of them, the viewer's eye is more drawn to the buildings. Only one work has a few tiny human figures. Indeed, they emphasize just what Hitler suggested, nature and buildings. Two of the watercolors are of scenes which include mountains and bodies of water. Hitler appeared to be concerned with his understanding of atmospheric perspective. On the other hand, the painting technique he used in the third landscape is quite impressionistic.

Hitler failed the second portion of the examination because his sample works included "two few heads." Yet, "there exists today studies for portraits drawn at this period which would undoubtedly have satisfied the Academy's requirement."[77] Their existence makes it impossible to refrain from an indulgence in speculative history. Many have asked, as Maser asked, "what the world might have been spared if Hitler had included a few more heads in his portfolio." It will be recalled that Hagmüller testified that, as early as his years in Leonding, Hitler drew heads of people of different races.[78]

It is frightening and perhaps too simplistic to suggest that the academicians who denied Hitler admission to the academy contributed to the catastrophe which occurred under Hitler's leadership as Fuehrer of the Third Reich. Yet, such thoughts are inevitable. When examining three of Hitler's competition drawings, de Jaeger found them "agreeable to look at, pleasant enough scenes, but without much imagination."[79] Perhaps never has history been so affected by a few unimaginative little paintings.

While the examiners of the academy did not find Hitler's painting skills sufficient for his admission to the General School of Painting, Siegmund L'Allemand, the Rector of the academy, did advise Hitler to take up architectural design. Hitler had not completed Realschule, however, and this was a prerequisite for application to the Architecture Academy.[80] Rather than pursue his Realschule diploma, Hitler elected to study painting and retake the admission examination for the academy.

In Mein Kampf Hitler related how confounded he was by the negative decision of the Academy. A retired professor of the Academy, who took the examination with Hitler, stated that Hitler went into a rage when he heard he had been rejected. Hitler called the examiners "fossilized Bureaucrats devoid of any understanding of young talent."[81]

Hitler's disappointment with his failure in the admission examination was overshadowed by news of the worsening condition of his mother's health. He returned to Linz in November to care for her, and Kubizek witnessed his proud, explosive and sometimes difficult friend become quiet, solicitous, and gentle.

When Klara Hitler was buried on Christmas Eve after her death on December 21, 1907, Adolf could hardly leave his mother's grave. Dr. Bloch testified that "In all my career I have never seen anyone so prostrate with grief as Adolf Hitler."[82] Several days later, the children of Klara went by to pay the doctor for his services. Adolf looked into the eyes of the kindly doctor and said, "I shall be grateful to you forever."[83] Binion suggested that on a conscious level Hitler loved Dr. Bloch like a kindly father, but unconsciously, he became anti-Semitic because his mother had died while under the care of a Jewish doctor.[84] Nevertheless, Hitler later sent Dr. Bloch carefully painted postcards expressing his gratitude. While other historians have been critical of Bloch's treatment of Klara, even Gestapo investigators of Klara's death had nothing but praise for Dr. Bloch.[85] Indeed, he was permitted to leave Austria in 1938 with his savings.

Starting in January, 1908, Adolf received twenty-five kronen a month as an orphan's pension in addition to the fifty-eight kronen per month he had received as patrimony since he turned eighteen. He may also have received a sum from his mother's estate. His monthly income, therefore, was at least eighty-three kronen. By comparison, an experienced lawyer of that time might receive seventy kronen per month after one year of practice.[86] Langer must be considered incorrect, therefore, in his suggestion that Hitler's income was insufficient for survival without other work during this period of his life.[87] Kubizek knew Hitler had a little capital at his disposal, "which would enable him to keep his head above water."[88] With relative financial security, therefore, Hitler returned to Vienna in February, 1908, to fulfill his dream of being an artist.

Hitler had long implored Kubizek to join him in the pursuit of a career in Vienna. In 1907, Kubizek developed bronchial catarrh and could no longer tolerate working in the dust in his father's upholstery shop. He had to find another occupation. Early in March, 1908, Kubizek joined Hitler in Vienna and began his studies at the Academy of Music. He shared a room with Hitler which was just large enough for Kubizek's rented grand piano, two beds, a few other pieces of furniture, including a small table for Hitler's art work, and floor space for three long steps where Hitler paced during his monologues. This was hardly what they had planned in their youth in Linz—someday winning the lottery and renting the entire second floor of a large house across the Danube, or building the spacious house which Hitler had designed for them.[89]

As a music student of the Academy, Kubizek received some free tickets to music performances in Vienna. Either with these tickets or ones purchased with their limited resources, Hitler was able to attend the opera, which Payne called the drug that kept him alive.[90] Hitler saw operas by Mozart, Beethoven and Verdi, Gounold's *Faust* which he regarded as vulgar, and operas by Tchaikovsky and Smetana, for which he showed no enthusiasm.[91] Hitler also continued his love affair with the operas of Wagner. Kubizek observed that when Hitler listened to Wagner's operas:

...he was transformed. His violence left him, he became quiet, submissive, tractable. His gaze lost its restlessness, and his daily preoccupations were as though they had never been. His own destiny, however heavily it weighed upon him, no longer appeared to have any importance. He no longer felt lonely, an outlaw, a man kicked around by society. He was in a state of intoxicated ecstasy. Willingly he allowed himself to be carried away into a legendary world more real to him than the world he saw around him every day. From the stale, musty prison of the room at the back of the courtyard, he was transported into the blessed regions of German antiquity, which was for him the ideal world, the highest goal of all his endeavors.[92]

During the months they lived together in Vienna, Kubizek saw Hitler write poetry, envision a play about the painter Murillo, begin dramas based on plots lifted from German mythology, and begin a play based upon the years when Christian missionaries first took their faith to Bavaria. Kubizek recalled a state setting for the latter in which the background showed:

...the Holy Mountain. In the foreground a huge sacrificial stone overshadowed by grand oaks. Two formidable warriors grasp the black sacrificial bull firmly by the horns, and press the heavy head of the sacrificial beast toward the hollow of the stone. Towering behind them stands the priest in a light-colored raiment. He grips the battle sword with which he will sacrifice the bull. All around him solemn bearded men, leaning on their shields, their lances at the ready watch the festive scene with steady gaze.[93]

Hitler's devotion to the Romantic tradition and his love of Wagner also stimulated him to compose an opera. This occurred when Kubizek informed him that an outline for a musical drama based on *Wieland the Smith* had been recently found among some of Wagner's papers. Hitler immediately set about writing an opera based upon this legendary hero of the Norse sagas. According to the myth, after:

...Wieland the Smith was lamed by the king he served, he avenged himself by raping the king's daughter and killing her two brothers and drinking out of their skulls before flying away on wings he had hammered out in his smithy.[94]

The opening scene of Hitler's opera was set in Iceland, with Wieland and his brothers seen fishing in Wolf Lake. In the background Hitler planned volcanoes, glaciers, huge rocks, and three Valkyries floating out of the clouds. For this scene he composed lively music which he wanted played on ancient Teutonic instruments. With Kubizek's persuasion, he "decided in favour of a modern symphony orchestra, reinforced by Wagnerian tubas." Hitler attempted to pick out the melodies on the piano. Kubizek copied them down and added harmonies. For weeks Hitler composed, designed costumes, and drew stage scenery in charcoal. After awhile, his creative flame died out. Hitler's musical drama, which Kubizek called "second hand Wagner" was never completed.[95]

It was while Kubizek and Hitler were together in Vienna that Hitler broadened his musical tastes in symphonic music. Kubizek was able to provide Hitler with free concert tickets, which he used two or three times a week. As his love for orchestral music grew, Hitler became determined that there should be a traveling orchestra to take music to the Austrian provinces. He and Kubizek discussed at length the proposed size, conductor, and program for the orchestra. As Hitler attended performances, he kept a list of works he believed suitable for the orchestra's repertoire.[96]

Hitler was not partial to virtuoso performances by soloists, but he did like Mozart's and Beethoven's piano and violin concertos, Mendelssohn's Violin Concerto in E Minor, Schumann's Piano Concerto in A Minor, and Grieg's Piano Concerto in A Minor.[97] Hitler finally decided that the program of the traveling orchestra, which eventually expanded to ten orchestras, would have programs from the music of German composers, including Johann Sebastian Bach, Gluck, Handel, Haydn, Mozart, Beethoven, the beloved Bruckner, and modern composers, whom he would select. Only music by German composers would be included on programs of Hitler's proposed "Mobile Reichs Orchestra."[98]

In July, 1908, Kubizek went home for the summer. Several letters and postcards, which Hitler sent to Kubizek during these months, have survived. Of particular importance for this study, were comments in which Hitler shared his concerns about architecture and his view of himself as an architect. For example, Hitler asked Kubizek to mail him a copy of Krakowitzer's *Guide to the Danube Town of Linz.* This request reflected his continued concern about the plans for the city. He also told Kubizek how stupid it was that the Parish Council decided to patch-up rather than rebuild the theatre in Linz. He suggested that if his handbook of architecture did not look so miserable, he would send it to the Council.[99] While Jetzinger makes much of the foolishness of such remarks by Hitler,[100] they may best be viewed as pent-up adolescent frustrations and not as signs of *dementia.* Kubizek knew he probably had no suitable designs for the Linz Council, but he did know of Hitler's dreams for the city and doubtlessly accepted his remarks in that context. Evidence for such speculation includes a design for a new concert hall in Linz and a sketch of the acoustical properties of the hall, which Kubizek had among his memorabilia of this period.[101]

In the autumn of 1908, Hitler again took the entrance examination at the Vienna Academy of Fine Arts. The same rector and faculty members gave him the second examination. Maser said Hitler did not pass the first portion of the examination, and, therefore, he could not submit the works he had painstakingly prepared under the tutelage of Panholzer, a Viennese sculptor with whom he had studied in preparation for the examination in 1908.[102] Maser suggested that several factors contributed to Hitler's second failure. He had lost his mother, had cut himself off from the rest of the family, and had taken "unwontedly rigorous and conventional training" from Panholzer "which had held back rather than developed his natural artistic talent."[103]

Kubizek assumed when he went to Vienna that Hitler was an art student at the Academy. He was unaware of Hitler's failure in the examination of 1907. The second examination was taken while Kubizek was away for a brief spell of military service following summer holidays. When Kubizek returned to Vienna, in November, he surprisingly found that Hitler had moved out of their apartment. Hitler:

...did not even leave an address, but fled the world that had known him and hid himself where none could find him—not least the Austrian military authorities who were thus unable to conscript him into the army.[104]

Hitler was evidently too ashamed of his failure to face Kubizek. It must have been difficult for him to give up the one true friend of his youth, but he did, and they did not see each other again for thirty years.

Even though he could not be a student at the academy, Hitler remained in Vienna until 1913. These, the saddest years of his life, were critical for the tempering of Hitler's world view.[105] By failing to accept him as a student, the state of Austria, vis-à-vis the Academy, had fulfilled the fears of his youth. For, as he said, in *Mein Kampf,* "Did we not know, even as little boys, that this Austrian state had and could have no love for us Germans?"[106]

Hitler claimed that he became a nationalist while at the *Realschule* in Linz and admired the Pan-Germanism movement founded by Ritter George von Schonerer. Many of Schonerer's beliefs paralleled interests of the young Hitler. Schonerer "venerated Wagner," rejected "the uncertainties and changes that characterized modern life," and "glorified the eternal verities represented by home, soil, Germanic culture and the Volk."[107] Schonerer and his followers were also anti-Semitic, but Hitler denied that he was aware of "organized opposition to the Jews" while in Linz.[108] Kubizek stated, however, that when he "met Adolf Hitler first, his anti-Semiticism was already pronounced."[109] If so, Hitler's interest in the Pan-German movement may have been an early reinforcement of his hatred of the Jews.

Dr. Leopold Poetsch, the history teacher at the Linz *Realschule,* was one of the major figures of the nationalist party. Hitler stated that Poetsch "used our budding nationalistic fanaticism as a means of educating us, frequently appealing to our sense of national honor." Under Poetsch Hitler came to the realization that:

...Germanism could be safeguarded only by the destruction of Austria, and, furthermore, that national sentiment is in no sense identical with dynastic patriotism; that above all the House of Hapsburg was destined to be the misfortune of the German national.[110]

When Hitler moved to Vienna, therefore, he was already fascinated with its architecture, much desirous of attending its art Academy, but full of hatred for its government and ruling family.

Hitler's ambivalence about Vienna was not peculiar to him, for as Bruno Walter wrote of Vienna in his biography of Mahler, every:

...outstanding personality brought up in the peculiar intellectual atmosphere of Vienna lived ever after in a dialectical syncretism of love and hatred for the city which offered splendid potentialities for the highest accomplishments, as well as the most stubborn resistance to their realization.[111]

Had Hitler been accepted by the Academy, he might have spent years encapsulated in a limited environment with his energies dedicated to the development of his artistic skills. As it was, the lack of matriculation gave him endless hours to immerse himself in the wealth of the negative and positive aspects of this remarkable city.

Kubizek believed Hitler was increasingly concerned about the social injustices in Vienna. A social consciousness drove Hitler to an erratic program of self education as he wandered the streets. He observed the terrible housing of the working class, which sharply contrasted with the sumptuous mansions of the wealthy. Kubizek stated the rather innocent civil concerns Hitler had about Linz expanded in response to the seriousness of the complex social problems of Vienna.[113] In his reflections on this period in *Mein Kampf*, Hitler stated that:

...the visual instruction of the Vienna streets had performed invaluable services. There came a time when I no longer, as in the first days, wandered blindly through the mighty city; now with open eyes I saw not only the buildings but also the people.[114]

Hitler's increased interest in social reforms paralleled his acceptance of the ideology of Dr. Karl Lueger and his Christian Social Party. Lueger, the mayor of Vienna, transformed Hitler's views with regard to anti-Semitism. His Viennese awakening to the "Jewish Question" caused him to purchase anti-Semitic pamphlets, observe Jews in the streets, acquaint himself with liberal and Zionist factions, and come to believe that Jews, by their very nature, had a negative effect upon the press, art, literature, and the theatre.[115]

When Hitler went to Vienna in the early months of 1908, it appeared that he had sufficient funds to live on. Kubizek, however, stated that meals were often missed in order to have money for concert and opera tickets. It is possible that such avid attendance of musical performances did put a considerable strain on their budget, for Kubizek claimed that they went to a performance every day. Hitler refused to sit in the gallery, where he believed young wenches interested only in flirting were given the front seats.[116] They, therefore, usually stood for the opera performances, as they had done in Linz. No women were allowed in this section. Hitler also "was always boiling over with indignation" because officers, whom he believed attended performances only to meet and seduce young women, paid less for tickets than he and Kubizek had to pay. Whatever the cause, Hitler implied in *Mein Kampf* that during this period he lived in abject poverty.[117] If so, his financial situation must have changed considerably sometime during 1908.

Jetzinger suggested that the patrimony which he had received was probably depleted sometime during 1908. He continued, however, to receive twenty-five kronen per month as orphan's pension. He had a small sum from his mother's estate, and this sum did not run out until sometime in 1909.[118] While it is difficult to ascertain Hitler's exact income during this time, and while he may have exaggerated his poverty in *Mein Kampf*, it is generally accepted that he did not live well while he was in Vienna.

The literature on Hitler's life from the autumn of 1908 until the autumn of 1909 has provided vague and sometimes conflicting evidence of his activities. It is clear, however, that he lived for eight months or so at 22 Felberstrasse and moved frequently thereafter. His residences included a room at 58 Sechshauser Strasse, from August 20 to September 16, 1909, and later a room on the Simon-Denk-Gasse.[119] Such movement reflected the unsettled nature of his life at this time, and perhaps his diminished funds.

Konrad Heiden wrote that, during the unusually cold winter of 1909, Hitler sank into bitterest misery and slept a few nights on park benches and in cafés. Hitler, at the end of his resources, found his way to the Meidling *dosshouse*. The Meidling home was "largely made possible by the endowment of the wealthy Jewish Epstein family."[121] Their generosity, and that of others in 1911, provided 710,000 portions of soup and bread to over 380,000 unfortunates in this shelter.[122] The city asylum helped some 94,000 persons during this year, and there were other shelters offering assistance. In light of the abject poverty of so many thousands of people, Hitler's condition was not exceptional.

At the *dosshouse* Hitler was provided a bath, a bed with wire springs covered with two sheets, and bread and soup. He, like all residents, was expected to stay only a few nights and search for work during the days. The habituees of the home instructed Hitler how to extend his stay and find other sources of free food in Vienna. He worked for awhile at the Westbanhof carrying baggage for the passengers for a few pennies. In *Mein Kampf* Hitler stated that in his Vienna years, possibly during this period of his difficulty, he was "forced to earn a living, first as day laborer, then as a small painter." He also stated that he grew hard when thrown into a world of misery and poverty among those for whom he would later fight.[123]

At the Meidling refuge, he met Reinhold Hanisch, a down-and-out artist from Berlin. Whereas Kubizek described Hitler as "a strange, awkward, violent youth, brimming with ideas, composing an opera, writing poems, reading voluminously, studying architecture with a frightening intensity," one year later, Hanisch, a new friend, found him a "little more than the husk of himself." Hanisch stated that Hitler had on one occasion "approached a drunk and begged for a few pennies," but in a statement drawn up in 1914 to explain why he had failed to register for military service, Hitler stated that he was "too proud to accept it (help) from anyone, let alone beg for it."[124] He had never been so miserable in his life. In a mindless state, incapable of ordering his own life, he apparently forgot about his pension of 25 kronen per month, which would have permitted him to eat regularly.[125]

On August 22, 1909, Hitler complied with state regulations and registered his new residence on Sechshauserstrasse with the police. At that time he called himself a writer. He was evidently persuaded by the examination of 1908 that he would never be an art student of the Vienna Academy and decided to concentrate his creative energies on writing.

Sometime during those days at the Meidling *dosshouse*, however, Hitler had confided to Hanisch that he was a painter. Hitler was insulted when Hanisch assumed he was a house painter and assured him he should be able to find work in that trade. Hitler informed Hamisch he was an academician and artist. Hanisch urged Hitler to write to his family for money to buy art supplies. His benefactor, probably his Aunt Johanna, replied with approximately fifty kronen. Hanisch promised to sell any pictures Hitler produced.[126]

Sometime in December, 1909, Hitler and Hanisch moved to the Maennerheim, a Home for Men, at 27 Meldemannstrasse, near the Jewish quarter known as Leopolestadt. Residents paid two kronen and eighty heller a week for one of the 544 cubicles which contained a bed with a mattress, a bolster stuffed with horsehair, two sheets, a double blanket and chamber pot.[127] They could eat in the vast dining room, which seated 352 men at once, enjoy lounges, a reading room, a writing room, a shower room, a laundry, and a canteen. They could cook their own meals in a communal kitchen, have their clothes repaired and cleaned by a resident tailor, and store their valuables in a basement locker.

The major inconvenience of the home was the requirement that the bedrooms be used only for sleeping during the night hours, unless one was employed during the night hours. This arrangement forced residents without jobs to go to other facilities of the home or into the streets during the daylight hours. Hitler's job, largely due to the insistence of Hanisch and the financial support of his Aunt Johanna, became painting. Since the Mannerheim would not permit Hitler to paint in his room during the day, he set up a work area near a window in the lounge. There, he made detailed copies of postcards and prints. A partially finished watercolor of Neulenback Castle, dated 1912 (?) by Price, possibly gives some insight into Hitler's painting process.[128] The unfinished portions are sketched in pencil. The finished portions show that Hitler's had great control of his techniques—filling in the predrawn lines. Payne believed that "to give them a pleasant old-fashioned quality he would hold them near a fire until they turned brown or sepia."[129] Most of his works of this period are of buildings, but he also did landscapes, portraits in oil, ink or watercolor and further, advertisements for cosmetics, shoes, shoe polish and even ladies' underwear.[130] By his own estimate, Hitler painted between 700 and 800 works in Vienna.[131] Most of them, without a doubt, were painted at his work table in the Maennerheim lounge.

As late as 1942, Hitler insisted that "real artists are not the product of traditional academic schooling, but training in the shops of the great masters."[132] Hitler, unable to go to the Academy, created his private "shop of the masters" by the window in the Maennerheim lounge. Although he claimed his style "was not the product of any single influence, but rather the sum of all that came before him, his style consciously reflected works of earlier artists." The masters he copied were artists of the nineteenth century. Of these, he called Rudolf von Alt his teacher. [133] As Chancellor of the Third Reich, he collected works by Alt to be hung in the great museum he planned to build in Linz and arranged for Alt's family in Vienna to receive a state pension. [134]

In *Mein Kampf* Hitler suggested that he painted during this period merely as a way to have free time to read and study so one day he could fulfill his dream of being an architect. As he said:

I painted to make a living and studied for pleasure. Thus I was able to supplement my visual instruction in the social problem by theoretical study. I studied more or less all the books I was able to obtain regarding this whole field, and for the rest immersed myself in my own thoughts.

Amid all this, as was only natural, I served my love of architecture with ardent zeal. Along with music, it seems to be the queen of the arts: under such circumstances my concern with it was not 'work,' but the greatest pleasure. I could read and draw until late into the night, and never grow tired. Thus my faith grew that my beautiful dream for the future would become reality after all, even though this might require long years I was firmly convinced that I should some day make a name for myself as an architect. [135]

Hitler was particularly impressed with architecture which exhibited "eternal values." Structures with such values "contained mixed elements of classicism, the Renaissance and the Baroque—all of which were amalgamated in the 'Vienna Ring Style.' "[136] This style was employed by architects of "a vast complex of buildings and private dwellings" occupying "a broad belt of land separating the old inner city from its suburbs."[137] This land had been opened by the abolition of the city's ramparts which Emperor Franz Joseph had ordered in 1857. Between 1860 and 1890 twelve important public buildings were erected along the Ringstrasse. These massive expressions of 19th century imperial power had captured Hitler's attention during his first trip to Vienna in 1906. There can be little doubt that the impact of the Ringstrasse Style upon Hitler was potent, and it "may well have been the most significant architectural experience of Hitler's youth."[138]

With great care he repeatedly painted Ringstrasse buildings such as Gottfried Semper's Burgtheater, Heinrich Ferstel's Votive Church and University, Friedrich Schmidt's City Hall, Theophil Hansen's Parliament, and other Viennese buildings.[139] Hanisch hawked Hitler's works in antique shops and in restaurants in the Prater pleasure grounds. He also sold Hitler's pictures to a framer, who wanted pictures to showoff his frames, and to furniture dealers, who inserted the postcard size paintings in the backs of chairs and love seat and varnished over them.[140] Most of Hitler's pictures of this period sold for five kronen to a dealer, and occasionally, an original Hitler work brought ten kronen. Profits had to be split with Hanisch, however.

It has been estimated that by the beginning of March, 1909, Hitler was turning out two or three works a day. Hanisch complained that Hitler was lazy, would only work when he wanted to do so, and would not respond to his prodding to be more productive.[141] Evidently Hanisch had little trouble selling Hitler's works and could have sold more had Hitler been more willing to increase his output. Their partnership, based upon splitting the profits equally, lasted eight months and ended when Hitler had Hanisch arrested for cheating him out of his share of a painting of the Parliament Building, which he believed to be worth fifty kronen, and another watercolor worth nine kronen. He also maliciously informed the court that Hanisch was living under an assumed name, a point irrelevant to the case but indicative of a vindictive attribute in Hitler's character.[142]

Hanisch spent eight days in jail, but Hitler withdrew the charge regarding the watercolor worth nine kronen when it was proven Hanisch had sold the work and appropriately shared the profits. The fate of the painting of the Parliament Building is unclear, but a painter named Greiner, who lived in the Home for Men with the parties concerned, testified that the work was certainly not worth Hitler's estimated value of fifty kronen.[143]

Hitler's last encounter with Hanisch came in 1913, when Hitler was delivering a watercolor to a customer. Almost twenty years later Hanisch sold libelous stories to journalists which eventually reached Konrad Heiden, an early Hitler biographer.[144] Hanisch also provided information for a pamphlet entitled "Hitler wie er wuklich est!," which was published by the *Verlag Novina* in Bratislava, and which apparently denounced Hitler.[145] When Hitler seized power in 1933, Hanisch approached NSDAP members with insinuations that he could help them please the Fuehrer by providing them with knowledge of Hitler's artistic tastes and his great appreciation of Gottfried Semper. In 1936, Hanisch was arrested by the Gestapo. Maser suggested that the cause for his arrest was the libelous stories he spread about Hitler. Smith believed, however, that Hanisch was arrested because he had copied Hitler's paintings and sold them throughout Europe through a man named Jacques Weiss. Hanisch was found dead in his cell on February 4, 1937, apparently from a heart attack. There were rumors both that he had been killed on orders "from Berlin" and that "he had hanged himself."[146]

It is difficult to say with regard to the Hitler-Hanisch relationship who was used and who was the user. What can be said is that it was Hanisch who made it possible for Hitler to say:

In the years 1909 and 1910, my own situation had changed somewhat in so far as I no longer had to earn my daily bread as a common laborer....I painted to make a living...[147]

Hitler's position at his work table in the Maennerheim lounge made him readily available for discussions or arguments with other residents. Occasionally, Hitler took the opportunity to orate on the virtues of Wagner or his own views on art. It was also not uncommon for Hitler to take part in discussions about schemes for "separating the public from its money."[148]

Increasingly, however, Hitler engaged in debates related to his renewed interest in politics. For example, his fascination with the film entitled *The Tunnel*, which dealt with the success of a demagogue, led to much haranguing with his companions in the home.[149] Hitler was, at this time, working out his own political views and reevaluating Lueger's Christian Social Party. He was overcome with emotion as he watched the funeral procession of Lueger on March 10, 1910. Hitler had been fascinated with Lueger, who advocated social reform and possessed great gifts in controlling a party which appealed to the masses. The evolution of the party under Lueger's lieutenants provoked much debate in the Maennerheim reading room. Evidence indicates that during these great Vienna discussions, Hitler violently denounced the Social Democratic Party, the party he would work to eradicate with his rise to power.[150]

The companions of the reading room, like Kubizek before them, gave opportunities for Hitler to test his oratorical skills and his powers of persuasion. He was not always well received, he was often insulted, but he never desisted. Hanisch said when he returned home in the evenings, he often had to take the T square out of Hitler's hand because "he would be swinging it over his head making a speech."[151]

Joseph Neumann, a Jewish part-time art dealer, often came by the Maennerheim to buy paintings and other art goods produced by its residents. Hitler and Neumann became friends and at one point discussed going to Germany together.[152] They did stay together for one week in another hotel, supposedly so Hitler could briefly escape Hanisch's persistent taunting for more of Hitler's paintings. Once the Hitler-Hanisch partnership was dissolved, Neumann sold some of Hitler's works.[153] Hitler also sold his works to Jewish dealers named Altenberg, Morgenstern, and Landsburger. To this list of dealers Price added the name of Schwertfeger.[154]

Peter Jahn, an art historian and art dealer, helped the NSDAP locate Hitler's paintings after his rise to power. Jahn found some of Hitler's works in Altenberg's Art and Frame shop, but Morgenstern was particularly helpful in this party venture. Jahn found that "Morgenstern's shop was Hitler's major source of income" in his Vienna years, and "the dealer was very fair to him." Hitler himself told Jahn that "Morgenstern had been his 'savior' and had given him many important commissions.[155] Hitler was doubtlessly referring to such commissions as the *Salzburg Land Cycle*, seventeen of which are shown in Price's collection.[156] These works are dated 1909 and must have been a commission which Hanisch arranged with Morgenstern. Jahn pointed out that "Hitler did some of his finest work for Morgenstern's customers, including a particularly lovely watercolor of the Karls Church, and others of the Scotch Church, St. Stephens, the City Hall, and the Opera." Price's collection contains many copies of each of these buildings, several of which have Morgenstern's stamp on the back.[157] There are only two works in Price's collection which are views of the interior of buildings. One of these, *Interior of the Franciscan Church*, was commissioned by Morgenstern.[158]

In the period of 1910 and 1911, Hitler's financial situation was so secure that he was in danger of exceeding the limit of 1,400 kronen annual income for Maennerheim residents. He was once more receiving his orphan's pension of twenty-five kronen a month and his paintings were providing a monthly income of about seventy kronen. His half-sister, Angela, had evidently learned that Adolf had received an inheritance from his Aunt Johanna Poelzl and had suggested to the court that she needed Adolf's pension to care for Paula.[159]

It may have been Hitler's financial security, stemming essentially from the sale of his paintings, which encouraged him to once more approach the Academy. He went with portfolio in hand to Professor Ritschel of the Hofmuseum and asked the professor to recommend his admission to the Academy. The works which he presented to Ritschel were done "with great architectural precision." There is no record of a formal application to the Academy in 1910.[160]

Hitler stayed at the Maennerheim for nearly three years after his break with Hanisch, and continued to paint at his regular spot by the window. He was:

...generally respected by his companions because he was a veteran in the home and had some of the mystique of an artist. He was polite to everyone, but his politeness never gave way to familiarity. He was reserved, and he was also remote, letting no one come too close. When spoken to, he replied courteously; when someone was in trouble he responded, but in general he was content to paint and mind his own business.[161]

This calm demeanor was often broken, however, by violent harangues over some political issue.

In May, 1913, with eighty kronen in his pocket, he crossed the border into Germany bound for Munich. Scholars have given much attention to Hitler's reasons for leaving Vienna and his reasons for the selection of Munich as his new home. Payne thought Hitler left Vienna because a man:

...can go mad after living three years in the Maennerheim, and indeed he was close to madness, fits of depression alternating with periods of manic excitement, violent speeches, sudden quarrels. There were days and weeks when he could no longer paint postcards or go on his rounds to the Jewish art dealers who bought his works out of pity and were not able to conceal their pity. By the autumn of 1912 he was once more in financial difficulties[162]

Hitler led Karl Hanisch, a companion at the Home for Men, to believe that he planned to "apply for admission to the Art Academy" in Munich. In *Mein Kampf*, however, he stated that he left Austria "primarily for political reasons," as he "did not want to fight for the Habsburg state."[163] Fest suggested that since Hitler moved to Munich, rather than Berlin, the capital of the Reich, "he was guided by romantic and artistic impulses far more than political motives."[164] It is true that Hitler saw Munich as the "Metropolis of German Art." He was attracted to Munich's "wonderful marriage of primordial power and fine artistic mood." He was glad to be away from

Vienna, "the Babylon of races," and among Lower Bavarians, who spoke the dialect of his childhood. He would later call his time in Munich before the war, "the happiest and by far the most contented of my life."[165]

In Munich, Hitler took lodgings with Josef Popp, a tailor. The tailor's children "liked the nice man who lived upstairs." His room, which cost twenty marks a month, "was pleasant, well furnished, and had a private entrance from the street." The Popps testified to Hitler's solitary existence during his Munich years. According to them, Hitler usually spent his time "at home with his nose buried in heavy books. In between times he painted."[166] Frau Popp once asked him "what all his reading had to do with his painting. He smiled, took her by the arm, and said: 'Dear Frau Popp, does anyone know what is and what isn't likely to be of use to him in life?' "[167]

Hitler set up his work table by the window in his room and copied photography, most often in watercolour but occasionally in oils. He sold his pictures mostly to the Kunsthandlung shops on the Maximilianstrasse. A baker, whose shop was near Hitler's dwelling, and who purchased two of his paintings, stated that Hitler's works sold for ten to twenty marks each.[168] He sold numerous pictures of the municipal registry office behind St. Peter's Church to newly wed couples leaving the building.[169] Among the surviving works of Hitler's Munich years is a commissioned oil floral arrangement, which he painted for a Dr. von Doebner. Upon delivery of the work, it was criticized for its brightness, but Hitler received his money when he convinced von Doebner the work was appropriate for the location for which it was painted.[170]

Most of the works from Hitler's Munich period which appear in Price's collection, are of buildings in and near Munich. These include several watercolors of the Royal Opera, the Munich Registry, the Hofbrauhaus, the Munich Old Courtyard, in whose fountain Hitler reputedly washed his brushes, and various buildings around the Marienplatz, such as the Old City Hall, St. Peter's Church, and the Felderrnhalle.[171] These works, and others which have survived from his Munich years, reflect no essential change in Hitler's painting technique from the work done in Vienna. He was not a part of the artistic experimentation of other artists who also lived in the Schwabing neighborhood, such as Vassily Kandinsky, Franz Marc, and Paul Klee.

Hitler was summoned to present himself for military service in Linz, on January 20, 1914. The Austro-Hungarian Consulate-General had been requested by the Linz Police to assure Hitler's response. The summons was not served until January 18, when he was promptly arrested. He then requested a postponement until February 5. The negative response to his request was not received until after January 20. Hitler then wrote a long letter to the Linz Police pleading poverty of funds to reach Linz and permission to report instead to Salzburg. The letter was signed, "Adolf Hitler, Artist." A cover letter by the Munich Consul-General confirmed Hitler's poverty and included the suggestion that Hitler believed himself unfit physically for service. Indeed, that was just the findings of the Salzburg Recruitment Panel when Hitler reported there on February 5, 1914.[172]

In 1938, with the annexation of Austria, Hitler demanded that the Gauleiter of Linz locate the dossier on his successful avoidance of conscription into the Austrian army. Upon discovery that the file was missing, the Gestapo was given responsibility for its location. Jetzinger, later author of *Hitler's Youth*, was a professor in Linz during that time. He was interrogated about the file, falsely reported it contained nothing unfavorable about Hitler, and later found the file in his own attic. Jetzinger realized the Gestapo would not have believed its discovery after the fact, and, therefore, he kept silent about evidence which Hitler believed would have proved him a draft-dodger.[173]

On June 28, 1914, a young Serbian shot Archduke Franz Ferdinand and set in motion the chain of events that brought about World War I. The remarkable change in Hitler's attitude toward military service which then took place appeared to validate his assertion that he avoided military service because he "did not want to fight for the Habsburg State."[174] A picture taken in the Odeonplatz in Munich, on August 1, 1914, showed Hitler, "his eyes shining, his face radiant with gladness and excitement," as he greeted the news of the declaration of war.[175] He decided to "leave his books," and on August 3, 1914, he submitted a petition to King Ludwig III in which he requested permission to enter a Bavarian regiment.[176] On August 16, Hitler joined the List Regiment. Following a training period he was posted to France in mid-October, where he served as a runner between the regimental staff and the advanced positions.

During lulls between dispatches, Hitler "could be found with his sketch pad on his knee and a T square and a box of watercolors within reach."[177] Most of Hitler's paintings of the war years show buildings devastated by shelling with roofs caving in and the streets littered with rubble. Not unlike his 1913 copy of Walter Hoy's *Convent Ruins*, are six views of the cloister ruins at Messines, which he did in 1914 and 1915.[178] Interestingly, four of these works, three in pencil and one in pen and ink, were drawn on field postcards. There are works in this period such as his pen and ink with a colored wash of his *Quarters in Fournes*,[179] which shows a continuance of his careful handling of linear detail. In general, however, his landscapes, sketches, and drawings are more spontaneous and may even be called impressionistic. Certainly, his view of the trench near Wytschaete, where his regiment had its bloodiest battle on October 20, 1914, is thoroughly impressionistic. The change in his style may have been due to the "presence and perhaps encouragement of ten academic painters in his Munich regiment."[180] An examination of several of his early landscapes also shows that his work may have been moving back to use of impressionistic techniques.[181] Whatever elements of this style were apparent in his early period, they had been increasingly pushed aside as he copied older, realistic artists' works to make a living in Vienna and Munich. His military service relieved his talent of economic strictures and his style became more natural and spontaneous.

Scholars generally accept evidence that Hitler was a good soldier in World War I. On August 4, 1914, he received the Iron Cross Second Class, along with an orderly named Bachmann, for protecting with his own body the life of Lieutenant Colonel Engelhart. In September, 1917, he was given the Cross of Military Merit, Third Class, with swords. In May, 1918, he was granted the regimental certificate for bravery in face of the enemy. The greatest of his medals, awarded on August 4, 1918, was the Iron Cross First Class, which was "seldom awarded to enlisted men." Only a few days after he received the Iron Cross First Class, he was given the Medal of Military Service Third Class.[182]

He was wounded sometime early in October, 1916, when a shell splinter hit his face, and a second wound, later that month, sent him back to Germany in a hospital train. Hitler had been fighting continually for two years. On March 1, 1917, he returned to his own regiment. On October 13, 1918, a drumfire of gas shells spilled chlorine gas into the trenches. He carried his last dispatch back to regimental headquarters the next morning. Within days, he was completely blinded and sent to the Pasewalk hospital near Stetlin. His four years of dehumanizing trench warfare were over.[183]

The doctors at Pasewalk were able to get Hitler past the initial burning in the eyeballs and to the point of seeing shapes and outlines within a week. By November 21, he was discharged from the hospital. During his stay there, the war-weary Reich began to fall apart, domestic revolutions broke out, Germany surrendered in defeat, the German imperial monarch was deposed, the Fatherland became a republic, and Hitler decided to go into politics.

Scholars have given considerable attention to Hitler's reaction to the gas poisoning and the turn of political events. Binion, for example, presented a lengthy unsubstantiated account of Dr. Edmund Forster, ranking psychiatrist at Pasewalk, who "officially put Hitler's blindness down to psychopathic hysteria."[184] Binion himself believed Hitler's politics was his anti-Semitism and his anti-Semitism was caused by:

...his reaction against his guilt for his mother's agony of 1907 following Bloch's ministrations that he prompted. That reaction, long repressed, was released by a gas poisoning reminiscent of his mother's agony—a reminder of traumatic intensity that impelled him to relive the unassimilated experience behind it. Such traumatic reliving involves patterned revisions of the original experience—reversals, and tendencies both to undo the outcome and to carry it to its final consequences. Poisoning the poisoner was a reversal; to undo mother Germany's demise was Hitler's ostensible aim; the culprits of 1907 both came to grief the second time around. But these revisions were subordinate to Hitler's straight reliving through his dire false cure for Germany's supposed mortal ailment. That reliving was no less straight for his assuming Bloch's old role on top of his own, beginning with the 'operation' he ordered in 1938 'to cleanse the German world of the Jewish poison.'[185]

However, both Maser and Payne reject insinuations that Hitler's blindness was hysterical. Maser argued that "some 400 such cases were admitted within the space of a few days." Payne admitted, however, that Hitler probably suffered more psychologically than physically during this time, and he:

...fell into a deep depression characterized by fits of weeping and periods of withdrawl, when he simply turned his face to the wall and spoke to no one, terrified by the thought that he might never see clearly again, that he had lost whatever usefulness he once possessed, and that he had nothing to live for. The war was coming to an end in total defeat for Germany, and the thought of all the vain sacrifice of countless troops only deepened his depression.[186]

In *Mein Kampf,* Hitler described his feelings about his blindness and his reaction to Germany's defeat. His eyes had begun to improve, although he was sure he would never draw again, when "the monstrous thing happened." On November 10, a pastor came to the hospital to psychologically prepare the patients for the imminent surrender of Germany and the establishment of a German republic. Hitler listened to the pastor until, as he said:

...I could stand it no longer. It became impossible for me to sit still one minute more. Again everything went black before my eyes; I tottered and groped my way back to the dormitory, threw myself on the bunk, and dug my burning head into my blanket and pillow.[187]

As Toland concluded, this relapse into blindness appeared to have no medical origin.[188] It may logically be accepted that his second period of blindness was induced as a result of the traumatic news announced by the visiting pastor. His beloved Germany was defeated, and so was he.

In 1906, with Kubizek, Hitler had stood on the Freinberg hill with the music of Wagner's *Rienzi* swirling in his head and had spoken of the day he would be called by his people to lead them out of slavery to freedom. In 1918, blinded, with the pastor's words of Germany's defeat burning in his head, he once more heard the messianic call. His fate became known to him. As he stated, "The great vacillating of my life, whether I should enter politics or remain an architect, came to an end. That night I resolved that, if I recovered my sight, I would enter politics."[189] As Toland stressed, on "That night in the lonely ward at Pasewalk the most portentous force of the twentieth century was born. Politics had come to Hitler, not Hitler to politics."[190] Fest believed the disillusionment Hitler suffered because of Germany's defeat:

...was as sudden and incomprehensible as had been his failure to win acceptance into the Academy. He magnified it into a legend and made it one of the basic themes of his career. Later he ascribed his resolve to enter politics to this moment. In virtually every major speech Hitler would ritualistically refer to the November revolution. He would speak of it as if his whole life dated from that event. This obsession has led some analysts to suggest that the revolution triggered the great political awakening of his life.[191]

At this moment in his life Hitler believed as his beloved Wagner had believed, that whenever "the statesman despairs, the politician gives up, the socialist vexes himself with fruitless systems, and even the philosopher can only interpret but cannot prophesy," then the artist will intervene to save the situation.[192] In autobiographical reflection he would later write in *Mein Kampf* "It nearly always takes some stimulus to bring the genius on the scene. The hammer-stroke of Fate which throws one man to the ground suddenly strikes steel in another."[193]

Prior to his entrance into political life, it is beyond dispute that Adolf Hitler thought of himself as an artist. It was a dream that sustained him during his lonely, alienated youth and a pose by which he identified himself to the world. The dream of being an artist was also the source of his greatest disappointments and frustrations during his youth. It led to conflict with his father, alienation from his beloved mother, when he went to Vienna, and pain and frustration, when he was twice rejected by the Vienna Academy. It was during this period that Adolf Hitler's artistic *Weltanschauung* was found. As will be seen later, this *Weltanschauung* was responsible, at least in part, for the monstrosity that was the Third Reich.

By any standard of aesthetic judgment, Adolf Hitler was not a great artist or perhaps even a good artist. What one sees in his work is merely the result of an above-average commercial artist. Adolf Hitler was a competent draftsman who was quite facile in working with the difficult medium of watercolors. His works are consistent over the entire picture area and show painstaking attention to subtle details. From a sample of Hitler's watercolors reproduced by Price, one can deduce that Hitler worked section by section rather than on the entire picture area at once. It must be remembered that much of Hitler's work was not done from nature but from pictures he copied while living in Vienna and Munich. They were the type of sentimental works that were used to fill out a picture frame or to decorate a recessed section of a sofa. His repetitious, hurriedly turned out works were often sold on the streets and, in Munich, to newlyweds leaving the licensing bureau.

The subjects of his compositions are not original. While they allowed him to utilize to the fullest his abilities as a draftsman, they are devoid of any of the influences and directions usually associated with the schools of modern art. Hitler's works are petit-bourgeoise as this was understood in Austria during the last half of the nineteenth century.

To the end of World War I, Hitler's paintings reveal no signs of psychological difficulties. They do reveal, as he was told by the Academy judges, that he was unable to execute human figures at the same level of competence with which he painted buildings and landscapes. This may indicate a psychological inability to relate or to empathize with people. This in itself is consistent with his early life as a shy, introverted youth. However, this in itself is no indication of psychopathology. It simply means he was unable to or did not prefer to execute human figures. If it is indeed true, even within wide limits, that art reveals the artist, Adolf Hitler was not at this point psychopathic or psychotic. As will be seen later, the trauma that produced the monster of the Third Reich is often associated with the defeat of his beloved "Mutterland" in World War I. The classical Freudian analysis of Adolf Hitler cannot grow out of what is known of his early life or his paintings. It is much better and certainly more consistent with his life and art to understand him by means of an Adlerian model which views his behavior as an effort to compensate for an inferiority complex.

Hitler delighted in referring to himself as an architect, and even during the last days of the Third Reich he still used architecture as a mental escape mechanism from his impending doom. Prior to World War I, it is known that he designed houses for the beloved Stefanie and another for himself and Kubizek. He also drew sketches for other structures in Linz and Vienna. None of these exhibit the megalomania and monumentality quite apparent in certain public structures of the Third Reich. As will be seen later, Hitler was quite prepared to build or accept plans for private homes and factories which were modern and functional, during the Third Reich. If megalomania and monumentality are to be taken as signs of mental aberration, one may assert that these do not appear in the work of the prepolitical Adolf Hitler.

Musically, there was nothing exceptional in the life of the young Adolf Hitler. When he attended the school attached to the Benedictine monastery in Lambach, he became fascinated with the ecclesiastical music and took singing lessons so he could sing in the choir. He particularly enjoyed the ritual and ceremony of the services. In these early years he became enamored with Wagner's operas as an example of the ceremonial and symbolic use that could be made of music. Hitler was not only enthralled personally by Wagner's operas but also saw in them the very pulse of the German people. Throughout his life, he listened to music, utilized it to advance his political career, and sought to use it to create his vision of the Volkish Gemeinschaft. As a youth he briefly studied piano. He used these skills when he tried to write an opera based on a subject which Wagner had worked on but not completed. There can be little doubt that Wagner was the major musical force of his life. His classical musical taste was limited primarily to great operatic and orchestral works by German composers. As will be seen later, he enjoyed certain types of lighter music as well.

This artistic *Weltanschauung* of the youthful Adolf Hitler provided the soil out of which grew, in the years after World War I, the fullbodied artistic *Weltanschauung* of the Chancellor of the Third Reich. It is now necessary to turn to a discussion of Hitler's artistic development during the period of the *Partei-Kampf* and his rule during the Third Reich. These years altered, modified, and sharpened his artistic *Weltanschauung* and saw its imposition on the Third Reich.

Chapter 3
The Artist-Politician

On November 19, 1918, Adolf Hitler was discharged from Pasewalk Hospital, where he had made a firm decision to enter politics. The following year, he found a political party which he gradually molded to suit his political ideology and which, by 1933, brought him to the Chancellorship of Germany's Third Reich. He carried into the years of the *Partei-Kampf* a well-defined *Weltanschauung*, which was further refined by like-minded individuals with whom he came into contact. His Volkish ideology found an immediate response among those Germans who wanted to believe in Aryan cultural supremacy and were willing to see the Jews as the cause of Germany's humiliating defeat in the World War. His oratorical power, his Wagnerian sense of the dramatic, his artistic skills, his understanding of propaganda, and his organizational skills, all played a part in Hitler's ascent to power.

Hitler left Pasewalk Hospital with orders to report to the replacement battalion of his regiment in Munich. His excellent war record resulted in his retention in the German army, the Reichwehr, which by the stipulations of the Versailles Treaty of June 28, 1919, was limited to 100,000 members. In February, 1919, he volunteered for guard duty at the prisoner-of-war camp at Traunstein and was then transferred to 2 Demobilization Company of 2 Bavarian Infantry Regiment. By early March, the camp was closed and Hitler was back in Munich.

Several of Hitler's army friends so praised his front-line art works, that sometime in 1919, he went to Max Zaeper for an opinion of his recent works. Zaeper, a well-known and highly esteemed artist, was so impressed by Hitler's work that he sought a second opinion from Professor Ferdinand Staeger, who stated Hitler's paintings showed exceptional talent. There is no evidence that the comments on his work by Zaeper and Staeger encouraged Hitler enough to cause him to further pursue a career in painting, but Maser mentioned that after 1918, his works were sometimes sold by his former army friend, Hans Mend.[1] Price's collection of Hitler's art works contains only two works which may be from the year 1919, and they appear to be unworthy of Staeger's praise. In later years, Hitler bought six of Staeger's works, but he never met the artist until he came to power. At that time, Staeger painted Hitler's portrait.[2]

Hitler's company commander, Captain Karl Mayr, had meanwhile selected Hitler to be a member of a so-called Enlightened Commando unit, which was organized to investigate subversive political activities among the troops and to infiltrate workers' organizations.[3] Between June 5 and 12, 1919, he took an anti-Bolshevist education course at Munich University in Civic Thinking, in preparation for his new duties. There, Hitler met politically like-minded comrades who agreed with his view that only an entirely new movement could answer the needs of the country.

Hitler's ideology was reinforced by the lectures delivered by the Munich historian, Alexander von Müller, during the training course.[4] Both Müller and Hitler believed that all positive products of civilization are rooted in the soil. Hitler and Müller both used the Bavarian dialect and expressions with emotive content such as "rooted in the soil," "the ardent German," and "the demoralizing influence of Jewry."[5]

Hitler also attended lectures by Gottfried Feder, whose "interest slavery" theories reinforced his anti-Semitism.[6] Feder's influence was apparent in a letter which Captain Mayr asked Hitler to write in response to questions raised by Adolf Gemlech, who had attended the course of study with Hitler. In his letter, dated September 16, 1919, Hitler stated that the Jewish lust for money and power had caused citizens to be yoked with interest payments, which in turn had aroused anti-Semitic feelings. He argued that the emotional reaction to anti-Semitism only resulted in pogroms, but the logical reaction should be "the systematic combatting and elimination of Jewish privileges," while "the ultimate goal would implacably be the total removal of the Jew." Although the expression "total removal" should not be equated with the Nazi's "final solution" for the Jewish people, its use, nevertheless, revealed the depth of Hitler's anti-Semitism at this time.[7]

In September of 1919, Hitler began his assigned duty as an investigator of the nearly fifty organizations which had sprung up in Munich with programs for political and social change. He twice was ordered to attend meetings of the German Workers' Party which was founded by Anton Drexler and Hermann Esser. At the second meeting, he spoke out vehemently, for fifteen minutes, against a professor's suggestion that Bavaria should be separated from Prussia. Drexler was profoundly impressed with Hitler's logic and oratorical skills, and as Hitler left the meeting, he pressed into Hitler's hand a forty-page pamphlet which he had compiled on his political beliefs. During that sleepless night, as he watched the mice in his room feed on the morsels of food he had placed on the floor for them, Hitler read Drexler's pamphlet and found his political mooring. Unimpressed by the next meeting, he remained undecided about joining the group. Nevertheless, he continued to be drawn to the basic beliefs of the party and saw its lack of solidification as an opportunity for him to mold it to suit his own political needs. High ranking military officials encouraged Hitler to join the organization, even though members of the new army were legally denied party affiliation. They believed Germany's military power could only be built with the help of the workers, and they wanted Hitler to build up the party to that end.[8]

In the next few months, Hitler was put in charge of party propaganda and became the driving force for the growth of party membership and funds. He personally helped with the preparation of invitations to party meetings, stressed the value of announcements of meetings in the *Münchener Beobachter*, developed the use of party slogans and leaflets and, in a radical move, insisted on the collection of a one mark fee for attendance at the meetings. With the increased funds and the financial support of Captain Mayr, Hitler acquired a party office and a paid business manager. He gradually changed the small debating society into a political party.

The first major step in the development of the party came on February 24, 1920. On that date, almost 2,000 people attended a meeting in the *Festsaal* of the *Hofbräuhaus* on the Platzl in Munich.[9] The presence of an estimated 1,000 Communists and Independents provoked shouts and skirmishes, which were gradually suppressed by Hitler's war comrades, other supporters, and Hitler's oratory. During a two and one-half hour speech, he presented a twenty-five point program which he and Drexler had drawn up. Hitler skillfully presented the program, point by point, and asked the audience to pronounce personal judgment on each item. Hitler understood that in a mass meeting the individual:

...while becoming a supporter of a young movement, feels lonely and easily succumbs to the fear of being alone, for the first time gets the picture of a larger community, which in most people has a strengthening, encouraging effect.[10]

Point twenty-three of the program which Hitler presented stated:

We demand legal action against those tendencies in art and literature that have a disruptive influence upon life of our folk, and that any organization that offends against the foregoing demands shall be dissolved.[11]

Point twenty-five called for a central authority to promulgate the laws which would be needed to uphold the demands of point twenty-three. The kernal of the artistic policies of the Third Reich thus appeared in the earliest days of Hitler's political life.

The night this twenty-five point program was passed was a joyful night for Hitler, for his political views had found approval. He knew he had kindled a fire "from whose flame one day the sword must come which would regain freedom for the Germanic Siegfried and life for the German nation."[12] One week later, the name of the party was changed to the *Nationalsocialistische Deutsche Arbeiterpartei* (NSDAP).

On April 1, 1920, Hitler left the army determined to seize the leadership of the NSDAP and to build the party according to his own ideas. It is assumed that he lived on money from the party funds, but he spent little on himself. He moved into a two-room apartment on Thierschstrasse, which had a bed, a table, two chairs, a bookcase and little more. He lived in these two rooms, reached by climbing a creaking stairway to the second floor of a rundown house, until 1929. Although he supposedly had given up art for politics, his friend Hanfstaengl visited his apartment and reported seeing "a lot of illustrations and drawings on the wall."[13]

In the early years of the party, several key figures made varied and critical contributions to Hitler and his rise to power. Dietrich Eckart was an early party member who had a profound personal effect upon Hitler and who, among other things, made a musical contribution to the party. Eckart was a poet, a playwright, and a journalist by profession. His early works included romantic poems and a successful translation of *Peer Gynt*.[14] The defeat of Germany in World War I made him a violent chauvinist. Thereafter, he produced such essays as *Thoughts on the Chaos of Our Time* and brochures such as *That Is the Jew*. In 1918, he began publication of a weekly paper called *Auf gut Deutsch*. He became a member of the Thule Society, which used the swastika as its official symbol and had as its racist motto "Remember that you are German. Keep your blood pure."[15]

In 1919, Eckart spoke at a meeting of the German Workers' Party and soon joined the group. He befriended Hitler and took him under his wing. He improved Hitler's appearance and manners and introduced him to wealthy and influential people with the whispered comment, "This is the man who will one day liberate Germany."[16] With 30,000 marks from various prominent people, 60,000 marks from General von Epp, and his personal note of 100,000 marks for the paper's debts, Eckart arranged for the party to purchase the *Völkische Boebachter,*, formerly the *Münchener Beobachter,* for 180,000 marks. On December 17, 1920, it became the official newspaper of the party, with Eckart as the editor. Sometime after 1922, Hanfstaengl loaned a thousand dollars to the party, which "enabled Hitler to purchase two American rotary presses and turn the weekly *Völkischer Boebachter* into a daily."[17] Hitler decided the newspaper should have an American format. He also "designed the title-head of the paper, using the unusual Antiqua type, as a contrast to the block capitals used by the majority of other papers" in Germany. Hitler mistakenly believed that this type originated in an earlier, purer Germany.[18]

Echart also wrote and personally delivered broadsides on party philosophy, lectured on party ideology at every opportunity, arranged party rallies, and composed marching songs. His best known work, *Germany Awake!*, or *The Storm Song*, was the earliest National Socialist musical composition, and its refrain, "Germany Awake!," became a major party slogan. The text of the song was:

> Storm, storm, storm!
> From tower to tower peal bells of alarm.
> Peal out! Sparks fly as hammers strike.
> Comes Judas forth to win the Reich
> Peal out! The bloody ropes hang red
> Around our martyred hero dead.
> Peal out—that thundering earth may know
> Salvation's rage for honour's sake.
> To people dreaming still comes woe.
> Germany, awake! Awake![19]

Before Echart's song, the party used songs they had taken over from the Freikorps repertoire.[20]

Hitler called Eckart, twenty-one years his senior, his "fatherly friend," and himself "Eckart's disciple." Indeed, Mosse credited Eckart with the further development of an already prominent anti-Semitic strain in the party and in Hitler. Eckard deepened Hitler's belief in the connection between the "removal of the Jewish menace and the resuscitation of the Volk." Such views served as the basis for *Der Bolshewismus von Moses bis Lenin: Zwiegespräch zweischen Adolf Hitler und Mir*, published in 1924, shortly after Eckart's death.[21] In this conversational meander through history, all political, economic, and intellectual aberrations are traced to the Jews, who allegedly had world destruction as their goal. Eckart and Hitler, like many nineteenth-century German intellectuals, sought an explanation for what they perceived as cultural decline—the European adventure coming to an end. Wagner, among others, had this sense of impending doom. Gutman wrote that, in his last years, Wagner:

...was alarmed to observe natural selection working against its distinctive Aryanism...Something was terribly wrong; the evolutionary machinery was malfunctioning, confusing the fit with the unfit. Instead of working toward endless improvement and Aryan perfection, it was producing racial corruption.[22]

In light of such nineteenth-century influences, Eckart saw German art— painting, sculpture, music, and literature—as rooted in Germany's racial distinctiveness. To Eckart, there was art that was world-denying and art that was world-affirming. He asserted significant artists dedicated themselves to the latter, and, in doing so, projected the basic heroic trait of the German people.

Ernst Roehm, according to Fest, did more for the NSDAP than anyone else.[23] Roehm was not only ideologically attracted to the party but also felt a blood tie with Hitler because they had both been front-line fighters in the war. After the war, Roehm became a professional freebooter and swashbuckler, with a contempt for what he saw as the pharisaism and hyprocrisy of Wiemar society. He became Hitler's superior in the Reichwehr, replacing Captain Mayr, and brought to the young NSDAP party followers, arms, and funds. It was Roehm's men who often suppressed violence in the early party meetings. Roehm also helped the party by introducing Hitler to important military and political figures.[24]

Alfred Rosenberg was another of Hitler's mentors. He joined the NSDAP in 1919 and met Hitler through Dietrich Eckart, whom he eventually succeeded as editor of the party paper, the *Völkische Boebachter*. He was the son of an Estonian mother and a Lithuanian father, who were both of Baltic German extraction. He had studied engineering in Riga and architecture in Moscow. After the Russian revolution, he fled to Paris and then to Munich. His membership in such groups as the Thule Society reinforced his obsession with the nefarious role of Jews, Bolsheviks and

Freemasons. He wrote tracts supporting his thesis that there was a Judeo-Masonic conspiracy that sought to undermine the foundations of Germany's existence. He established himself in the 1920s as the guardian of the National Socialist *Weltanschauung*, as a leading theoretician, and chief cultural propagandist. Later, however, Hitler declared Rosenberg's book, *The Myth of the 20th Century*, was not to be regarded as an expression of the official doctrine of the party. Hitler was not alone in this denial of Rosenberg's position as spokesman of National Socialist ideology, for "none of the twenty-one defendants at the Nuremberg Trial of Major Criminals had read the book."[25]

Hermann Goering joined the party in the early 1920s. He was considered a prize recruit for the young party due to his aristocratic background and his prestige as a war hero. He was the son of a judge who was sent by Bismarck to be the first Resident Minister Plenipotentiary of South-West Africa. In the war, Goering distinguished himself as an air ace by shooting down twenty-two Allied aircraft. He was awarded the *Pour le Mérite* and the Iron Cross First Class. After the war, he was a barn-stormer in Denmark and Sweden, where he met Baroness Karen von Fock-Kantzow, whom he married in February, 1922. He was drawn to the NSDAP by its "promise of action, adventure, comradeship and an outlet for his unreflective, elemental hunger for power."[26] Goering provided Hitler with the support of a nationally known war hero who had commanded the squadron of Baron von Richthofen after Richthofen's death. Further, Goering was the first commander of the SA and was quick to use it to protect Nazi rallies by the use of force. He was totally loyal to Hitler until he committed suicide following his sentencing at Nuremberg.[27]

Ernst (Putzi) Hanfstaengl attended his first National Socialist Party meeting in 1922. He befriended Hitler and became an active party member. Hanfstaengl was the wealthy heir-apparent of an art publishing business in Munich. He had attended Harvard with plans to manage the New York branch of the family business, but he returned to Germany after his graduation and spent a year in the Bavarian army. His life would have been full had he never met Hitler, for he claimed friendship with the young Franklin D. Roosevelt and visits to his home by such persons as Pierpont Morgan, Toscanini, Henry Ford, Caruso, Santos Dumont, Charlie Chaplin, Paderweski, and the daughter of President Wilson. After he joined the National Socialists, Hitler benefited from Hanfstaengl's contacts with wealthy and influential people.[28]

Besides his monetary support of the party and his introduction of Hitler to influential supporters, Hanfstaengl composed a dozen or so marches for the party. He fascinated Hitler with his descriptions of the hypnotic effect marches and cheering had at Harvard sports events. He told him of thousands of spectators being whipped up with enthusiasm through cheers of "Harvard, Harvard, Harvard, rah, rah, rah!" Hanfstaengl played Sousa Marches and his own *Falarah* on the piano and showed Hitler how German tunes could sound when given a buoyant beat like American brass-band music. Hitler shouted with enthusiasm, "That is it, Hanfstaengl, that is what we need for the movement, marvelous, and he pranced around the room like a drum majorette." He had the SA band practice the technique and Harvard's "rah, rah, rah!" became "Sieg Heil! Sieg Heil!"[24]

In 1920, Henrich Hoffmann, a party member, and Hitler became close friends. Hoffmann too had wanted to study art, but his father had insisted he join him in the family's photographic business. Hoffman became Hitler's personal and official photographer and, as such, he added an important visual dimension to our understanding of the Third Reich and its propaganda. Hitler insisted Hoffman photograph him in all his uniforms, he approved all of Hoffmann's photographs which were released to the public, and Hoffmann taught Hitler about effective photographic representation. All official photographs of Hitler, during the Third Reich, were, therefore, Hoffmann's presentation of Hitler.[30]

Other early supporters in the party included Emil Maurice, Hitler's friend and "a typical barroom and meeting-hall brawler," Christian Weber, a "paunchy former horse dealer who worked as a bouncer in a notorious taproom," Ulrich Graf, "a butcher's apprentice," who served as Hitler's bodyguard, and Max Amann, Hitler's former sergeant, who became business manager for the party and its publishing house. These members often met with Hitler at "the Osteria Bavaria or the Bratwurstglöckl near the Frauenkirche, or talked for hours over coffee and cake at the Café Heck."

The influential and wealthy patrons, whom Eckart and other party members introduced Hitler to, were from among the elements in Munich society which feared a Bolshevik revolution and hated the Weimer Republic in Berlin. This group included such prominent people as Elsa Bruckmann, wife of the publisher of the racist writings of Houston Stewart Chamberlain, Chamberlain himself, who was Wagner's son-in-law, Winifred Wagner, his daughter-in-law, and Helena Bechstein, wife of the piano manufacturer. Elsa Bruckmann made something of a protégé of Hitler. The relationship was maternal on her part, for she was considerably older than Hitler. Besides their political compatibility, they shared a love of Wagner and Bayreuth. Frau Bechstein also developed a motherly interest in Hitler. She became convinced that she was going to marry her daughter Lotte to Hitler. She worked to make his clothes suitable to her social level, and he followed her suggestion to acquire a dinner jacket, starched shirt, and patent leather shoes.[32]

After Hitler left the Reichwehr, in April, 1920, he devoted all his creative energies to the party. Stierlin insisted that henceforth Hitler's creative worth must not be determined by his watercolors and drawings but by an examination of his "art of power politics, played on the smallest and largest scales; the art of political stagecrafting; and the art of myth-making or better, myth-selling." In these areas, Stierlin found Hitler like Wagner, "who also uniquely integrated musical compositions, playwriting, and stagecrafting into a *Gesamtkunstwerke*, thus creating a new art form."[33]

Quite early, Hitler developed a special theatrical style for his public appearances. He used sound trucks and posters to announce great meetings. He combined elements borrowed from the circus, grand opera, and the church such as banners, march music, repetitious slogans, communal singing and repeated cries of 'Heil.' This sense of stagecraft and drama was apparent in his preparations for party meetings. He:

...studied the beer halls for their acoustics, their colors, the best places from which to speak, the entrances and exists....He learned the advantages of arriving late, keeping the audience in suspense...He would appear from some totally unexpected direction and then march across the hall with a fixed and frozen expression on his face, with a wedge of bodyguards in front of him and another behind him, like an army.[34]

These tactics were not arrived at intuitively but were deliberate and conscious. In the 1920s, Hitler took lessons in speaking and mass psychology from a man named Hanussen, a practicing astrologer and fortune-teller. He was a very clever individual who taught Hitler about the importance of staging meetings to obtain the greatest propaganda effect.[35]

Hitler's theatricality was linked to his oratorical force. He was persuasive with small groups, but he electrified large audiences. Waite asserted Hitler learned many of his techniques for imposing his will on his listeners from reading Gustave Le Bon's work called *Psychologie des Foules*, which by 1908 had been translated into German. Indeed, in *Mein Kampf*, Hitler reflected Le Bon's thesis that the masses react emotionally like a woman and want to be dominated.[36] This thesis supported Le Bon's belief that the effective leader must not appeal to the audience's reason but to its emotions. Hitler began his speeches slowly and waited for the moment when his remarks struck a responsive chord and then would launch into a fierce attack on Germany's enemies that electrified his audience. He then played on the emotions of hate and rage and closely resembled a conductor before an orchestra.[37] Following his speeches at the Hofbräuhaus, Wagner's memory was often invoked by the playing of the overture to *Rienzi*—much to the pleasure of artists and intellectuals present. Von Maltitz asserted this use of Wagner narrowed the gap between the party members and the German intelligentsia as it was acceptable to both and provided a common meeting ground for them.[38] On other occasions, when Hitler was finished with a speech, the band played *Deutschland über Alles*. Hitler would salute and leave while the music was being played. He usually reached his car before the music ceased.

Le Bon also believed that huge theatrical meetings were most effective, and that constant repetition of simple themes was essential. Hitler repeated the same ideas over and over in his speeches. They were the leitmotifs of his speeches, like Wagner's musical monograms. Mayer called Wagner's repeated melodies his tricks for capturing the attention of the audience, and, in principle, Hitler's repetition of basic ideas served the same purpose. His "recognizable themes were hammered in through endless repetition." Of Hitler's dramatic and repetitious speeches, Flanner wrote Hitler's oratory would "wilt his collar, unglue his forelock, glaze his eyes; he was like a man hypnotized, repeating himself into a frenzy."[34]

Hafstaengl often played the old upright piano in the hallway of Hitler's Thierschstrasse apartment. Hitler loved the *Meistersinger* prelude, and Hanfstaengl drew parallels between Hitler's speeches and the prelude. He believed the:

...whole interweaving of leitmotifs of embellishments of counterpoint and musical contrasts and arguments, were exactly mirrored in the pattern of his speeches, which were symphonic in construction and ended in a great climax, like the blare of Wagner's trombones.

Hanfstaengl also gave musical descriptions of Hitler's oratorical gestures. The most striking movement, he said:

...was a soaring upward movement of the arm, which seemed to leave infinite possibilities piercing the air. It had something of the quality of a really great orchestral conductor who instead of just hammering out the downward beat, suggests the existence of hidden rhythms and meaning with the upward flick of the baton.

Hanfstaengl found "the first two-thirds of Hitler's speeches were in march time, growing increasingly quicker and leading up to the last third which was primarily rhapsodic." Hanfstaengl first heard Hitler speak in 1922. He found Hitler's early speeches unmatched in innuendo and irony, and believed no one:

...who judges his capacity as a speaker from the performances of his later years can have any true insight into his gifts. As time went on he became drunk with his own oratory before vast crowds and his voice lost its former character through the intervention of microphone and loud speakers. In his early years he had a command of voice, phrase and effect which has never been equalled...

Hanfstaengl believed an especially effective aspect of Hitler's speech making was his ability to sound like "a neighbor of his audience." He never talked down to his listeners, and he had the "priceless gift of expressing their own thoughts." Often he directed his remarks to women in the audience, commenting on problems they faced regarding food shortages and other domestic difficulties, and they would cheer him riotously.[40]

Hitler's artistic energies were also given over to creative uses of the swastika, which was made the official NSDAP symbol in 1920. It will be recalled that he first became familiar with this symbol when he attended the monastery school in Lambach during his youth. He later saw this ancient symbol on anti-Semitic magazines and pamphlets, which he read while in Vienna. He also saw the symbol used by such anti-Semitic organizations as the Thule Society, and the Order of the Holy Cross, which J. Lanz-Liebenfels established about 1900. In 1919, Friedrich Krohn had recommended the swastika be made the symbol of the National Socialist party, and the next year he designed a swastika flag for the founding meeting of the Starnberg

Ortsgruppe, the local party meeting. The first known use of the swastika, after it became the official party symbol, was on arm bands which Hitler designed for the *Ordunungsleute*, those who kept order at the meetings.[41] Herzstein believed Hitler selected the swastika as the party symbol because it had been used as a sun symbol or good luck sign by the ancient Aryans, ancestors of the modern Germans. He also suggested that Hitler believed the swastika had always represented anti-Semitism and would be a perfect sign for the Aryan man.[42]

In *Mein Kampf*, Hitler discussed at length his selection of colors for the swastika flag. He decided to use black, white and red because they had "the most brilliant harmony in existence," because he had been a soldier under these colors, and because in their aesthetic effect they were most compatible with his feelings. He rejected all designs which were submitted to him in favor of his own design—a red background, a white disk and a black swastika in the middle. He stated that the red meant the social ideal of the movement, white stressed the nationalistic idea, and the swastika represented the mission of the Aryan race. In midsummer of 1920, the new swastika flag, stitched by "a faithful woman party comrade" was seen in public for the first time.[43]

Hanfstaengl later tried to get Hitler to change the colors of the Party flag. He thought that, since the swastika was a sun symbol, it would be red and not black. Hitler informed him that, if the swastika were red, the background could not be red, and he had learned in the Berlin Lustgarten at a big Socialist demonstration that "there is only one colour with which to attract the masses and that is red." Hanfstaengl then suggested that the swastika be placed in the corner of the old black, white and red flag of the Second Reich, that they keep the swastika on a red background as a war flag, and have the swastika on a white background as a peace flag. Hitler responded that, "If I put the swastika against a white background we are going to look like a charitable organization, and this is the right thing and I am not going to change it."[44]

In addition to armbands and flags, Hitler also designed a Roman-type standard, which, along with the Roman-style salute, may have been inspired by Benito Mussolini.[45] The flags and standards became an extremely important aspect of the life of the party. Hoffmann reported that on January 27, 1933, he "watched hundreds of SA-men parade on the Marsfeld, to receive from Hitler's hands four standards which he himself had designed."[46] Hitler also designed posters for the party. He carefully selected different sizes of type and turned many of them into miniature, written speeches. Red was prominently used on the posters, and, when the swastika was used, it was placed on a white circular field. He also spent a great deal of time hunting through old art magazines and the heraldic department of the Munich State Library to find the eagle to be used as the official stamp of the party.[47]

Meanwhile the Weimar Republic was awash in turbulence occasioned by both the right and the left. On March 13, 1920, Dr. Wolfgang Kapp proclaimed himself Chancellor of the German Reich. He was supported by two brigades of the *Freikorps* under the leadership of Captains Ehrhardt and Von der Goltz. Their attack on Berlin was essentially a right-wing reaction to the Allied Commission's order for the Freikorps units, stationed uncomfortably close to the Reich capitol, to disband. This initial success of the Freikorps units stimulated the military to take charge in Munich, where the new government was headed by Ritten Gustav von Kahr. Hitler was then selected to be the liaison officer between the two military forces. He set out with Dietrich Eckart in a military plane, but the pilot lost his way and landed the plane forty miles outside of Berlin. Using disguises, in Hitler's case a goatee, they passed themselves off as a merchant and an accountant, for they could have been shot if their true mission had been revealed. Hitler and Eckart arrived in time to see the collapse of Kapp's five-day-old regime due to a general strike. Before the defeated Freikorps units marched singing out of the city, the troops clubbed and stomped a young boy to death who had hooted them and then turned their guns on a horrified crowd. Hitler admired the brigades, however, and believed the failure of the Kapp Putsch was due to the weakness of Kapp, who did not carry out his threats to shoot the strikers and raid the state treasury. He returned to Munich convinced that the path to power lay in a putsch and in the next two and a half years he sought to create a putsch that would take the form of an uprising in Munich followed by a march on Berlin.

In Berlin, Hitler observed that Ehrhardt's men had used swastikas on their helmets. They also sang a marching son, set to an old English melody, which had a chorus which read:

> Swastika on helmet
> Colors of Red, White, Black,
> The Ehrhardt Brigade
> Is marching to attack!

When Ehrhardt's men joined Hitler's National Socialists, they changed the words "Die Brigade Ehrhardt" to "Sturmabteilung Hitler." The dress of Ehrhardt's men probably inspired a drawing by Hitler of 1920, which shows a soldier wearing a helmet with a swastika on it and holding a swastika flag in his hand. Interestingly, Hoffmann reported that Hitler himself never wore a steel helmet, not even during the war.[48]

In January, 1921, the party decided to sell promissory notes to increase party funds. Hitler participated in making the design of the notes and drew the border and swastika at the bottom of the picture which appeared on the note. Other art works of his 1921-1923 period include drawings of public buildings, theaters and warships, caricatures, a bookcover design for a text called *Fundamentals of National Socialism, Vol. I, the Revolution,* a Portrait of Dr. Schweyer, Bavarian Minister of the Interior, and several doodles.[49]

In the early months of 1921, Drexler and other early party members challenged Hitler's position in the party. To demonstrate his power, Hitler left Munich for six weeks. Within a short time, they clamoured for his return because no one else could run the daily business of the party, design posters, and fill the meeting halls. When, on July 11, 1921, he returned and threatened to resign from the party, Drexler and the others gave in to his demand for dictatorial power. This was the first appearance of the concept of the *Führerprinzip,* the leadership principle of absolute obedience to a commander.

Although there had always been disturbances at the party meetings, violence increasingly became a part and parcel of party activities. Music played at least some part in the increased violence. On weekends, for example, Nazi members often undertook propaganda drives through the countryside. Wearing the armbands and carrying knobby walking sticks, they marched through the countryside singing songs that had a bloodthirsty ring. On these adventures, they collected donations for "the massacre of the Jews" and often broke up meetings or concerts that displeased them.[50]

On September 14, 1921, Hitler personally participated in an act of violence. He, Hermann Esser, Oscar Koerner, and their bodyguards physically attacked Otto Ballerstedt, a leader of the Bavarian Monarchists, as he spoke to his party. The police were called and the three men, Hitler, Esser and Koerner, were charged with creating a public nuisance and causing severe bodily injury. For this act of violence, Hitler served one month of a three-month sentence in Stadelheim Prison, in Munich.[51]

In the months before he served his token sentence, however, several significant events took place. In October, 1921, Hitler began to organize a private army under Ulrich Klintzsch, a twenty-two-year-old former member of Ehrhardt's Brigade. On November 4, 1921, Hitler had his forty-two member army primed to fight Communists who heckled him with the Communist slogan *"Freiheit!,"* as he spoke at the Hofbräuhaus in Munich. Under their new leader, Emil Maurice, the soldiers hurled themselves repeatedly against the seven hundred Communists until the Communists were driven from the hall. This bloody night would later be viewed as the foundation date of the *Sturmabteilungen,* the SA. This group became the prime force for movement of the National Socialists out of the meeting halls and into the streets, where they confronted the Social Democrats and the Communists. To the Nazis, political power not only in Munich, but in the state, became synonymous with domination of the streets. At that time, Hitler saw the storm troopers as the force which would ultimately bring the existing government to its knees.

Hitler, therefore, wanted the storm troopers to be visible. They soon began to march, usually to the accompaniment of small bands. They often paraded in separate units, but at a Munich rally of August 16, 1922, they marched into the Königsplatz with their banners and two bands. Hitler had been invited to speak about a "Law for the Protection of the Republic," which was directed against extremist organizations. Hitler took this opportunity to call for a law to protect the German people against the government in Berlin. This was no small opportunity, for the audience numbered 40,000. His speech ended with the party slogan extracted from Eckart's song, " *Deutschland erwache!*"[52]

On October 14 and 15, 1922, the SA had its first real test of strength. Earlier, Kurt Lüdecke, a new convert to National Socialism, had encouraged Hitler to copy Benito Mussolini's political techniques. His fascist Blackshirts had recently occupied Ravenna and other Italian cities. Lüdecke went as Hitler's representative to see if Mussolini might be an ally. He graciously received Lüdecke and impressed him, and later Hitler, with a confident statement that the Fascists would succeed due to their determination.[53] With this encouragement, memories of the Kapp Putsch, and his SA units built up, Hitler decided to make a show of force at the German Day celebration in Coburg. On October 14, 1922, he left Munich in a special train with six hundred SA men. They piled on the train to the music of a forty-two piece brass band. By the time they reached Coburg, the SA numbered eight hundred. Coburg was a predominantly socialist and Communist town and Hitler went there to drive them out. His troops stepped into formation on the station platform and the band struck up a lively march. They paraded to the Hofbräuhauskeller, in the inner city, and the gates were locked. Hitler, however, insisted that they be housed in a shooting gallery near the edge of town. When the angry crowd of workers hurled cobblestones at them, Hitler cracked his whip and eight hundred SA men attacked them with rubber bludgeons. The next day the citizens of Coburg lined the streets and cheered as the National Socialists paraded by. On October 28, Mussolini's Blackshirts took Rome and four days later Esser introduced the Fuehrer at the banquet hall of the Hofbräuhaus by saying "Germany's Mussolini is called Hitler!" Hitler perpetuated the memory of that successful day in Coburg by designing a Coburg Medal, which was given to NSDAP members as a designation of a particularly high achievement.[54]

In addition to the incitement to a show of force, Hitler was indebted to Mussolini for many other things, including the use of uniform-colored shirts, the arm extended salute, the victor's bundle, and the death's head emblem. Mussolini's *Squadristi* were an example for Hitler's *Sturmabteilungen*. The Italians swore an oath to the Duce before Germans swore an oath to the Fuehrer. Hitler's district party leaders, called Gauleiters, were much like Mussolini's *Federale*. Mussolini preceded Hitler in consecrating flags, and holding quasi-religious services which preserved the names of the fallen dead. Hitler and Mussolini both organized women and youth into separate political organizations and established secret police.[55]

On January 11, 1923, French and Belgian troops went into the Ruhr Valley on the excuse that Germany had failed to fulfill her reparations obligations. This act inflamed nationalists and caused the mark to plunge from 6,750 to the dollar to 50,000 to the dollar in just two weeks. The invasion in the Ruhr, inflation, and increased unemployment brought new followers to the National Socialists. This change in the political and economic climate caused Hitler to defy the police and announce twelve public rallies for January 27, the First Party Day of the NSDAP.[56]

Throughout 1923, the mark continued to fall in value and the desperation of the German people grew apace, as did political radicalism. On November 8, 1923, Hitler attempted a dramatic coup. He tried to place himself at the head of all anti-republican groups in the Bavarian capital. On that day, he went to a meeting of about 3,000 government officials held in the Bürgerbraukeller, leaped on a table, fired a gun in the air and declared "The national revolution has broken out." The next day, believing he had the support of leaders of several local factions, including General Otto von Lassow, the military commander of Bavaria, and Colonel Hans Ritter von Seisser, commander of the Bavarian state police, he placed himself at the head of a crowd, which eventually numbered several thousand, and marched into the Munich Odeonplatz beside the Feldernhalle. There they were met by police, and, in an exchange of fire, sixteen of Hitler's followers were killed. The other nationalists had not joined Hitler at the Odeonplatz, and his plans for a collective march on Berlin had failed.[57]

On the evening of the abortive revolution, Hitler, Dr. Walter Schultze, and two other National Socialists stayed at Hanfstaengl's home. Hitler had a dislocated shoulder, caused when Max Erwin von Scheubner-Richter, whose arm was linked with Hitler's, was shot and killed. Hitler was in great pain, but his shoulder was not set until three or four days later, when he arrived at Landsberg prison. Hanfstaengl, always tempted to compare Hitler with one of Wagner's operatic figures, stated that even with his dislocated shoulder, Hitler spent two days "behaving like Tannhäuser in the Venusberg."[58] In Wagner's opera, *Tannhäuser*, the minstrel Tannhäuser was lured to the abode of Venus, Venusberg. For over a year the goddess bestowed her love on him, but he grew weary of the place and longed for the simple pleasures of earthly life. Hitler was strongly attracted to Hanfstaengl's wife and perhaps this is why Hanfstaengl drew the parallel between Tannhäuser and Hitler. He was locked up with his Venus, but he longed for freedom. There were plans for Hitler to escape to Austria in the Bechstein's car, but this was prevented by his arrest by "a lieutenant and two gendarmes," who received a tongue-lashing from Hitler about their "conniving at the splitting of Germany."[59] Two of Hitler's followers did escape to Austria. Goering was wounded in the attempted coup, treated at a Munich hospital, and smuggled across the border. Hanfstaengl fled to Austria where, in his enthusiasm for the Bayreuth master, he took the name Georg Wagner. He soon abandoned the name, however, when a friend informed him there was a standing warrant for a forger by that name.[60]

While awaiting trial, Hitler suffered from deep depression and went on a hunger strike. Interestingly, he said, "Anyone who has the deaths of as many people on his conscience as I have must die himself. I have no other course left than death by starvation. And that is what I shall do." Payne claimed that Hans Knirsch, a Sudenten German, who founded a National Socialist Workers Party in Bohemia before World War I, visited Hitler and persuaded him to break his fast.[61] Hanfstaengl, however, believed his wife, Helene, convinced Hitler to eat. She had wrested a gun from Hitler's hand when he attempted suicide while hiding at the Hanfstaengl's before his arrest. She sent Hitler word in prison that she had not saved him to let him starve to death.[62]

Early in December, Hitler's sister, Angela, reported his "spirit and soul were at a high level." During her visit to the prison, a count "brought a Christmas package from Villa Wahnfried, the Wagner's home in Bayreuth." A few days later, Winifred Wagner sent him a book of poetry. She still believed that in spite of everything, Hitler would "pull the sword out of the German oak.[63] This is perhaps a reference to Siegmund, of Wagner's opera *Die Walküre*, who is able, when others fail, to pull the sword from the ash tree and save Sieglinde from an unwanted husband. Winifred may also deliberately have wedded the sacred sword to the German oak, the most sacred tree of primitive German times, which was thought of as the tree of freedom.

There is considerable evidence that Wagner's family and works were much on Hitler's mind during the months prior to the November, 1923, putsch. In April of that year, Hanfstaengl traveled with Hitler to Berlin to raise funds for the party. Hanfstaengl confessed that he enjoyed such trips with Hitler because Hitler often passed the time by whistling or humming long passages from Wagner's operas. On this trip, they visited the Berlin War Museum and the National Gallery. Hanfstaengl recalled that Hitler particularly enjoyed seeing Rembrandt's *Man in a Golden Helmet*, with the heroic, soldierlike expression. Hitler believed that this work proved that, in spite of the many works Rembrandt painted in the Jewish quarter of Amsterdam, he was a true Aryan and German.[64]

They stopped by Bayreuth on their return route and visited the festival theater where the stage set for a performance of Wagner's *Flying-Dutchman* had been left undisturbed since August, 1914, when World War I broke out. Hanfstaengl took that opportunity to tell Hitler about his great-grandfather, Ferdinand Heine, who did much work at the Dresden Opera House where Wagner's *Flying Dutchman* was first performed. Heine and Wagner became fast friends, and, besides the *Flying Dutchman*, they produced *Rienzi*. Hitler was very impressed by this visit to Wagner's theatre.[65]

On September 30, 1923, Hitler visited Wagner's Villa Wahnfried in Bayreuth. The master's eighty-six-year-old widow, Cosima, kissed Hitler, while Winifred and Siegfried greeted him warmly. He also met Wagner's English-born son-in-law, Houston Stewart Chamberlain, the author of *Grundlogen des XIX Jahrhunderts*, published in 1899. The thesis of this book stressed a racial theory of history and the superiority of Aryans, who had the duty to civilize the world. Chamberlain worshipped his father-in-law and saw in Hitler hope for Germany's future. A few days after Hitler's visit, Hitler received a letter from Chamberlain in which he said, "With one blow you have transformed the state of my soul...that Germany, in the hour of her greatest need brings forth a Hitler that is proof of her vitality."[66] Winifred later reported that Hitler "visited the Master's grave alone, and came back in a state of great emotion, saying, 'Out of *Parsifal* I make a religion.' "[67] While it is impossible to know exactly what Hitler meant by this statement, an examination of the *libretto* of Parsifal provides some insight into the problem.

Wagner based *Parsifal* upon the legendary story of a brotherhood of knights who protected the Holy Grail, the cup which Christ drank from at the Last Supper. To help the knights with their task, they were given the lance with which the Roman soldier pierced Christ's side when he was on the cross. The lance was supposed to protect them from evil men such as the sorcerer, Klingsor, to whose abode knights were lured by maidens such as Kundry, who mocked Christ as he hung on the cross.

The opera opens after Titurel, the old ruler of the knights has appointed his son Amfortas to succeed him. Amfortas intended to rid the knights of the sorcerer, Klingsor, by killing him with the Holy Lance. Klingsor had Kundry seduce Amfortas, however, and he dropped the lance. Klingsor then picked up the lance and wounded Amfortas. The brotherhood was then told that the wound would not heal until one who was free of guile, and full of compassion, regained the spear and touched it to Amfortas's wound. Nevertheless, the knights and the repentant Kundry continued to search for a cure.

A youth named Parsifal was brought before Gurnemanz, a veteran knight, for having killed a swan with an arrow. Kundry told the old knight that he was Parsifal, the son of a knight who was killed before the boy was born and a woman who died of grief because the boy left home. Gurnemanz believed Parsifal was perhaps the innocent who was destined to heal Amfortas. He took Parsifal to a communion service where the Holy Grail was used. Parsifal saw Amfortas suffer agony as he consecrated the blood of Christ and saw his wound break forth afresh. Gurnemanz realized that Parsifal could not help Amfortas, so he sent him away.

Klingsor, however, recognized Parsifal as the order's salvation, and sent Kundry to seduce him. Klingsor wanted to inherit the Grail by destruction of Parsifal. Kundry, transformed into a beautiful siren, wooed Parsifal with memories of his childhood and his mother. When she tried to kiss Parsifal, he realized what had happened to Amfortas. Klingsor hurled the sacred spear at Parsifal who caught it in mid-air. Klingsor's domain vanished and Kundry cursed Parsifal to wander hopelessly in search of Monsalvant, where Amfortas still suffered from his wound.

Years passed before Parsifal stumbled upon Gurnemanz who recognized the Holy Spear and realized who Parsifal was. He and the penitent Kundry removed Parsifal's armor, and Kundry washed his feet and dried them with her hair. The day was Good Friday, and they headed toward the castle where bells announced the burial of the old king, Titurel. In the Hall of the Grail, Amfortas, who was no longer able to uncover the chalice, begged the knights to end his life. Parsifal touched Amfortas's chest with the sacred lance, and he was healed. Parsifal raised the Holy Grail and accepted the homage of the knights as their new king. Kundry, who was earlier baptized by Parsifal, fell dying. The brotherhood of the Holy Grail was saved.[68]

Robert Gutman believed the message of *Parsifal* was not Christian but Wagner's call for the racial regeneration of Germany. The composer simply used trappings of the Christian church to "set forth a religion of racism under the cover of Christian legend." Amfortas, an Ayran, lost control of his will and was corrupted through sexual contact with Kundry, a racial inferior. He thus ceased to be herioc and his contaminated blood caused a wound that would not heal. Parsifal controlled himself, however, when Kundry tempted him through thoughts of maternal intercourse. He heroically reclaimed the spear, the holy apparatus of Aryanism, which was appropriated by Jewry in the form of the sorcerer Klingsor. With this symbol of Aryanism he healed the Aryan blood of Amfortas. The baptized Kundry was granted "the ultimate reward of heraldry—the bounty of death." The evil, non-Aryan Klingsor simply vaporized in the presence of true Aryanism.[69]

Meanwhile, the date for Hitler's trial had arrived. Hitler's trial, held in June, 1924, was covered by major German newspapers and the world press.[70] It became a forum for Hitler to propagandize party and personal views. In his speech, he paid tribute to Wagner and recalled his visit to Wagner's grave. He stated that:

The first time I stood in front of Wagner's tomb my heart was filled with pride...I was proud that this man, and so many men in German history, were satisfied to leave their name to posterity, not their title. It was modesty that made me want to be the drummer. That is of utmost importance, the rest is a bagatelle.[71]

Hitler wanted to be a "drummer," like he believed Wagner was when he called for a Parsifal to heal Germany's wounds by the removal of contaminated inferiors. In truth, Hitler saw himself as Parsifal, a savior of Aryan blood, much as he saw himself as Rienzi in his youth in Linz. He was to answer Wagner's call for a new Barbarossa, a spiritual reincarnation of Siegfried or Parsifal, who would save Germany.

Hitler was tried for high treason, a crime which would carry the death penalty. Hitler, however, received a reduced sentence of five years in Landsberg prison. From the beginning it was understood he would not serve the full sentence. He lived in what was essentially a small suite of rooms and was allowed to have visitors and receive gifts. Frau Bruckmann was one of the most generous donors, but food and money were also sent by Siegfried and Winifred Wagner. For his thirty-fifth birthday, April 20, 1925, gifts came from all over Germany, until his cells took on the appearance of flower, fruit and wine shops.

In Landsberg Prison, Hitler began work on a book which he originally called *Four and One Half Years of Battle Against Lies, Stupidity and Cowardice: Account Settled*. Max Amann, financial director of the party publishing house, convinced Hitler to change the title to *Mein Kampf*.[72] He nearly finished volume one during his stay in prison. According to Waite, this work was the fulfillment of a promise Hitler had made to himself in Vienna to one day write a great political work and design a cover for it.

Emil Maurice initially served as his secretary, but Hess soon replaced him and pecked out the pages on a decrepit Remington portable typewriter. It was typed on paper which Winifred Wagner supplied, while a gramaphone thundered Richard Wagner's music.[73] The first volume of *Mein Kampf*, completed after Hitler was released from prison, was dedicated to Dietrich Eckart. The second volume was dictated in Upper Salzberg with the collaboration of Max Amann. Several well-educated men, including Hangstaengl, read the proofs, but had little success in rectifying the estimated 164,000 errors in German grammar and syntax.[74] The original manuscript was sent to Hitler's motherly patroness, Frau Bechstein.

Mein Kampf was "partly a biography, partly an ideological tract and partly a plan of action." The central theme "around which all the other conceptions were grouped, was a vulgar Darwinism, which saw the fundamental law of life as a merciless struggle of each against all, as the victory of the strong over the weak. Fest believed the real purpose of the book was Hitler's "attempt to substantiate on literary and philosophical grounds his claim to leadership within the movement."[75] Hitler resigned the leadership of the party while he was in prison. Part of the reason was that he wanted to assure the government that he need not be exiled as an undesirable alien from Austria. He also knew the factions within the party would fight among themselves, and, upon his release, he would be considered the only one capable of revitalizing the party, and he was right.

The interest here is Hitler's brief references to the arts. In *Mein Kampf* Hitler bemoaned the state of German culture since the turn of the century. He was especially disappointed with the way the great art of the past was "besmirched and effaced." While the age of Pericles seemed embodied in the Parthenon, Hitler found the Bolshevistic present embodied in a cubist monstrosity. He believed "such diseases could be seen in Germany in nearly every field of art and culture."[76] Hitler revealed his plan for ridding Germany of this Bolshevik disease, this decay of her culture and disregard for the art of the past. His plan was much like points twenty-three and twenty-five of the German Workers' Party program which he worked out with Drexler in 1920. In *Mein Kampf* he stated that "it was the business of the state, in other words, of its leaders, to prevent a people from being driven to the arms of spiritual madness." These leaders should "remove what is bad or unsuitable and continue building on the sound spot that has been laid bare."[77]

While dictating *Mein Kampf*, Hitler did one or two drawings a week for the prison newspaper, *The Honorary Landsberg Citizen*. He also drew a portrait of General Field Marshal Mackensen.[78] However, *Mein Kampf* was his primary creative outlet during his imprisonment.

On December 20, 1924, Hitler left Landsberg prison and returned to his small Thierschstrasse apartment, which his Munich friends had filled with flowers. They placed a laurel wreath on the head of their returning hero, sang his favorite songs, and feasted on sweet cakes, fruit, and wine. A little later, a woman came to the door collecting donations for the organ fund of Saint Anne's Church. Hitler looked at the list of donors and the small sums they had given her. Because he had no money, Hitler asked his rich friend Adolf Mueller and others to donate fifty marks to the organ fund. Payne called this fund raising Hitler's "first political act on his release from prison."[79] Later that day Hitler went to Hanfstaengl's new home in the Herzog Park quarter of Munich. Almost immediately upon arrival, Hitler asked Hanfstaengl to play the "Liebestod" from Wagner's *Tristan and Isolde* which he did with Lisztian embellishment on his grand piano.[80]

The National Socialist Party was reorganized and the *Völkischer Beobachter* was revived on February 25, 1925. Two days later, Hitler spoke at the Bürgerbräukeller where he had launched the putsch. He spoke to 4,000 people—1,000 were turned away. Hitler's speech that night clearly reestablished the unity of the NSDAP and his position as Fuehrer. Afterwards, Hitler was physically and emotionally drained. He and his aides left Munich with Winifred Wagner and stayed overnight at her home in Bayreuth. This was the beginning of Hitler's frequent visits to Wahnfried, often under the pretense of fleeing from assassination attempts. He always stopped by the nursery at Wahnfried and fascinated the master's grandchildren with stories of his adventures.

Heinrich Held, head of the Bavarian government, became alarmed by Hitler's success and the inflammatory nature of his speech. It had included such phrases as "Fight Marxism and Judaism not according to middle-class standards but over corpses!"[81] Hitler was, therefore, on March 9, 1925, banned from speaking in Prussia, Baden, Saxony, Hamburg and Oldenburg, but he could speak in Württemberg, Thurengia, Brunswick and Mecklenburg-Schwerin. The period following this silencing of Hitler in certain regions of Germany has been called the "years of stagnation." During this time, however, Hitler laid the foundation for what amounted to a shadow state. He established within the NSDAP departments which paralleled the structures of the ministerial government. This structure kept power within the party divided and ultimately within his own hands. However, it gave the party a greater cohesiveness throughout Germany and served as a dress rehearsal for the day the National Socialists would take over the government.

In spite of the fine reception by his friends and followers and the reestablishment of the party and its paper, Hitler found that the basic appeal of the party had changed while he was in prison. Had Held not silenced him, he would have faced a decreased appeal due in part to the improved German economy. In late August, 1924, the Dawes Plan, drawn up by the American banker, Charles G. Dawes, set into motion Germany's payment of reparations linked to the rate of prosperity rather than in established sums. The improved economy, the seeming stability surrounding the election to the Presidency of Field Marshal von Hindenburg, the withdrawal of the French from the Ruhr and the decreased success of the Communists in the April, 1925, elections were detrimental to the fortunes of the NSDAP.

Although the party may have been suffering in 1925, Albert Speer believed Hitler's drawings of this period show he had a strong sense of self-assurance. Speer became Hitler's architect after he became Chancellor of Germany, and Hitler gave him his sketchbook of 1925. Speer believed Hitler's "political mission and his passion for architecture were inseparable," and found that the architectural sketches of 1925 exhibited a self-confidence missing in his earlier watercolors.[82] Price included in his collection twelve of the drawings from Hitler's sketchbook, including one for a grand hall and another of a triumphal arch. Most of the twelve are architectural drawings, but two are of naval ships, and one is of a tank.[83]

Hitler's voice may have been silenced in certain areas of Germany in 1925, but his ideology found a new spokesman at this time, Dr. Paul Joseph Goebbels. Goebbels became a party member in 1922 and was drawn into the North German wing of the Party. He was initially opposed to Hitler's leadership, and, to his later regret, at a party congress meeting in 1925, he demanded that "the petit bourgeois Adolf Hitler be expelled from the party."[84] He met Hitler shortly after the Hanover Congress, however, and promptly recanted. He was rewarded by being made Gauleiter of Berlin, a position he held until his suicide with Hitler in 1945.

Goebbels was born into a strict Catholic, working-class family from Rheydt in the Rhineland, on October 29, 1897. He was educated in a Roman Catholic school and, after attending several universities, completed his doctoral degree at Heidelberg University. Polio left him with a crippled foot, so he was rejected for service in World War I. He was tormented by his deformity, his small stature, and his inability to conform to the Aryan racial standards of the Third Reich. He overcompensated for his frailties with "his ideological rectitude and radicalism once he joined the NSDAP.[85] In 1925, he was made business manager of the party in the Ruhr district and soon founded the *Nationalsozialistischen Briefe (NS Letters)* and other publications. With his appointment by Hitler as Nazi district leader for Berlin-Brandenburg, Goebbels unified the northern branch and edited his own newspaper, *Der Angriff (The Attack)*. Like Hitler, Goebbels also prepared posters, invented his own invective type of propaganda and staged street battles and brawls to call attention to the Berlin branch of the party. His blood-red posters appeared everywhere on the walls and kiosks of Berlin. They were designed to attract attention through the use of dramatic color and typography. Small type was used to answer a question which was sketched out in bold type. They were always eye-catchers. Hitler recognized that Goebbels' success was due to his verbal facility and his intellect. In 1929, Hitler appointed him the Reich Propaganda Leader of the NSDAP.[86] This appointment prepared him for the position he would have in the Third Reich as enforcer of Hitler's cultural policies.

In February, 1929, the *Kampfbund für deutsche Kultur* was established as a national organization. Rosenberg had fathered this group of intellectuals during 1928, in order to extend the cultural influence of the party. Although it fell into disfavor and was boycotted after 1933, for more than three years before Hitler's rise to power it did much to combat modernism in German culture. Early meetings often dealt with literature, music, and the drama. Targets of their criticism included Krenek, Kurt Weill, Max Reinhardt and Heinrich Mann, whose works they believed exhibited chaotic elements which threatened German form. The *Kampfbund* was particularly repulsed by Krenek's Berlin review, "Johnny spielt auf," in which the leading role was played by a Negro. To counter these performances, the organization endowed prizes in literature and held concerts and poetry evenings where only German masters and poets were heard. They also sponsored exhibits of modern art with such titles as "Spirit of November," "Art in the Service of Sedition" and "Art Bolshevism."[87]

In this period, the *Völkisher Beobachter* printed editorials about the declining culture. The Negro Americans Paul Robeson and Josephine Baker were sharply attacked by the paper when they appeared in Berlin, and "in January of 1930 it published an article which summed up the party's entire cultural policy as 'Against Negro Culture.' "[88]

On January 23, 1930, Wilhelm Frick was elected Minister of the Interior in Thurengia. Six years earlier, Frick had been elected one of the first National Socialist deputies to the Reichstag. Through Frick's positions of power, Hitler's cultural *Weltanschauung* was imposed, at least on a geographically limited scale, several years prior to his coming to power as Chancellor of Germany. Hitler even announced, "I have selected Party Comrade Frick to take over the post of Ministry of Interior and Education...only to represent the ideas of our *Weltanschauung*."[89] Among Frick's cultural changes was the transformation of Walter Gropius's world-renowned Weimar Bauhaus into the *Vereinigt Kunstlehranstalten* (United Institutes for Art Instruction) with National Socialist Paul Schultze-Naumburg as its director. All twenty-nine faculty members of the Brauhaus were dismissed, and Gropius' Bauhaus was moved first to Dessau and then to Berlin. Gropius' ideas of international architecture and modern design were abandoned in Weimar, as Schultze-Naumburg, a "traditionalist of racist, nationalistic (Alt-Völkisch) conviction: promoted crafts, local art, and Germanic ornamentation."[90]

This devastation of the Weimar Bauhaus was followed by a decree on May 4, 1930, called "Against Negro Culture—For Our German Heritage." Films by Eisenstein and Brecht and Pabst's film of *The Threepenny Opera* were banned, Piscato's Berlin theater company could not enter Thurengia, Hindemith and Stravinsky's music was struck from concert programs, and Oskar Schlemmer's frescoes in the stairwell of the Weimar Bauhaus building were destroyed. Also, at the Schlossmuseum in Weimar, seventy works by modern artists, such as Ernst Barlach, Otto Dix, Lyonel Feiniger, Erick Heckel, Wassilly Kandinsky, Paul Klee, Oscar Kokoschka, Wilhelm Lehmbruck, Franz Marc, Johannes Molzahn, Emil Nolda, Oskar Schlemmer, and Karl Schmidt-Rottluff were removed.[91]

The Nazi attack on modern art was more than a tactical device to secure the support of the German masses. It represented the sincere conviction that art not only reflected, but actually determined the moral life and value of the nation and the Volk. Hence, modern art, which was destructive, narcissistic, individualistic, even anarchistic and nihilistic, had to be itself destroyed. Allowed to exist, it would sap the very substance of the Volk. Not yet in a position to patronize the arts with state funds, the Nazis, whenever and wherever possible, attacked and removed such modern works.

Schultze-Naumburg's term lasted a little over a year and his policies were almost entirely destructive. Frick finally came into conflict with the federal government and the Thuringian Landtag, so his ministry was brief. However, both men became heroes to the party. The party paper, which had in 1927 contained articles in praise of Gropius and others who standardized building methods, and employed modern technology in the construction of public housing, began to call the Bauhaus a stronghold of bolshevism. Schultze-Naumburg became the *Kampfbund's* major speaker and he helped them build a campaign against the new architecture beginning in 1931, when they sponsored a series of lectures by him entitled "The Struggle over Art."[92] There can be little doubt that Rosenberg's association with the *Kumpfbund* and their attack on new architecture caused the *Völkischer Beobachter* to publish, by 1932, an average of three major articles on architecture each month. By March 5, 1933, six of ten issues of that year carried full-page attacks on radical architects and their works.[93] The propaganda for electing Hitler became increasingly directed toward the preservation of German culture by ridding it of cultural bolshevism, and Rosenberg and the *Kampfbund* envisioned Hitler's success as a mandate for the birth of a new age in which they would assume dictatorial power over German culture.

On February 23, 1930, the National Socialist Party lost a member, but, due to the propagandistic genius of Goebbels, it gained a martyr. His name was Horst Wessel. This son of a Protestant military Chaplain had distinguished himself as a party speaker and an SA commander who waged aggressive street battles against the Communists. On January 14, 1930, Wessel was shot by Ali Hoehler, a Communist, in the room where Wessel lived with a former prostitute named Erna Jaenicke. The Communists labeled Wessel a pimp.[94] Since Erna admitted at the trial of Wessel's killer that she had previously had an affair with Horst Wessel's murderer, it could have been labeled a crime of passion. Goebbels preferred, however, to make political capital out of Wessel's suffering, and he transformed Wessel into a "Nazi Christ" fighting Communists. Goebbels took political advantage of the weeks it took for Wessel to die in Friedrichshain Hospital. During this time, every issue of the twice-weekly newspaper *Der Angriff* contained reports on Wessel's condition and called for public concern.

Wessel earlier had written a poem called *Raise High the Flag*, which was published in *Der Angriff*. The poem was later set to a melody which Hanfstaengl believed was a popular "Vienna cabaret song of the turn of the century."[95] As part of the transfiguration of Wessel from lover to working-class Jesus, Goebbels had the song sung for the first time at a mass meeting of nearly ten thousand people, on February 7, 1930.[96] It soon became the official party song, was sung at all party functions, and during the Third Reich was second only to the national anthem, *Deutschland über Alles*[97]

Goebbels' planned a magnificent funeral for Wessel. Thousands of people wearing black armbands and giving the Hitler salute watched the funeral cortege on its way to the cemetery. Hitler, for reasons of safety, did not attend and speak as Goebbels had intended. Rather, Goebbels himself spoke eloquently of a commission of Wessel from the grave and "dramatically called the roll:'Horst Wessel?';the storm troopers shouted back 'Present!' " As if on cue, and to Goebbel's great satisfaction, the Communists hurled stones over the cemetery wall. Goebbels had taken a simple murder and given the party a martyr, a new party anthem, and new workers to the cause, who would eventually help Hitler secure the chancellorship.

Meanwhile, Hitler continued his bid for power by campaigning for the election of NSDAP members to the Reichstag. Hanfstaengl traveled with Hitler on many of these campaign trips. He found Hitler generally unconcerned with the day-to-day political scene. Hitler simply "wanted power, supreme and complete, and was convinced that if he talked often enough and aroused the masses sufficiently, he must, in due course, be swept into office." Hanfstaengl found the trips much like accompanying a musical artist on a concert tour. Hitler would "give his performance, have his bags packed, and be off to the next town." Hanfstaengl often played the piano for Hitler at night during the campaign trips. He would start off with a little Bach and Chopin or some of the marches to get his fingers warmed up, but in the end he always had to play *Tristan* and *Meistersinger*, while Hitler sat in a half doze with obvious delight.[98]

In January, 1931, the new party headquarters, the Brown House, was opened. Between his release from Landsberg Prison and 1931, the party business had been headquartered in twelve rooms of a very ordinary building at 50 Schellingstrasse. Early in 1929, Hitler acquired the Barlow Palace on Briennerstrasse as a headquarters, in order to showcase the substance and reliability of the NSDAP, at a time when German economic conditions were approaching disaster. The purchase was made possible by special contributions by party members, wealthy supporters, profits from Hitler's rallies, and party dues. Hoffmann said subscriptions "poured in so Hitler could design and furnish the house to his own taste."[99] Hitler's approval of the decoration of his large office in reddish brown, which, along with other decorative uses of this color, contributed to the name of the palace being changed to the Brown House.

The major renovation of the Brown House was undertaken by the architect Paul Troost. Of Troost Hitler said:

I first learned what architecture is from Troost. When I had some money, I bought one piece of furniture after the other from him. I looked at his buildings,...and always gave thanks to fate for appearing to me in the guise of Frau Bruckmann and leading this master to me. When the party had greater means, I commissioned him to remodel and furnish the Brown House...What trouble I had on account of it! Those philistines in the party thought it was a waste of money. And how much I learned from the Professor in the course of that remodeling.[100]

Indeed, Hitler spent many hours with Troost and personally "sketched furniture, doors, and designs for marquetry" for the new headquarters. Price's collection of Hitler's works includes samples of his sketches of furniture.[101]

Throughout the Brown House, Hitler paid tribute to his heroes of the *Partei Kampf*. In his office, he placed a painting of Frederick the Great, one of the historical figures who profoundly affected his nationalistic views. He also placed there a bust of Mussolini, from whose examples Hitler had taken profound encouragement, and a picture of his old regiment in Flanders. The presence of this picture in the new party house supported Binion's thesis that the Nazi's "carried forward the spirit of the national battle of 1914-1918."[102] Other art works were placed in the adjoining Senate Hall. There was a bust of Bismarck, the "Iron Chancellor" with whom Hitler believed he had common characteristics such as a brutal will, artistic hands, pale blue eyes, and similar cranial measurements. There was also a bust of Dietrich Eckart, who had by then become one of the patron saints of the movement. In the canteen in the cellar of the Brown House, a seat for Hitler was reserved beneath a large portrait of Eckart.

In the entrance hall of the Brown House, Hitler placed bronze tablets bearing the names of those who died in the November putsch. He also designed two new flags for the entrance. Price's collection of Hitler's works contains a pencil on cardboard design of a standard by Hitler, which is dated around 1929, and which Price believed Hitler drew for the flags of the Brown House entranceway.[103] The new party house also enshrined the blood flags, those carried during the November putsch. These flags were used at special ceremonies, when Hitler was present, to consecrate new party flags by touching them to those carried during the November putsch when blood of the party knights was spilled. Such a ritual was not unlike the touching of the holy lance, which had born the blood of Christ, to Amfortas' wound in Wagner's *Parsifal*.

At this time, Hitler was also designing the building he intended to erect when he gained power. In 1931, Munich's Glass Palace was destroyed by fire along with its collection of German Romantic art. Hoffmann and Hitler hurried to the scene and watched the hopeless effort to save the building. Not long after that, Hitler met with Troost and declared that the first building project when he came to power would be a new gallery for German art. Troost set about making plans for the museum on a site which Hitler personally selected.[104]

Before proceeding further, it is necessary to mention another event of 1931 which had a profound psychological effect on Hitler's life. In 1929, Hitler had purchased a large apartment on the Prinzregentenplatz in Munich. He then invited his half-sister, Angela Raubel, to act as his housekeeper. She brought her two daughters with her. One of them, Geli, particularly arrested his attention. By most accounts, she was a charming and attractive girl, and Uncle Alfi, as she called Hitler, came to idolize her. With Geli, Hitler was relaxed, gentle, and happy. He took her on picnics, on shopping trips, to the movies and to the opera. She was nineteen years younger than him and gave him a sense of youth. To Hoffmann, he confessed, "I love Geli and I could marry her, but you know my views that I am determined to remain a bachelor."[105] Waite stated that she became, as once Stefanie had been, his female ideal. Fest believed Geli was Hitler's "great love, a tabooed love of Tristan moods and tragic sentimentality."[106] It has never been established that Hitler had a sexual relationship with her.[107]

Geli, with Hitler's encouragement, took singing lessons, first with Adolf Vogel, then Hans Streck. Neither found her to possess any exceptional talent. Streck complained Geli was lazy, missed lessons, and showed little progress. Hitler often sat outside the studio during her lessons. When it became apparent Geli was not likely to become an opera singer, Hitler hoped she would be able to sing *lieder*.

Gradually, the relationship began to change. Geli became smothered by Hitler's excessive protectiveness. She had an affair with Hitler's chauffeur, Emil Maurice, which sent Hitler into a rage. Hoffmann's wife, Erna, believed Geli was actually in love with an artist who lived in Vienna, and that finally, Geli made plans to go there under the pretense of studying singing. On September 18, 1931, Geli and Hitler argued, and, after he left with Hoffmann on a tour, she shot herself. Hitler was devastated and had to be physically prevented from committing suicide. He went into seclusion with Hoffmann as his silent and supportive guardian. Later in the evening of the day Geli was buried, Hitler, with a special dispensation to spend twenty-four hours on Austrian soil, visited Geli's grave in Vienna.[108]

There has been much speculation about Geli's death. The murder theories include speculation the SS killed her because she distracted Hitler from his political work[109] or because Himmler believed her to be an obstacle to his ascendancy in the party.[110] It has also been suggested Hitler killed her because of her promiscuity or because he had gotten her pregnant.[111] Waite insisted, however, that "all responsible evidence" indicated Geli had committed suicide.[112] Hanfstaengl insisted she committed suicide after Hitler discovered she was pregnant due to a liaison with a Jewish artist from Linz.[113] The suicide, according to Fest, represented a desperate desire to escape her uncle's tyranny.[114]

It is certain that Hitler was shattered by Geli's death. Geli's room, next to Hitler's, was made a shrine to her memory. His housekeeper, Annie Winter, was ordered to keep the room as it was when Geli died and place fresh flowers in the room every day. Adolf Ziegler was commissioned to paint her picture from photographs, and it was given a place of honor in the reception room at Obersalzberg. Joseph Thorak was commissioned to carve a bust of Geli, and it was given a place of honor in the Berlin Chancellery which Hitler later built. Hitler also carried Geli's photograph with him as he did one of his mother. The pictures and the sculpture all played a part in the cult in honor of Geli. No one but Hitler was ever allowed to mention her name. Hitler spent Christmas Eve alone in her room for a number of years. Goering asserted to an attorney at the Nuremberg Trial that the suicide completely changed Hitler's relationship to all others.[115] Payne believed that it was Geli's suicide that freed Hitler from all claims of morality and caused him to be utterly ruthless and merciless—It placed him "beyond good and evil."[116]

Hitler submerged himself in frantic political activity to assuage his grief. The NSDAP had become a national party and Hitler a major political figure. This increased importance was due to more than the effective use of propaganda. Hitler had developed a Volkish ideology that, as the economic depression of Germany deepened after 1929, increasingly struck a responsive chord among Germans, especially those of the lower middle-class.

Hitler's Volkish ideology was a descendant of romantically irrational and emotional nineteenth-century Volkish thought. In that era, Europeans were shaken by the rejection of the discipline of the Enlightenment, the ideal of revolution, and the movement away from the concept of a comprehensible God toward the acceptance of a pantheistic view of the universe.[117] They were also profoundly frustrated by the bewilderingly rapid industrialization, which strengthened the individual's sense of isolation from his society. Men found it increasingly difficult to use reason to fit into the new social order, and, therefore, delved into their emotional depths for answers.[118] They found both a desire for self-identity and "a contradictory urge to belong to something greater than oneself." The romantic pantheistic concept of nature became the individual's mode for expressing unity with the Volk. This was possible because nature was viewed as having a "life force which corresponded to the emotions of man," and a soul which could be in rapport with man's soul.[119] Individuals could, therefore, be linked with the Volk through a common emotional experience with nature, which increasingly became defined as the landscape. German Volkish thought eventually came to express rootedness with the soil as possible only in an individual's native landscape.

Romantics also came to see the Volk as "a historical unit that had come down to the present from a far and distant past."[120] Writers on Volkish thought romanticized the medieval past both in an effort to lend an enduring quality to the Volk and to stress the destructive nature of modernity. They idealized the medieval division of estates into peasantry and nobility and saw the bourgeoisie as the disruptive element that had challenged these estates. The ability, however, of the bourgeoisie to trace their roots to their inauspicious beginning along side the peasantry gradually caused writers to integrate them into the Volk. They also presented the same argument for bonding the working class with the Volk. In their hands, the industrial worker was transformed into a rooted artisan. The proletariat did not fair so well, for they became identified as a pariah caste, "the product of modernization," and "the enemy of the vanquished."[121] While Hitler may have accepted this thesis, he came to realize that he needed financial support from the bourgeois. The anti-bourgeois emphasis was slowly diminished, and a distinction was made between the native and the Jewish bourgeoise. The movement, therefore, left its anti-capitalist direction and retrenched into anti-Semitism.[122]

The position of the uprooted proletariat as the enemy of the Volk was, therefore, gradually usurped by the Jew. This was encouraged by literary works such as Wilhelm von Polenz's Der Büttnerbauer (The Peasant from Büttner) of 1895, in which "the Jew was identified with modern industrial society, which uprooted the peasant, deprived him of his land, caused his death, and thereby destroyed the most genuine part of the Volk.[123] The Jew became the hated moneylender, upon whom the peasant relied for support during difficult times. The Jew became identified as the cause of the German people's misfortune, the enemy of the peasant, the embodiment of rootlessness, and the most antagonistic force to Volkish values.

Scholars have long attempted to locate the source of the anti-Semitic dimension of Hitler's Volkish ideology. While some assumed that Hitler was influenced by anti-Semitic writers such as Guido von List and Lang von Liebenfels, Mosse stressed "there is no evidence that Hitler read all the literature on the subject of the Volk and the Jew."[124] It will be recalled that Hitler himself claimed his awareness of Jews began in Vienna when he encountered Eastern Jews in the streets. Although he was in contact with Volkish groups in Vienna and later in Munich, it was not until after the war that Hitler became a Volkish orator. Hitler's embitterment about the loss of the war, which in his eyes was due to the revolution led by the Jews Karl Lebnecht and Rosa Luxemburg, caused him to later write in Mein Kampf that:

If at the beginning of the war and during the War twelve or fifteen thousand of these Hebrew corrupters of the people had been held under poison gas, as happened to hundreds of thousands of our very best German workers in the field, the sacrifice of millions at the front would not have been in vain.[125]

Mosse believed, however, that Hitler's Volkish ideology was not crystallized until his contact with Dietrich Eckart, in 1921. Eckart not only "reinforced Hitler's abhorrence of Jews," but he also "connected the removal of the Jewish menace with the resuscitation of the Volk."[126]

There can be little doubt that Richard Wagner's racist views were also supremely important to the development of Hitler's Volkish ideology. Hitler himself said that any who sought to understand National Socialism "must first know Richard Wagner," and boasted that he had read everything the master had written. "I have the most initiates familiarity with Wagner's mental processes," he said, and "at every stage of my life I come back to him." Hitler believed that "with the exception of Richard Wagner he had 'no forerunner,' " and confessed that a hysterical excitement overcame him when he realized his own psychological kinship with Wagner.[127]

Waite, who found strong parallels between Wagner's and Hitler's anti-Semitism, pointed to Wagner's essay, "Judaism in Music," as a possible source of Hitler's early statements abut removal of the Jews. In that essay, Wagner called for the destruction of Ahasuerus, the wandering Jew of Volkish legend, "who had infected the German people with cholera and syphilis." Indeed, Hitler's ideology paralleled Wagner's thesis that Jews were incapable of artistic creation. Both men were physically repelled by Jews, believed Jews had no religion, thought Jesus was not a Jew, and believed that Christian baptism could not remove Jewishness, which was rooted in blood.[128]

Fest supported the thesis that Wagner's operas and writings formed:

...the entire framework for Hitler's ideology: Darwinism and anti-Semitism (I hold the Jewish race to be the born enemy of pure humanity and everything noble in man), the adoration of barbarism and Germanic might, the mystique of blood purification expressed in *Parzifal*, and the general historic view in which good and evil, purity and corruption, rulers and ruled, stand opposed in black and white contrasts. The curse of gold, the inferior race grubbing underground, the conflict between Siegfried and Hagen, the tragic genius of Wotan—this strange brew compounded of bloody vapors, dragon slaying, mania for domination, treachery, sexuality, elitism, paganism, and ultimately salvation and tolling bells on a theatrical Good Friday were the perfect ideological match for Hitler's anxieties and needs. Here he found the 'granite foundations' for his view of the world.[129]

Wagner's greatest contribution to Hitler's Volkish ideology may well have been the concept of the unchanging, inner substance of the Volk. For this reason, the saga remained eternally relevant to the German Volk. Wagner, like Hitler, desired to restore the purity of the Volk and, in the face of the modern fragmentation of the national community, viewed his operas as a means to that end.

In 1887, Ferdinand Tönnies produced a study of two contrasting types of society, the *Gemeinschaft and the Gesellschaft*, which is instructive at this point.[130] This dual typology of Tönnies was not entirely original. Plato had depicted his ideal republic of the Guardians in contrast to the oligarchic society common in his day. Augustine had equally contrasted the "City of God," of which he approved, with the earthly city of Rome, of which he was critical. While it cannot be demonstrated that Hitler read Tönnies, it is clear that the Volkish ideology embodied many of the elements, concepts and relationships which Tönnies summarized in his discussion of the *Gemeinschaft*.

The German medieval society was a prime example of a youthful society in which the *Gemeinschaft* model predominated. Then, society enjoyed a unity based upon sympathetic relations between kinfolk and old acquaintances bound together by a shared natural will (Wesenwille) which arose out of a shared language, religion and relationship with the soil. The family was a microcosm of the larger society, which through ties of clan, tribe and blood became one's extended family. Then, there was a hierarchy of authority which proceeded from the father of the family upward to the supreme authority of the group. This authority expressed itself as a solicitous paternalism. Just as the father represented the authority of age, force and wisdom in the family, the communal leader acted as the father of the society. Similarly, as the father exercised power for the benefit of the family, the communal leader exercised power for the benefit of those of lower levels in the group. The leader became, in effect, a mythical common ancestor of the Volk.

In the *Gemeinschaft*, human economic ties were met by home production and barter with kith and kin within the community. Exploitation and competition were a violation of the natural will and community spirit. Products of labor were in harmony with the collective spirit of the group and reflected its ties of blood and shared soil. Handicrafts served the needs of the community and revealed its creative, formative, and artistic genius. The *Gemeinschaft's* architecture, sculpture and paintings retained the memories of the deities and eminent persons of the Volk and kept that which was noble and eternal before their eyes.[131]

Conflict or war, when it came, interrupted what was the norm of peace and was severely limited in its intensity by the realization one was fighting one's own people. The intellectual will was harmonious with one's subconscious, emotive nature and expressed the learned and inherited modes of thought and behavior common to the community. Conflict was thus expressed within a shared set of values, beliefs, and spirit.

The *Gesellschaft*, on the contrary, was seen by Tönnies as the representative of an aging, mass society based on a capitalistic, trade economy in which industry predominated. The original or natural relationships of human beings were replaced by a system in which one's value and position were determined solely by what one produced and consumed. The individual was viewed as continually striving for his own interest in perpetual competition with aliens and strangers. No actions arose from an *a priori* and existent unity but always from selfish interest. Even the family became an economic unit governed by economic ties.

The nation, therefore, loses its original unity, as the nation is perceived as nothing more than a market for goods or a base of production of superfluous goods exportable to other, foreign markets. As profit becomes the sole motive, the noncommercial values and worth of the Volk are ignored. The *Gesellschaft*, in mature form, promotes internationalism in which economic contracts for profit supersede the racial ties of the community.

Art in all its forms reflects the value system of the *Gesellschaft*—production for profit, atomization, individualism, and internationalism. It loses its organic tie with the community and ceases to promote that which is noble and eternal in nature and mankind.[132]

The *Wesenwille* is replaced in the *Gesellschaft* by the *Kürwille*, in which the will is dominated by rational thought divorced from one's emotions, feelings and organic conscience. Healthy nationalism is censored and replaced by thought directed at gaining one's personal ends. The state becomes a contract system dominated by those special-interest groups able to impose their will on others through force and possession of wealth. Law ceases to be paternal and benevolent and exists only to protect the selfish interest of the rulers. Science, applied dispassionately by depersonalized authority to society, depersonalizes all individuals in turn. Thus, when conflict thus comes, it produces mass slaughter.

Although Tönnies called the *Gemeinschaft* an earlier and the *Gesellschaft* a later stage of society, he implied that the process could be reversed and the *Gemeinschaft* restored to something of its pristine nature. Any such change could take place only if *Kürwille* were replaced by *Wesenwille*. Romantic sentimentalizing of the past was ineffective and foolish. The *Gemeinschaft* could be created only through the realization of the organically united community.[133]

In the case of art, all creations divorced from the community, that which is displeasing and without restraint, all creations contrary to tradition, would have to be abhorred and rejected. The organic relationship between art and the cult of the community would need to be reunited with its economic life. Art and religion would have to be taken as the highest and most important functions of the community and its government. Tönnies has been discussed at length as he so succinctly described the type of *Gemeinschaft* desired by Volkish ideologues.

Hitler's view of the Germanic culture sprang from this same Volkish ideology. To Hitler, Aryans were the bearers of human cultural development. Fate had provided Aryans with the proper soil, climate and subject peoples to allow their abilities to develop. Lower human helpers were "the first technical instruments in the service of a developing culture." But, as the subjugated peoples began to better themselves, the division between the master and the servant fell. Then:

The Aryan gave up the purity of his blood and, therefore, lost his sojourn in the paradise which he had made for himself. He became submerged in the racial mixture, and gradually, more and more, lost his cultural capacity until at last, not only mentally but also physically, he began to resemble the subjected aborigines more than his ancestors.[134]

Hitler thus saw the responsibility of the new government as ridding the culture of racial impurities, as removing the chaff from the Volk.

Hitler believed it was still possible to reestablish a *Volksgemeinschaft*, a racially pure community, because a "self-sacrificing will to give one's personal labor and if necessary one's own life for others is most strongly developed in the Aryan."[135] The common good was to take precedence over the good of the individual in the *Volksgemeinschaft*, but this submission of individualism would not produce democratic rule. On the contrary, Hitler believed:

. . . the folkish state must free all leadership and especially the highest—that is, the political leadership—entirely from the parliamentary principle of majority rule—in other words, mass rule—and instead absolutely guarantee the right of the personality.[136]

Hitler's call for subordination of the individual for the communal good given in *Mein Kampf* reflected many of his earlier speeches and several points of the German Workers' Party, which he helped Drexler develop in 1920. Point ten, for example, stressed the duty of citizens to work mentally or physically and forbid individuals to do any work that offended against the interest of the community to the benefit of all. On a practical level, point sixteen called for the communalization of large stores which would be rented cheaply to small tradespeople. Point eighteen called for the death of those who worked to injure the common welfare. Point twenty-three threatened the closure of newspapers which transgressed against the common welfare, and point twenty-four stated, "a lasting recovery of our folk can only come about within on the principle: COMMON GOOD BEFORE INDIVIDUAL GOOD."[137]

In a "Proclamation to the German People," dated February 1, 1933, Hitler made it clear that the years of struggle to power had strengthened his dedication to the Volk. He stated:

We men of this government feel ourselves responsible before German history for the reconstruction of an ordered folk community and with it for the definite elimination of that crazy class warfare. We do not represent one class, but all the German people, the millions of farmers, city folk, and workers, who will either together overcome the troubles of these times or succumb to them.[138]

Later, the organizational book of the National Socialist Party stressed the necessity for understanding that:

...the value of work is determined...by the inner attitude with which it is performed. Therefore, the main elements of education for the Work Corps are a military bearing, a closeness to the soil, a positive attitude toward work, and a communal spirit.[139]

Hitler was thus not so much the creator but an heir and adapter of decades of Volkish thought. Neither was he the originator of the identification of the Jew as the cause of national problems. He understood, however, that the mass of Germans would be highly receptive to a peculiarly Volkish anti-Semitic definition of the nation's problems. He understood because he too embraced Volkish anti-Semitism. Hitler thus became their leader, at least in part, because he successfully politicized their Volkish ideology and found large segments of the population ready for his message.

Until the Reichstag election of September 15, 1930, Hitler and his NSDAP were generally regarded as insignificant right-wing fanatics both in Germany and in the foreign press. Street battles between Nazis and Communists were regular occurrences, but few believed this would bring Hitler to power. Nazi propaganda utilizing mass parades, pomp and meetings appeared to be meeting little success. As there were no national elections and few state elections between 1928 and 1930, the increasing support of the NSDAP by the lower middle-class and peasantry was largely overlooked.

However, the deepening depression produced thousands of new converts to the party. By January, 1930, Nazi party rolls listed 200,000 members. On July 18, Chancellor Bruening dissolved his cabinet and scheduled elections for September 15. In the ensuing campaign, some 34,000 NSDAP election meetings were held across Germany. Hitler threw himself into the campaign with boundless energy and fury. While it was generally expected that radicals of both the right and the left would gain in the election, the final results were astounding. The NSDAP leaped in one bound from insignificance to the second largest party in Germany with a total of 107 deputies in the Reichstag.

The new Reichstag promptly became deadlocked and Hindenburg ended by allowing Bruening to rule under Article 48 of the Weimar constitution, which permitted Bruening to govern essentially by decree. Bruening reacted to the still deepening depression with austerity measures that drove increasing numbers of Germans to desperation and the NSDAP. In the presidential election scheduled for March 13, 1932, Hindenburg was opposed both by Hitler and the Communist Ernst Thaelmann. When the results were announced, Thaelmann had polled 13.2%, Hitler 30.1%, and Hindenburg 49.6% of the vote. Nazi strength had increased by 5,000,000 since September, 1930. In the required run-off election, Hindenburg won another term as president, but Hitler had increased his support to 36.8% of the votes cast.

With the Reichstag deadlocked, Hindenburg forced the resignation of Bruening and on May 31, 1932, appointed Fritz von Papen chancellor by presidential decree. Reichstag elections were scheduled for July 31. Hitler lead the NSDAP into frenzied campaigning. Added to the previous methods of mass rallies, parades, and effective pageantry was Hitler's and Goebbels's masterful use of the new media of radio. The NSDAP won almost fourteen million votes, elected 230 deputies to the Reichstag and, overnight, became the largest party in Germany.

Von Papen decided to rule by decree and ignore the results of the election. However, he was unable to reduce the level of political violence or alleviate the growing economic distress. Reichstag elections on November 6, 1932, saw Nazi strength drop to 196 deputies—nevertheless, it remained by far the strongest party in Germany. When von Papen failed to muster parliamentary support, Hindenburg replaced him with Reichswehr Minister Kurt von Schleicher, who became chancellor on December 2, 1932. Von Schleicher, however, alienated Hindenburg by his agricultural policies and became the object of intrigues led by von Papen. On January 29, Hindenburg demanded and received von Schleicher's resignation. Von Papen suggested to Hindenburg that Hitler be appointed chancellor in a cabinet dominated by non-Nazis. So it was that:

The man who had failed to graduate from high school, who had been refused admission to the Academy of Fine Arts and who had lived as a tramp on the streets of Vienna was Chancellor of Germany on the thirtieth day of January, 1933.[140]

Chapter 4
The Imposition of Hitler's Artistic Taste
on the Third Reich

In his speech in the Reichstag on March 23, 1933, Hitler defined the cultural aims and tasks of his new government. The political purification of the country would be accompanied by a "thorough moral purging of the body corporate of the nation." All means would be used to maintain the essential character of the people. Hitler stressed that:

Art will always remain the expression and the reflection of the longings and the realities of an era. The neutral international attitude of aloofness is rapidly disappearing. Heroism is coming forward passionately and will in future shape and lead political destiny. It is the task of art to be the expression of this determining spirit of the age. Blood and race will once more become the source of artistic intuition.

Hitler affirmed the government was responsible for the security of "man's inner life and a nation's will to live" through the promotion of a culture which was rooted in appreciation of traditions of the past.[1] He spent much of the remainder of his life attempting to purify German culture of what he considered to be destructive elements. He was determined to establish a culture, based upon the heritage of the past, which he insisted would last for a thousand years.

The full range of Nazi cultural and propagandistic activities undertaken in the Third Reich in order to implement Hitler's *Kulturgemeinschaft* almost beggars description. These activities were conducted by a plethora of ministries, party organizations, institutes, leagues, and academies.

Initial efforts to establish regulations over the arts in the Third Reich began when Frick, who became Reich Minister of the Interior when Hitler came to power, appointed a system of art commissioners whose task it was to implement the cultural views of the government in art institutes and in the various ministries dealing with culture. Their activities were guided by the views of the *Kampfbund für Deutsche Kultur* and the *Fuehrerrat der Vereinigten Deutschen Kunst* (Fuehrer's Council of United German Art and Cultural Associations).[2] In 1933, the latter organization published in *Deutscher Kunsthericht (German Art Report)* a five-point manifesto entitled "What German Artists Expect from the New Government." This manifesto was not an official document, but it did set the tone for the future policy of the party. It began militantly:

What German artists expect from the new government! They expect that in art, too, there will be only one guideline for action from now on, and that guideline is a philosophy drawn from a passionate national and state consciousness anchored in the realities of blood and history! Art shall serve the growth and strengthening of this folkish community...They [artists] expect not only that materialism, Marxism, and Communism will be politically persecuted, outlawed, and eradicated but also that the spiritual battle...will now be taken up by the people as a whole and that Bolshevist nonart and nonculture will be doomed to destruction. Here it must be the sacred duty of the state to place in the front lines those soldiers who have already proved their mettle in cultural battle. In the visual arts, this means:

1. that all products of cosmopolitan or Bolshevist nature will be removed from German museums and collections. First they should be brought together and shown to the public, and the public should be informed how much these works cost and which gallery officials and ministers of culture were responsible for buying them. Then only one useful function remains to those works of nonart. They can serve as fuel for heating public buildings.

2. that all museum directors who sinned against a needy nation...by their shameless waste of public funds...who opened our art galleries to everything un-German...be immediately 'suspended' and be declared forever unfit for public office...

3. that from a certain date on the names of all artists subscribing to Marxism and Bolshevism no longer appear in print. We must abide...by the old law of an eye for an eye, a tooth for a tooth!...

4. that in the future we in this country will not have to look at apartment blocks or churches that look like greenhouses with chimneys or glass boxes on stilts and that ways will be found to claim restitution from the criminals who grew rich perpetrating such insults against our native culture...

5. that sculptures that are offensive to the national sensibility and yet still desecrate public squares and parks disappear as quickly as possible, regardless of whether these works were created by 'geniuses' like Lehmbruck or Barlach. They must give way to the scores of artists loyal to the German tradition. The conscientious care and nurturing of all existing impulses toward a new flowering of art will have to go hand in hand with the radical negation that will free us from the nightmare of the past years! The people's love for art, immobilized by the terror of artistic Bolshevism, will reawaken...[3]

Following this manifesto, on May 10, 1933, books considered to be un-German were ceremoniously burned by students in cities throughout the Reich. In his "Speech of Justification" Goebbels stated:

When you students take upon yourselves the task of casting this unworthy filth into the flames, then you must also take upon yourselves the duty of replacing it with a real German spirit of the street.[4]

This statement epitomized what would be the Third Reich's approach to the arts. Un-German cultural elements would be purged and replaced by pure German works.

On June 30, 1933, Hitler issued his decree for the *"Gleischschaltung* (Coordination) of All Activities in the Third Reich." The Ministry of Public Enlightenment and Propaganda was already in the hands of Goebbels. He was now directed to coordinate the press, radio, art, music, theater, and cinema. Each area was to promote, foster and nurture the Nazi image and standards set by Hitler. The essence of the decree was that Nazi Germany was to simply reflect the personal views and wishes of Hitler. Because Hitler passionately admired Wagner, Wagner's work was to be especially promoted. Because Hitler rejected modern art, it was to be labeled *entartet Kunst* and purged. Because Hitler hated Jews, German culture had to be cleansed of all Jewish contributions.[5] Goebbels henceforth became the primary spokesman and implementer of Hitler's policies.[6]

On September 22, 1933, a new law established a Reich Chamber of Culture with Goebbels as its president. Seven subordinate chambers were set up concerning literature, music, films, radio, theater, fine arts, and the press. Each of these chambers had its own administrative apparatus that reported directly to Goebbel's ministry. While preserving the appearance of autonomy, the chambers were, in fact, part of a single propaganda machine.

The preamble of the law which put the Reich Chamber of Culture in place stated that it:

...is the duty of the State to combat all influences which are detrimental to culture and to encourage, on the other hand, those that are valuable, comfortably with the consciousness of its responsibility toward the national community. The same criterion applies to the creations of the artist himself, which within this limitation may remain individualistic and independent. But the pursuit of a German cultural policy in the true sense of the word renders it necessary to unite artists, authors, and journalists, in a common will under the direction of the Reich.[7]

Thus, the nation became a *Kulturgemeinschaft* with artists, authors, and journalists in service to the common good.

The new Reich Chamber of Culture was inaugurated in the Philharmonic Hall in Berlin, on November 15, 1933, in the presence of Hitler. In his opening speech Goebbels stated:

Culture is the highest expression of the creative forces of a nation and the artist is its qualified inspirer. It would be a fallacy to suppose that he could fulfill his mission without reference to his own nation, since the mission is in reality destined for the latter and since the force thanks to which the artist has laboured is derived from his nation. We have once more liberated the creative forces of the German nation, which can henceforth develop freely without let or hindrance, and thus abundantly fertilise the soil on which new generations will be reared.[8]

In order for an individual to be involved in any artistic profession, membership in the Culture Chamber was compulsory. Members were not permitted, however, to belong to a Chamber of Industry, Commerce, or Handicraft, or to the German retail trader's organization, thus ensuring the purely cultural character of the new institution. During this initial year of the Chamber's operation, the explusion of all non-Aryans from its various component Chambers was decreed and their transfer to the Jewish cultural association mandated.

A complementary decree of November, 1933, gave the Chamber of Culture and its subdivisions state power. The president of each division of the Chamber of Culture could exercise powers which were equal to and as binding as state laws. They could refuse anyone membership in their particular chamber or withdraw it, if the individual proved not to possess qualifications necessary for the exercise of activities in his field. They could also impose fines up to 100,000 Reich Marks upon members or non-members who contravened regulations. This same decree obliged the police to enforce measures taken by the presidents of the various divisions of the Reich Chamber of Culture.

In 1934, one year after the establishment of the Chamber of Culture, Goebbels praised the effectiveness of the Chamber in a speech before the Chamber of Arts. He announced that the orders he issued earlier against the severe and unornamental style of the post-war period had enabled many sculptors and painters to obtain jobs on public building enterprises. He also announced the opening in large cities of galleries where artists could sell their works and receive a fair price. Goebbels stated that in the art industries "unfit" persons, non-Aryans, would be replaced with qualified artists and craftsmen. German artists would, according to Goebbels, be expected to conform to an aesthetic code which demanded inspiration be drawn from their own race and native soil.[9]

In 1935, non-Aryan art dealers were ordered by Goebbels to close their doors. More than seventy firms were affected in Berlin, Munich, Dresden and Frankfort-on-Main. Their licenses were suspended, their bank accounts were sequestered, and they were told they could not sell their works in Germany nor abroad. One Aryan connoisseur claimed the art dealers' profession in Germany needed to be purged because many dealers had no art education, although, in fact, many had thirty to forty years experience in the business.[10]

Goebbels also moved to mute all criticism of the artistic policies of the Nazi state. On November 11, 1936, Goebbels issued a "Decree Concerning Art Criticism." He declared that he had granted German critics four years after the National Socialist assumption of power to adapt themselves to the new principles. Since no improvement in that direction had been made, he simply abolished all art criticism. He stated artistic criticism was to be replaced by "art reporting." All comments on works of art were to be only descriptions, to which the author signed his full name. In order to edit a journal concerned with art, special permission had to be obtained. Applicants for such permission had to be over thirty years of age. Kurt Karl Eberlein, an art historian and literary critic, supported the official policy which Goebbels expounded and summoned Volkish ideology to defend his position when he said, "The rural family (and the peasant is the primordial image of the Volk) does not 'judge' art, but accepts it and lives it...if this art is of the right Germanic kind."[11]

As late as March, 1944, Hitler continued to justify this action against art critics. He recalled that the ancients had disregarded art critics and judged a work as they found it for themselves. In Hitler's mind, this was the "natural method of selection." He resented the power which a critic had to destroy the aspirations of an artist, such as E.R.A. Hoffman, who had "prejudiced the chances of success of *Der Freischütz.*" Wagner, too, he stressed was "torn to bits for ten years by critics and so was the opera *Carmen.*" He rejoiced in the fact that the critics of such masterpieces were "utterly forgotten, but the works live on."[12]

Annual installments of *Das Recht der Reichskulturkammer (The Law of the Reich Chamber of Culture)* kept all concerned apprised of the Chamber of Culture regulations. Such details included even the fees allowed to textile dealers and the opening times for an antique dealer's fair. Detailed records were kept of the membership of suspect groups such as Masonic Lodges and Rotary Clubs. The chamber records assisted in the establishment of proof of a member's Aryan descent.

A sense of the enormity of the Chamber of Culture may be grasped by a look at the membership statistics for a single division in late 1936. At that time, the Chamber of Visual Arts (Fine Arts) had about 42,000 members. Among the members were "15,000 architects, 14,300 painters, 2,900 sculptors, 2,300 people working in arts and crafts, 4,200 graphic artists, 1,260 designers and 2,600 art publishers and art dealers."[13]

All areas of the arts were profoundly affected by Hitler's rise to power. Architecture, however, was dearest to his heart and received his personal and devoted attention throughout the twelve years of the Third Reich. As early as 1920, Hitler told an audience at the *Hofbräuhaus* that "a strong Germany must have a great architecture, since architecture was a vital index of national power and strength." His attitude toward architecture did not change during that decade for, in 1929, he promised that when the party was in power, "out of our new ideology and our political will to power we will create stone documents."[14] He reiterated this in a speech of 1935, when he said that even when a nation's life is denied, the visible demonstration of a people's highest values remain as a witness of a people's moral right to life. When "unfortunate people have closed their mouths in death, then the stones will speak again." He believed it was the task of the Reich to help the people understand its greatness through achievements in the field of architecture.[15]

Prior to coming to power, the party promised supporters the architects Gropius, May, Taut, Wagner, and about twenty other leading modern architects, would be purged. They also insisted the new government would insist on a 'German' or 'national socialist' style in building. Naturally, the *Kampfbund* believed it would direct this process and would shift emphasis to architecture of a rural, rather than an urban character. Part of these exceptions were fulfilled in the spring of 1933, when the first rank of architects of *Der Ring* style of architecture in Vienna lost their jobs in schools, building societies, municipal governments, and professional organizations.[16] No law was passed, however, preventing them from taking commissions, and many of their assistants and students retained positions in the new government.

Hitler himself never publicly criticized modern architecture before 1933. It was in a speech before the Party Congress on September 1, 1933, that he first condemned "those who think that the representatives of the cultural decadence. . .can be the standard bearers of the future." He stated that "today's tasks require new methods." Hitler seemed to have proposed a compromise between the conservative Rosenberg clique and the modernistic Goebbels factions of the party. A few weeks later, he insisted that "there be no wrangling or small selfish quarrels among the brothers of the great German Fatherland."[17] In an effort to resolve these problems, Hitler set up the *Kulturkammer* with Goebbels as its director. For nearly two years, Goebbels and Rosenberg debated in speeches and articles their individual concepts of Reich architecture. Rosenberg was finally removed from control over cultural affairs by assignment to the party's foreign policy bureau and, in 1934, he assumed the post of "Custodian of the entire intellectual and spiritual training and education of the party."[18] Goebbels, in triumph, took the middle-of-the-road approach to architecture that Hitler had suggested.

The *Kulturkammer* division in charge of architecture was the *Reichkammer der bildenden Künste*. The first president of this chamber was Eugen Honig, a member of the *Kampfbund*, and German Bestelmeyer, another member, was appointed to the governing body of the organization, the *Reichskultursenat*. These men were, however, only moderate opponents of 'architectural bolshevism.' The chamber demanded membership for architects who wished to practice and passed a law which required building designs that exhibited proper architectural views. Surprisingly, however, the law was used only to preserve a consistent roof line in the historic sections of cities or occasionally to prevent the erection of ugly signs and billboards.[19]

Lane claimed that no architect was denied membership in the *Reichkammer der bildenden Künste* on the basis of the style of his work, and, while the chamber was set up to control style, it was used as a means to exclude Jews from practice.[20] The radical architects were not terrorized, imprisoned, nor deprived of the right to practice. After 1933, however, they simply did not receive new commissions. Gropius, Mendelsohn, Mies van der Rohe, Wagner, and Ludwig Hilbersheimer emigrated to England and America, while May and Taut were prevented from returning to Germany from Russia. Of those who remained in Germany, some retired, some taught and others took subordinate positions in large firms.[21]

The National Socialist building program was extensive and impressive. There never developed a unified "Nazi" style of architecture, however. Many styles they used had roots in architectural designs which existed long before Hitler came to power. There was, however, a united sense that building would develop the bonds of the German community. Each style played a part in expressing or supporting the volkish concept. The half-timbered cottages symbolized the unity of the German people with "the soil." The new monumental structures expressed the triumphal strength of the unified volkish community.[22]

Hitler never provided a stylistic control of Reich architecture. Instead, in his speeches on art, he praised each type of architecture as an index of national creativity, which he supported in the Reich through a propaganda campaign. While the most obvious ideological styles were energetically publicized, even those with lesser ideological significance were praised with great ceremony and celebration. Taylor believed the lack of stylistic unity in Third Reich architecture was symptomatic of Hitler's indifference to any architecture other than the monumental and, additionally, of the eclectic, pragmatic theory of architecture that developed in the Reich. Hitler did not forbid any style as long as it could be rationalized as "German."[23] Hitler's tolerance of various styles may also have been rooted in his own eclecticism, for, while he preferred neoclassicism, he genuinely appreciated a wide variety of architectural styles.

While Speer claimed there was not a Fuehrer style of architecture during the Third Reich, there was a basic style Hitler preferred for public buildings. As was seen earlier, Hitler was much influenced by the buildings of the Vienna Ringstrasse. The neo-Renaissance and neo-Baroque styles of these buildings dominated his architectural aesthetic until the early 1930s. At that time, perhaps due to the influence of such architects as Paul Troost, Hitler's architectural commissions became thoroughly imbued with classicism. He was, therefore, a willing supporter of theories fostered by writers of the period who believed that the Dorian Greeks, who were responsible for major aspects of classicism, were Germanic peoples who had migrated from the north into the Mediterranean region. Hitler believed the ancient Greeks had a fresh and healthy view of life, which was expressed in their architecture. To Hitler, Greek architecture represented the supreme combination of beauty and function.[24]

Hanfstaengl stressed Hitler's admiration for the ancient Greeks and found Pericles, the great Greek architect-politician to be one of Hitler's idols. He pointed to A.W. Grube's nineteenth-century work called *Historische Charakterbilder* as Hitler's source of information on Pericles. Hanfstaengl also drew parallels between "the council of elders on the Areopagus hill, which Pericles had stormed" and "the corrupt bourgeoise forces the Nazis had sworn to liquidate."[25]

Joachim Winckelmann's *Kunst des Altertums* of 1776 was a prime transmitter of Greek classicism to the nineteenth-century German neo-classicism from which Hitler's architectural taste was derived. Winckelmann saw Greek classicism as ideal beauty. He espoused the classical thesis that beauty was predicated upon symmetrical proportion and unity. Winckelmann's classical aesthetics were compatible with Schiller's thesis that beauty was the unifying element in society. It united opposites into harmony and brought out the best in men. In order to achieve this purpose, Winckelmann, Schiller, and later, Hitler, believed beauty must never be chaotic.

Shortly after Winckelmann, Friedrich von Schlegel, in 1794, sounding much like Hitler, called for Greek forms in contrast to modernity. There followed construction of impressive nineteenth-century structures such as Leo von Klenze's *Walhalla*, near Regensburg, which is a Greek temple for statues of famous Germans. Other Greek-style architectural works of that century include *The Hall of Liberation of Kelheim*, the *Hall of Fame* and the *Gate of Victory* in Munich, the *Niederwalddenkmal* in the Rhineland, and the *Volkerschlachtdenkmal* in Leipzig. The classical tradition was also continued by the late nineteenth-century architect Gottfried Semper, whom Hitler came to appreciate during his association with Ludwig Troost. Speer attested to Hitler's love of Semper's classicism as well as that of Theophil Hansen, and among Hitler's sketches there survived a drawing of the interior of the Prinzregenten Theater in Munich by Hansen and Semper's famous theater in Dresden. Speer also reported he was sent to Brussels to look at the huge Palace of Justice by Poelaret, when German troops took the city in 1940. Hitler had raved about the building and he wanted Speer to give him a detailed description of it.[26]

The severe Prussian classicism of architects such as Schinkel and Gilly, however, seemed to have no appeal to Hitler. Speer gave Hitler a book on Gilly, whom Speer admired and strove to follow, but Hitler never even mentioned the book to Speer. He concluded that Hitler could not relate to Prussia because "he was Habsburgian, basically anti-Prussian."[27]

Several of these nineteenth-century works exemplified an amalgamation of the classical with the monumental. They served as visual expressions of nineteenth-century mass politics and nationalism. In the twentieth century, they inspired Hitler to design structures of super-dimensionality as expressions of his political views.

At least as early as 1933, Hitler began to include ancient Rome, as well as Greece, as an appropriate source of classical influence for the Germans. He said:

...each political heroic age in its art immediately seeks bridges to a not less heroic past. The Greeks and Romans suddenly become very near, because all their roots lie in a founding race, and therefore, the immortal accomplishments of the ancient peoples have an attractive influence on their racially related descendants.[28]

His already well-developed love of monumental structures was reinforced by his visit to Rome in 1938. At both the Pantheon and the Colosseum, he sent his retinue outside so he could concentrate on the structure undisturbed. He was also much impressed with the size of the baths of Caracalla. Hitler appreciated the heroic dimensions of ancient classical architecture as he did the monumental works of the nineteenth-century.

In a speech before building workers in January, 1939, Hitler justified his taste for grand-scale architecture by stating, "I do this to restore to each individual German his self-respect," and "In a hundred areas I want to say to the individual: we are not inferior, on the contrary, we are the complete equal of every other nation."[29] Helmer suggested that, while Hitler's monumental undertakings may "offend our sense of social justice," in the 1930s "it would not necessarily have affected most ordinary Germans in this way, hungry as they were for a renewed sense of National pride."[30] Viewed in this light, Hitler and his followers saw monumental works much as Moller van der Bruch had when he wrote in 1916, that such works represented dominance and manliness and recalled a time when man, hero and artist were identical. Speer, who worked with Hitler to design monumental works, added that Hitler "wanted to impress, and also to intimidate, the people by vast proportions," to psychologically secure his rule and that of his successors.[31]

The greatest evidence for his concern with monumentality came after his rise to power, but Fest pointed out that Hitler's love of large-scale structures began in his youth when he dreamed of extending "the 360-foot-long frieze on the Linz museum to another 300 feet, so that the city would have the 'biggest sculptural frieze on the Continent.' " This, Fest saw as only one example of Hitler's early obsession with record size, speed, and numbers.[32]

Perhaps, due to his love of the Roman Colosseum, Hitler approved of the clear proportions, practicality and force of the Romanesque style in architecture. He may also have accepted the thesis of some of his contemporaries that early Romanesque architecture was a Germanic style. These contemporaries thought the Romans had taken over Greek achievements to which the Teutonic tribes brought their energy and imagination, thus creating a "Nordic synthesis."[33]

Hitler judged the Gothic style of architecture, however, as Winckelmann doubtlessly would have, as exaggerated and excessive in its ornamentation. This condemnation of ornamentation was reflected in the structures Hitler built for the Third Reich. Schramm insisted that Hitler disliked the Gothic style because its vertical thrust offended him. He did approve of Strasbourg Cathedral but only because its nave was not as narrow as that of the typical Gothic structure. Further, its angels' columns stressed its horizontal lines and stood out in nearly full relief. Hitler planned to make the Strasbourg Cathedral into a monument to the Unknown Soldier of World War II after Germany's victory.[34]

Speer claimed Hitler was not fond of the baroque splendor of the Banz monastery, but he "showed unrestrained admiration for the monumentality of the architectural complex as a whole." On the other hand, Speer came to realize in Spandau Prison that Hitler was drawn to baroque architectural elements but had difficulty including them in his sketches for buildings. Speer was well aware, however, that Hitler's fondness for the neo-baroque elements of Vienna's Ringstrasse remained with Hitler "to the end."[35] His enthusiasm for this style evidently sprang from the Vienna Opera House and stimulated his love of the Paris Opera House, which Hitler believed had one of the most beautiful staircases in the world. He was also especially fond of the many late-baroque theaters built by Hermann Helmer and

Ferdinand Feller in Austria-Hungary and Germany. In Augsburg, Speer saw Hitler unnerved because the theater by Helmer and Feller had not been maintained. Speer recalled:

> ...Hitler went into rapture over the rich neo-baroque architecture of the galleries and boxes. For almost half an hour he hurried us down the rows of seats, up corridors, into stairwells, backstage, to show us every perspective, every detail, every ornament.

On the spot, Hitler declared he would thoroughly renovate and rebuild the theater out of his personal funds and promised to send his opera architect, Professor Baumgarten, to put the theater in first-class shape. He reiterated his epigrammatic sentence that, "The theater is the standard by which the culture of a city or civilization is measured."[36]

Although the works Hitler commissioned during the Third Reich reflected a taste for classicism in public architecture, Speer believed that Hitler was ultimately "drawn back to inflated neobaroque such as Kaiser Wilhelm II had also fostered, through his court architect Ihne."[37] While this may appear to contradict Hitler's love of classical architecture, it represents the other side of the aesthetic coin. The history of art is replete with the counterbalancing of the romantic and the classical, the emotional and the sober. Hitler's love of the neo-baroque style may reflect his romantic side, and his classical taste, his serene side.

Hitler, therefore, carried into his Chancellorship an eclectic architectural taste, which doubtlessly contributed to his tolerance of a variety of architectural styles in Third Reich architecture. Although he would never completely abandon his delight in baroque elements, he came to identify classicism as the appropriate style for architectural projects which he personally undertook. This taste for the classical was reinforced by the architect Paul Troost, who created for Hitler what Speer called an austere neo-classicism. This style became identified as the "Fuehrer Style," and the House of German Art, which Troost and Hitler designed together, became the standard-bearer of that style.[38]

The preference of Hitler for neo-classical architecture must be placed in a larger context than merely a German or Nazi setting. The *Jugendstil* movement in Vienna was representative of a growing appreciation of the neo-classical versus the heavy historicism of the latter part of the nineteenth century. By the 1930s, neo-classicism had taken hold internationally. The University of Rome building of Marcello Piacentrini, Auguste Perret's Museum of Public Works in Paris, and the Red Army Theater in Moscow by K.S. Alabyan and V.N. Simbirtzev all demonstrate elements of neo-classicism. The Russian pavilion at the Paris World's Fair in 1927 and Speer's German pavilion are complementary images of one another—even to the type of sculptural figures employed by each.[39] In Washington, the National Archives (1935), the Jefferson Memorial (1943), the Supreme Court Building (1935), and the National Gallery (1941) are prime examples of this trend in the United States. This tends to support Speer's assertation of the nonideological character of neo-classicism in Germany. It also undercuts any idea that neo-classicism was a "totalitarian" architecture.

The House of German Art was opened on July 18, 1937, and still stands on Prinzregentenstrasse, in Munich. This first major architectural project of the Third Reich was dedicated to art, a central force in Hitler's life. The design of the structure embodied a modernized neoclassical style, which conformed to Hitler's desire to display the Greek spirit in modern form. The cream-colored limestone building has only two storeys. It stands long and low with classical columns. The rectangular stones, which are laid horizontally, are emphasized through the use of recessed mortar. Horizontal steps running the length of the building serve to further emphasize this horizontal dimension.

Troost had insisted that the museum be not merely a showplace for painting but a representative structure, a temple of German art. The marble interior is symbolic of Troost's injunction. Although functional considerations appeared to be secondary, the building was well equipped with a heating and humidity-control system powered by gas and an underground air-raid shelter.[40] Of the structure, Hitler said:

This masterpiece is as notable for its beauty as it is for the functionality of its technical equipment, but no where do subordinate, technical requirements intrude on the design of the whole. It is a temple of art, not a factory, not a power plant, not a train station or a transformer station. With this building, we set ourselves a historic task. It is not only the great and unique artistic conception of this museum that has helped us fulfill this task but also the magnificent materials used and the exacting and conscientious execution of the design... The result is a house worthy of sheltering the highest achievements of art and of showing them to the German people. The building was also conceived of as a turning point that would put an end to the chaos of architectural dabbling we have seen in the recent past. This is the first new building worthy enough to take a place among the immortal achievements of our German artistic heritage.[41]

The overall design of the museum is neoclassical. However, the blocky masses and flat surfaces of the museum, the absence of ornamentation, except for minimal base and cornice projections, and the horizontal orientation of the building, proclaim Troost's and Hitler's debt to the twenties. This unity of neo-classicism with modernity was carried further in works Hitler commissioned from Albert Speer.

Trappings of Nazi art and artifacts were zealously removed from the building after World War II. Such was the fate of a saying by Hitler on a tablet on the front wall of the museum. It read, "Art is a noble and fanatical mission." Also removed were two large braziers which stood on pylons on either end of the facade. Surprisingly, a stylized swastika pattern in red and green tile may still be seen on the ceiling of the porch.

It appeared for awhile after Troost's death, in 1934, that Hitler himself would take control of the building of the House of German Art. In the end, however, Leonhard Gall, Troost's assistant and staunch supporter of Troost's style, was given the task, along with Troost's wife, Gerdy. It has also been generally assumed that after Troost's death, Albert Speer became Hitler's chief architect. Speer, however, warned his readers in *Inside the Third Reich* that ten or twelve architects worked for Hitler, and they were not subordinated to Speer.[42] Hitler was able to keep up with several architectural projects at once. Speer reported that Hitler possessed an ability to "grasp a sketch quickly and to combine the floor plan and renderings into a three-dimensional conception." He could monitor the progress in designs of ten to fifteen large buildings at once and showed restraint and civility in working out design problems with the architects.

Troost afforded an opportunity for Hitler's classical taste in architecture to find expression. Albert Speer, however, became his companion in the design of several party and public buildings which gave increased expression to Hitler's love of the monumental. Speer received his first major commission from Hitler in 1934. He was to replace the temporary bleachers on the Zeppelin Field in Nuremberg with a permanent stone installation. After some inward struggle, Speer designed "a mighty flight of stairs topped and enclosed by a long colonnade, flanked on both sides by stone abutments." Speer asserted his design was based upon the Pergamum Altar, and the dimensions went far beyond the scope of Hitler's request. It measured thirteen hundred feet long by eighty feet high. Hitler examined the model and drawings Speer prepared and simply said, "Agreed," presumably because Speer had conformed to Hitler's classical taste and his desire for the monumental.[43] Speer, however, believed that he did not abandon his own architectural desires for Hitler's. Rather, he thought Hitler had led him to find himself. He had never been drawn to the work of Gropius but to the feeling of solidarity, simplicity and craftsmanship of Tessenow, with whom he worked before he met Hitler.

Speer was also attuned to Hitler's *Volkish* ideology, for, as he said:

My distaste for big cities, for the type of person they produced, and even my incomprehension of the amusement of my fellow students, together with my passion for rowing, hiking, and mountain climbing—all this was part and parcel of the romantic protest against civilization. I regarded Hitler above all as the preserver of the world of the nineteenth century against that disturbing metropolitan world which I feared lay in the future of all of us. Viewed in that light, I might actually have been waiting for Hitler.[44]

With this confession, made during his imprisonment in Spandau, Speer himself laid to rest his earlier explanation that he was a victim of Hitler, the great seducer.

Hitler wanted his architectural projects to transmit his time and its spirit to posterity, and he believed that monumental architecture survived after people were gone. Monumental architecture also sustained a nation in periods of weakness. The success of Mussolini was stimulated by the exhortation to greatness by the surviving heroic monuments of the Roman empire. The works Hitler proposed were to speak to a future Germany. Therefore, they had to be a permanent type of construction. Speer, therefore, developed a "Theory of Ruin Value" for Hitler, in 1934. This theory dealt with the use of special materials and the application of certain principles of statics which would cause a building to look heroic even with decay and neglect after thousands of years. To exemplify his theory, Speer had a drawing of the Zeppelin Field done with crumbling walls and fallen columns which were overgrown with ivy. Hitler accepted the theory and ordered that "in the future the important buildings of the Reich were to be erected in keeping with the principles of the laws of ruins."[45]

In this work it is both unnecessary and impossible to discuss each of the major Nazi works in detail.[46] What is necessary is to discuss those buildings in which Hitler played the greatest personal role and which represent his personal interests and attitudes.

The Zeppelin Field served as the setting for one of Hitler's propaganda triumphs. For the 1937 party rally at the Zeppelin Field, Speer suggested a night parade. He asked for one-hundred and thirty anti-aircraft searchlights to light the Zeppelin Field. Goering objected to their use, but Hitler stated that "if we use them in such number for a thing like this, other countries will think we're swimming in searchlights." The lights created the illusion of columns which rose to 20,000 feet enclosing a vast room.[47]

Earlier, in 1935, Hitler had approved Speer's plans for the Nuremberg Party Rally site, of which the Zeppelin Field was one component.[48] In 1937, Speer's design was displayed as a model at the Paris World's Fair where it won the Grand Prix. The Zeppelin Field, which measured approximately 960 feet square, or roughly twice the size of Trafalgar Square, was an early example of Hitler's insistence on monumentality for public architectural works.[49] Designed to hold 240,000 spectators, it was bounded on all sides by stands dominated by the twin colonnades of the major stand on the north. Its low horizontal lines were intended to provide a sense of expanding space and distance. Overall, its basic design was neo-classical—as one might expect given Speer's use of the Pergamum Altar as his inspiration.

Psychologically, the overall impression was that of a fortress. Nazi writers lauded it as a recreation of the Tannenberg Memorial in East Prussia and, as such, the expression of the "living space of a community" bounded by the determination of the community to defend itself.[50] Speer subsequently described it as his best design.

At one end of the Nuremberg Complex lay Mars Field. Its name was selected not only to symbolize the war god Mars, but also the month in 1935 when Hitler introduced conscription for the first time since 1918. Inside its interior area of 3,400 by 2,300 feet, which may be compared to the Place de la Concorde, with its approximately 1,170 by 705 feet, the German army could actually conduct minor maneuvers. Speer planned for it to have twenty-four towers over one hundred and thirty feet high to punctuate the stands, which could hold 500,000 spectators. The processional avenue was a mile and a quarter long, 264 feet wide, and was paved with granite slabs that would support the weight of tanks. Hitler and his generals were to review the army from a stand opposite a sixty-foot colonnade, where regimental flags would be displayed.[51]

Hitler stipulated that the Luithold Stadium of the Nuremberg Complex was to be large enough to hold 400,000 people. Speer designed it to be 1,815 feet long, 1,518 feet wide, with stands three hundred feet high. Speer proudly pointed out that the volume of over 11,100,000 cubic yards was some three times more than the volume of the pyramid for Cheops. When Speer presented Hitler with the estimated cost of the stadium, Hitler declared the billion marks ($250,000,000 in 1969) to be less than two battleships of the *Bismarck* class. He also pointed out to Speer that warships would be scrap-iron in ten years, but the Stadium would stand for centuries.[52]

Hitler placed Speer in charge of construction of everything at the Nuremberg Complex except for the Congress Hall, which Ludwig Ruff designed in 1927-1928. Hitler approved of Ruff's plans, but he had them expanded to hold 60,000 people and ordered that construction begin in 1935. In order to improve the durability quotient of the structure, he decided it be built of "pure" granite blocks instead of Ruff's proposed concrete. This was a sixty-meter-high building with a curving facade which corresponded to the horseshoe shape of the interior stands and which had an arcade running its entire length. A free-standing roof was planned to stretch over the one hundred and sixty meter floor, which gave the impression of being outside due to large windows in the ceiling. Once again, a severe neo-classicism dominated the design. Only the Zeppelin Field was completed of the planned works.

The same desire for monumentality and propaganda effect was exhibited in Hitler's new Chancellery building. Late in January, 1938, Hitler called Speer to his office and asked him to have a new chancellery completed by January 10, 1939, in time for Hitler's next diplomatic reception. Largely Speer's work, Hitler, nevertheless, regularly checked the plans as they were drawn.

The new Chancellery repeated the same severe neo-classicist impulse characteristic of Speer's designs. It had generally horizontal lines with a heavy cornice intended to define the roof and so resembled an Italian Renaissance facade. What was most noteworthy about the building was its deliberate monumentality and theatrical interior. Walking through the rooms, according to Wolters, was to see "a magnificent play."[53] The visitor entered the grounds through huge gates, transversed an antechamber to the huge Mosaic Room, passed into the large Round Room, and finally entered the Long Hall. This hall was twice as long as the Hall of Mirrors of Versailles and particularly pleased Hitler by its sheer dimension—it was 480 feet long by approximately forty feet wide by thirty-two feet high.[54] Altogether, the visitor had to walk seven hundred twenty-five feet from the entrance merely to reach the Reception Hall of the Chancellery.

The construction of the Reich Chancellery took forty-five hundred workers laboring in two shifts to complete the work by Hitler's deadline. Reflecting on this several years later, Hitler said, "In Berlin, I think, people work harder than anywhere else. I know of no other city in which it would have been possible to complete the construction of the Reich Chancellery in nine months."[55] The dedication to completion of this project was due in part to the fact that it was to symbolize the revitalization of the German Volk. As such no other Nazi building received as much attention as the Chancellery. It provided an air of respectability to the regime. Additionally, it was intended to express the entire Volk community. The stone and wood were taken from every district of Germany.[56] German political discipline and military virtue were thought symbolized in the structure. Giessler insisted the building refuted liberal "materialism" by a return to authority and law.[57] As the very embodiment of Nazism, the building was totally razed after the war.

Not only was architecture a "hobby-horse" of Hitler, but, from his youth onward, he was concerned with the redesign of entire cities. This obsession began with his beloved Linz and was later extended to Berlin, Nuremberg and Munich. With the war at full speed, Hitler by personal decree, declared another twenty-seven cities, including Hanover, Augsburg, Bremen, and Weimar to be "reconstruction cities." Hitler's attitude toward these projects can best be seen by his statement on August 28, 1942, that "Some German towns must be protected at all costs—Weimar, Nuremberg, Stuttgart. Factories can always be rebuilt, but works of art are irreplaceable."[58]

In June, 1936, Hitler showed Speer his plan for the center of Berlin. With unusual patience, Hitler had waited four years for the mayor of Berlin to agree to the project. Finally, he ordered Goebbels, who had remained Gauleiter of Berlin, to replace Mayor Lippert. The actual plans for the city were a conglomeration of Hitler's ideas, Speer's designs and contributions of other architects, sculptors and painters called into Hitler's service. The work of contributors was thoroughly examined by Stephen D. Helmer in his 1980 publication, Hitler's *Berlin: The Speer Plans for Reshaping the Central City*. Helmer noted that Hitler contributed to the project "three key elements—the north-south boulevard, the Great Hall, and the Arch," and that "after entrusting his initial ideas to Speer, Hitler's direct involvement as a designer diminished greatly." Helmer admitted, however, that more important to the overall outcome was the broad philosophical influence the Fuehrer continually brought to bear on the rebuilding operation. His passion for architecture imparted an overall aesthetic bias.[59]

Hitler's increasing demand for surrealistic monumentality can be clearly seen in his plans for a great domed hall and triumphal arch to be built in Berlin. Hitler initially gave Speer two small sketches, dated 1925 in Price's collection of Hitler's works. Price also reproduced four additional sketches of the Great Hall from 1937.[60] However, under Hitler's urging, Speer increased the size of the Great Hall until it lost all semblance of human scale. As finally drawn by Speer, the dome was to "have the almost inconceivable diameter" of 825 feet and would have risen to a height of 725 feet, with an area of 410,000 square feet—a space large enough to have contained sixteen times the volume of St. Peter's Cathedral in Rome.[61] It would have provided space for an audience of 150,000-180,000 people. Like the Roman Pantheon, which served as Hitler's model, the dome was to contain an oculus 152 feet in diameter, and so, be alone larger than the entire Pantheon dome (142 feet) and that of St. Peter's (145 feet). The sheer size of the dome was an obsession for Hitler. He was "deeply irked" when he heard Stalin merely planned an enormous assembly building in honor of Lenin, but finally contented himself with the thought of the uniqueness of his dome.[62]

Hitler's projected design for his Triumphal Arch likewise revealed his loss of any sense of reality in his architectural planning. The arch was to have been 550 feet wide, 92 feet deep, and 386 feet high. The Arc de Triomphe in Paris is only 160 feet high and would have fitted into Hitler's arch 49 times. The arch was intended to have carved in its granite the names of Germany's war dead.[63] Except for its monumentality, there was nothing noteworthy about Hitler's arch.

Price's collection also contained Hitler's sketches for the Railway Station in Berlin.[64] This structure was to have been at the opposite end of the approximately four mile long boulevard from the Great Hall. Hitler invisioned that visitors would come up out of the station, look down the long boulevard, through the Triumphal Arch and see the Great Hall.[65] Other monuments he sketched for Berlin included a Pilot's Memorial, a Mussolini Memorial, and an Extension of the Winged Victory Column.[66]

During 1940, Hitler made a tour through Paris. He thought it was beautiful but insisted that Berlin must be made far more beautiful. He confided calmly to Speer that he had in the past considered the destruction of Paris, but then realized it would be only a shadow beside Berlin when the rebuilding was completed. The following year Speer requested permission to dedicate his energies only to the Berlin and Nuremberg projects. In order to carry out Hitler's orders regarding completion of Berlin, Goering diverted eighty-four thousand tons of iron annually from the war effort. The operation was camouflaged under the code name "War programs for waterways and Reich railways, Berlin section." To speed up the construction of the buildings which formed Hitler's power center around the Adolf Hitler Platz, the seven best German construction firms were called in. In July, 1941, while the German march into Russia was "still proceeding boldly," Speer suggested to Dr. Todt, who was in charge of the German construction industry, that "work be suspended on all buildings not essential for the war." Hitler would not hear of it. On the contrary, by September, "when the advance in Russia was already lagging," Hitler increased contracts for granite purchases from Sweden, Norway, and Finland for the Berlin and Nuremberg buildings. The Reich had, in fact, founded a transport fleet in June to transport the stone to Germany. Shipyards were set up in Wiemar and Berlin and plans were made for construction of 1,000 five-hundred ton cargo boats.[67]

The only known remains of the plans for the Great Hall of Berlin are a test sample of the concrete footing which was built near Berlin, drawings, and photographs of the models. Of the remainder of the building plans for the Berlin project there are numerous designs and photographs. The only portion of the completed segment of the structures which survived is a segment of the street plans called the Great Star.[68]

A drawing of the project was done by Speer in Spandau prison with the application of his "Ruin Value." In the drawing he tried to say, "The destroyed life work must not be allowed to become the end of all hopes. A wooden barracks symbolizes my new standards. The columns of the portico of the Great Hall were thirty meters high. I show them as ruins."[69]

In addition to rebuilding Berlin, Hitler also had plans for redesigning Linz on a monumental scale. Hitler's plan for rebuilding Linz began as early as his years of friendship with Kubizek and lasted the rest of his life. He spoke with Speer about a transformation of Linz so it could win its proper place. He wanted to build impressive buildings on both sides of the Danube with a suspension bridge connecting the two banks. Plans published in 1944, showed the so-called *Hitlerzentrum*. The cultural buildings were to be built along the Prachtstrasse, which ran from the Opera House on the main square to the railway station. His plans also included a large Gau House with a hall and tower. The tower was intended to contain his crypt. The plans also envisioned a library, armaments museum, exhibition building and monuments to the *Anschluss* and to Anton Bruckner.[70] Hitler did sketches for all of the structures,[71] but Speer was to design the picture gallery and the stadium. The latter was to be built on a hill overlooking the city, as was Hitler's residence for his old age. Hitler also sketched one of the towers of the historic fortification of Linz. He told Speer, "here was my favorite playground. I was a poor pupil in school, but I was the leader of our pranks. Someday I am going to have this tower made into a large youth hostel, in memory of those days."[72]

Speer collected altogether one-hundred and twenty-five drawings by Hitler. A few were prepared overnight, but most were hastily done in a few heavy strokes, but with accurate perspective, in Speer's presence. Of these drawings, "a good fourth of them relate to the Linz building project, which was always closest to his heart."[73] The Price collection of Hitler's works included both a ground plan and a facade drawing of what Price believed to be the Linz Opera House. These sketches were in the 1925 sketchbook which Hitler gave to Speer. Price's collection also includes the floor plan and facade of the Opera House which was drawn in Speer's presence at Obersalzberg in the spring of 1939. Three other architectural drawings in his collection show the Linz Theater on Laubenstrasse. Hitler told Hermann Giessler, who became the chief architect of the Linz program after Speer was granted permission to work exclusively on Nuremberg and Berlin, the columns were to be eliminated leaving an open hall of 400 square meters.[74]

On February 21, 1942, Hitler discussed his plan for an observatory at Linz on the Poestlingberg:

I can see it in my mind. A facade of quite classical purity. I'll have the pagan temple razed to the ground and the observatory will take its place. Thus, in future, thousands of excursionists will make a pilgrimage there every Sunday. They'll thus have access to the greatness of our universe. The pediment will bear the motto: 'The heavens proclaim the glory of the everlasting.' It will be our way of giving men a religious spirit, of teaching them humility—but without the priests.[75]

Hitler justified construction of the observatory in Linz simply because Kepler had once lived there.

Speer asserted Hitler's plans for Linz, the city of his retirement years, gradually assumed an escapist character. As the war neared its end, Hitler increasingly summoned Giessler to his headquarters in order to discuss the Linz plans—especially those of his tomb.[76]

The bridge which Hitler planned for Linz was the only portion of his designs ever constructed. Hitler called it the "Nibelungen Bridge" and planned sculptural works of characters from Wagner's operas to adorn either end of the bridge. A sculptor named Count Plettenberg did sculptures of the Wagner characters Siegfried and Kriemhild seated on chargers for the southern end of the bridge and Gunther and Brunhild for the northern end of the bridge. These were large scale works. Kriemhild's pigtail, for example, measured five feet. This sculpture project was never completed and the casts which Hitler viewed have been lost.[77]

Hermann Giessler was also employed to transform Weimar and Augsburg. Hitler was enthralled with Giessler's plans for Augsburg, when he added baroque ornamentation to the tower for that city. Together they thought of covering the tower walls with frescoes, reviving an old tradition of Swabian architecture.[78] The project was financed by placing a moratorium on all public housing, a step which Gauleiter Wahl justified on the grounds that houses "could always be built, but that monuments of such historic grandeur could only be constructed during the lifetime of the greatest German of the ages." Hitler sketched his conception of the city for Giessler to follow. He wanted this city not to feel inferior to the great city of art, Munich. Nevertheless, he planned an opera house for Munich which would seat 5,000 people.[79]

Hitler envisioned Nazi architectural works as political cathedrals for the Third Reich. In 1936, he confided to Speer that the Catholic Church and the Nazi movement were the only institutions in which a man from the lowest classes had a chance to rise so high. He believed the movement should learn from the church's method, its internal freedom, and its knowledge of psychology, but he told Speer:

...we shouldn't copy it or try to find substitutes for it. Rosenberg's fantasies about an Aryan church are ridiculous. Trying to set up the party as a new religion! A gauleiter is no substitute for a bishop; a local group leader can never serve as a parish priest....It isn't an easy thing to build up a tradition.[80]

While it appeared that Hitler was supportive of the church, further on in his monologue, it became evident that he saw the church as only one more element of German life over which the movement would take supremacy aided by architecture. He said:

...our great Movement buildings in Berlin and Nuremberg will make the cathedrals look ridiculously small. Just imagine some little peasant coming into our great domed hall in Berlin. That will do more than take his breath away. From then on the man will know where he belongs.[81]

Some six months after this conversation with Speer, Hitler planned the forum for Augsburg with a grand boulevard, a new Party Headquarters, and a tower which was deliberately made twenty meters higher than the tallest church steeple in the city and which had bigger and louder bells.

While this conversation with Speer seemed to indicate Hitler's bias toward supremacy of National Socialist architecture over that of the Christian church, it must be pointed out he essentially wanted Party architecture to dominate all its surroundings. He assured Speer that:

Large commercial towns like Ghent or Bruges, and Augsburg too, had thought in this way hundreds of years ago...That was the reason they put up such buildings as Elias Hall's six-story baroque town hall, the most beautiful in Germany. And that was also the reason that the Perlack Tower close by had been built to a height of seventy meters. Just as, in the Middle Ages, the cathedrals had towered over the homes and warehouses of the burghers, so the Party buildings must surpass modern office buildings.[82]

It was not surprising, therefore, that Hitler was against construction of high-rises and skyscrapers, for in his mind, the State belonged to the Party and not to banks.

Toward the end of the war, Hitler's hatred of America was manifested in fantasies of destruction of its major architectural contribution, the skyscraper, for which he had long ago expressed no aesthetic appreciation. Of these fantasies Speer said:

I never saw him so worked up as toward the end of the war, when in a kind of delirium he pictured for himself and for us the destruction of New York in a hurricane of fire. He described the skyscrapers being turned into gigantic burning torches, collapsing upon one another, the glow of the exploding city illuminating the dark sky.[83]

Such thoughts triggered a call for Saur to carry out Messerschmitt's scheme for a four-engine long-range jet bomber, which would have sufficient range to repay America a thousandfold for destruction of German cities.

Speer saw Hitler develop in time an almost maniacal passion for building opera houses. He believed all sizeable towns should have at least two theatrical buildings. All existing theaters had been built before the World War and in most towns the population had tripled. Therefore, he declared:

We will build opera houses almost exclusively. Opera is for the people; therefore, they must be big and have room for the masses at low prices. The youth must be brought into the opera houses. Not starting with the age of eighteen, but much sooner. That way they'll remain loyal devotees of the opera until old age. In Berlin I want to build at least five new opera houses in the various sections of the city.[84]

In 1942, the population of Berlin was about four million people and Hitler thought three opera houses were not enough. Also, Munich had only enough theater seats for 5,000 spectators and its population was nearly 900,000. Such figures justified his building projects in his own mind, but to offset criticism, Hitler always moved his defending monologues toward references to his own operatic experiences. Criticism of his plans would per force mean criticism of him. He also refused to accept criticism of his plans for building opera houses by pointing to critics of his Autobahn, who saw it as unneeded, but which had plenty of traffic once it was completed. There can be little doubt that this building project gave Hitler deep satisfaction and, as Speer reported, during the war, the destruction of an opera house pained him more than the bombing of whole residential areas.

The designs for his opera houses were much influenced by his architectural taste of the Vienna years. In 1944 he said:

...when I think of the Paris Opera House, I cannot help feel that those of Dresden and Vienna are in a very different category. The design itself of the Paris Opera is a work of genius but the execution from the artistic point of view, is very ordinary; and the interior is pretentious, overcrowded with decoration and devoid of all artistic taste. We must make sure that the new Opera House which we intend to build in Munich surpasses everything, in every way, that has ever gone before it.[85]

Mosse believed that Hitler's preoccupation with ceremony was reflected in his sketches for opera houses. This was apparent in the size of the grand staircases. He pointed to the huge stair wells of the Ringstrasse buildings in Vienna, including the Opera House, as sources of inspiration for Hitler's own stair designs. They were associated with his concept of the importance of monumental effect and appeared in his designs for all the official structures in Berlin.

One overriding characteristic of all National Socialist architecture was the rejection of ornamentation for its own sake. This dislike of superfluous ornamentation Hitler shared with the functionalists.

Ornamentation for Hitler's massive rectilinear public buildings, with their severe, unincumbered facades, was provided by the presence of sculpture. In some of his works, unimposing relief panels were planned. Such was the case in designs for his great Triumphal Arch, The Soldiers Hall, and the Fuehrer's Hall, all planned for Berlin. Other affixed sculptural elements included the traditional National Socialist symbols, including the eagle. The most imposing sculpture of the National Socialist period was, however, the free-standing, grand-scale, human forms, usually nudes, which Hitler commissioned and placed in open courts and foyers of his monumental architecture. The placement of sculpture in open spaces was in keeping with Hitler's belief that sculpture must be freed from the sterility of bare museum walls and placed in its proper place in the whole aspect of cities, in the square, on boulevards, and in the new civic areas for the people.

In his speech at the opening of the House of German Art in 1937, Hitler asserted it was the task of German sculptors to glorify the racial structure of the German people as the "ultimate fulfillment of the Greco-Nordic tradition."[86] They were to demonstrate that "never was humanity in its appearance and its feeling closer to classical antiquity than today." At the Nuremberg party rally two months later, Hitler insisted classical sculptors had described the human body in a "real" or "natural" manner according to what "later, so-called exact scientific research" found to be "correct" anatomically.[87]

In practice, this attitude led Hitler to insist on an idealization of nature in the classical tradition executed in contemporary manner. He had little difficulty in imposing this attitude upon the German people for it was an approach that already appealed to large numbers among the culture-conscious. Among sculptors, Hitler met little resistance as the idea lent itself to the vision of the key figures. Lehmbruck had died in 1919, Barlach had a limited following, as did Marcks and Gies, while Kollwitz only occasionally executed small pieces. The dominant sculptors were already Thorak, Breker, and Kolbe. Hitler was thus able to enlist already-established sculptors for his purposes. After receiving little or no patronage from the Weimar Republic, they found themselves swamped with commissions. Hitler's directives were clearly defined, widely propagated and quite palatable to the German masses.

If Hitler praised classical representation, that praise was not always tempered with the Greek reverence for sculpture of human scale. As in the case of the architecture which he inspired, Hitler again insisted on monumentality and larger-than-life works. He directed two fifty feet tall sculptures of Atlas and Tellus, a Roman earth-goddess, be prepared to flank the colonnade of the Great Hall in Berlin. As seen earlier, for the Nibelungen Bridge Hitler wanted statues so monumental that a single pigtail on Kriemhild measured five feet in length.[88] Further, Hitler preferred statues with an erotic, even lewd, nudity. He also favored an element of romanticism combined with classicism. Figures with a dramatic energy and mass, like the figures of the *Altar of Zeus*, were preferable to him. The works which Hitler commissioned, therefore, varied in their dynamic quality from the static to the energetic, and, in conformity to his prohibition against modern art, they avoided abstraction and expressionism in favor of representation. Sculptors who refused to conform to his directives were not only excluded from commissions but forbidden, along with Jewish sculptors, to work or exhibit their work.

Arno Breker, perhaps Hitler's favorite sculptor, amply demonstrated Hitler's concept of the purpose of statues. Breker's *The Party* was a heavily muscled male bearing a torch. His *Comrades* presented a similar heavy musculatured male with a defiant appearance supporting a wounded comrade.[89] These works not only met Hitler's sculptural ideals but were excellently suited to serve his social, heroic, and militaristic propaganda purposes.

Hitler was also protective of the Third Reich sculptor Joseph Thorak. In 1938, Adolf Wagner told him the sculptor's name was among a list of artists who had signed a Communist proclamation before the Nazi seizure of power. Hitler responded:

Oh, you know I don't take any of that seriously. We should never judge artists by their political views. The imagination they need for their work deprives them of the ability to think in realistic terms. Let's keep Thorak on. Artists are simple-hearted souls. Today they sign this, tomorrow that; they don't even look to see what it is so long as it seems to them well meaning.[90]

Hitler was, however, not tolerant of artists whose works he viewed as degenerate, modernistic or Jewish.

As early as April, 1933, *The New Republic* reported that painters, Jewish and gentile, were beaten on German streets because their pictures were modern.[91] This behavior reflected Hitler's desire to purge modern art from Germany. It also showed the writer's awareness that Jewish artists were under attack. Until this purge was completed to Hitler's satisfaction, he continued to condemn Dadaists, Cubists, Futurists and "vainglorious Impressionists: because their work made references to the form of expression of primitive folk." Hitler denied claims that their works were the expression of a naive, unspoiled soul and saw them rather as having a degeneracy which was utterly corrupt and diseased. While he acknowledged that art had always treated "the tragic problems of life...the useful and the harmful," he thought it was never created in order to allow the harmful to triumph, but to prove the necessity of the useful. Although Hitler believed negative subjects were appropriate within limits, he stressed it was not the function of art to:

...wallow in dirt for dirt's sake, never its task to paint men only in the state of decomposition, to draw cretins as the symbol of motherhood, to picture hunch-backed idiots as representatives of manly strength.[92]

There had been recent precedents in Austria and Germany for rejection of modern art. One such incident occurred in 1901, when the Kaiser unveiled statues of monuments to his Holenzollern ancestors and at an ensuing banquet declared "Art which transgresses the laws and limits laid down by me can no longer be called art."[93] Kaiser Wilhelm dismissed Dr. Tschude, director of the Berlin Nationalgalerie, for "aesthetic lèse-majesté in purchasing Impressionists, while the Austrian heir presumptive, Franz Ferdinand, wanted his batman to give Kokoschka the thrashing of his life."[94] The Dresden group called "Die Brucke" was accused by a Dresden newspaper of "fostering a cult of insanity," while a Munich newspaper called for the arrest of the "Blaue Reiter" painters. The Combat League of German Culture was aesthetically and politically repelled by the pacifist expressionists, and a half dozen associations protested to President Hindenburg that a 1926 Dresden exhibit of modern art was a slap in the face of the heroic army and its leader.[95] This was followed in 1930, by the short-lived ministry of Wilhelm

Frick in Thurengia, when the first flowerings of Hitler's *Kulturgemeinschaft* brought attacks upon modernism in all the arts.

The first artist to respond to Hitler's call for a purification of the arts was painter Hans Buehler, who was appointed academy director in Karlruhe. He set up an exhibit of "Government Art from 1918 to 1933" which was meant to discredit the support given to artists by the Weimar government. The artists included Max Liebermann, Lovis Corinth, Max Slevagt, Hans von Marées, and Edward Munch.[96] A sign of his lack of understanding about inappropriate art was the exclusion of works by Marées, whom the Fuehrer himself would later declare to be exemplary of the best in German painting.[97] This exhibit was followed by one in Stuttgart called "The Spirit of November: Art in the Service of Social Decay," which referred to November, 1918, the date when the German Kaiser was replaced by the Weimar Republic. Exhibited works were by such artists as Otto Dix, George Grosz, Max Beckmann, and Marc Chagall, all of whom would continue to be designated as degenerate artists.[98]

Gustav F. Hartlaub, director of the Mannhein school, was among the first museum directors to be dismissed. He had received word of what was brewing and hid several paintings in a cellar. They were found, however, put on a wagon and taken through the streets. Marc Chagall's painting of a Jewish rabbi was hung on one side of the wagon and on the other side was placed a photograph of Hartlaub and a poster which showed the amount the pictures had cost the citizens during the fantastic inflationary period of 1923.[99]

Hartlaub's dismissal was followed by other removals, which were termed "leaves of absence." These included museum directors such as Sauerlandt, Schreiber, Wiegand and Justi, and numerous government officials. It also included the entire Bauhaus faculty and the Bauhaus school, which had moved to Berlin after Frick's purge in Thurengia in 1929-1930. These early attacks upon the art world resulted in imprisonment for many artists and art scholars. Eventually, artists would be among the several thousand from the cultural sector who emigrated to cultural centers such as London, Moscow, Paris, Prague, Stockholm, Vienna, Zurich, and Palestine. Once the war began and many of these places were occupied by German troops, many then emigrated to the Americas.

Early attacks on the art world were viewed as "spontaneous popular reactions against 'smut and trash' " inspired by such groups as Rosenberg's Combat League and the Fuehrer's Council. Carl Einstein's *Die Kunst des 20 Jahrhunderts (Art of the Twentieth Century)* was used by such groups as a self-definition of their opponents in the visual arts. Troost, it was believed, used this book to explain Marxist elements in modern art to Hitler and Goebbels.[100]

More formal attacks came with the establishment of the Reich Chamber of Propaganda and Enlightenment, with its Department of Fine Arts, and the Reich Chamber of Culture, with its Reich Chamber of Visual Arts. An attempt was made to divide the responsibility for the arts between the Ministry and the Chamber of Visual Arts. The Fine Arts Division officially determined what was regarded as desirable and unacceptable in art. It was quite active in the *Kulturkampf* against the "decadent" trends in modern art. It provided exhibits across the Reich that conformed to official policy and encouraged and financed the production of Nazi art and artists. It also controlled the Reich Chamber of Culture. Established on September 22, 1933, the Chamber supervised the seven individual chambers that covered the entire field of *Kulturgüter*. Only its members were permitted to take part in the cultural life of Germany. In this manner, these organizations encouraged Nazi cultural ideology and excluded Jews and "decadents" who transgressed Hitler's view of culture.

Goebbels was directly responsible for all agencies in charge of the visual arts. He personally found it difficult, however, to conform to Hitler's desire for the purge of modern art from Germany's culture. in 1933, for example, he permitted an exhibition called "Thirty German Artists," which included works by modern artists like Barlach, Nolde, and Pechstein.[101] He tolerated a permanent exhibit of modern art in the National Gallery in the Berlin Kronsprinzen Palais, and, as late as July 21, 1936, he permitted the opening of an exhibit by modern painters and sculptors in Hamburg. This show was closed a few days later by the Berlin government, however, because "it constituted an act of provocation against the state."[102] Goebbels biographer stated that it was at this point "Goebbels gave up the struggle" to defend modern art.[103]

It seems highly unlikely, however, that Goebbels actually carried his support of modern art beyond the first months of the Third Reich. Early in 1933, Speer was given the assignment to refurbish Goebbels' house. He borrowed a few watercolors by Nolde from Eberhard Hanfstaengl, who was then the director of the Berlin National Gallery. Goebbels and his wife were delighted with the Nolde watercolors until Hitler expressed his severe disapproval. Goebbels then demanded that they be removed. In this case, some of those closest to Hitler had to be instructed by the Fuehrer regarding degenerate art. The problem with Nolde was his identification as an Expressionist. Many of the National Socialists saw Expressionism as "a typically German, 'Nordic' affair and therefore to be encouraged by party and state."[104] Even the National Socialist organ *Der Angriff* defended Expressionist artists such as Nolde. There was, in fact, a radical group in the party which sought to fuse Expressionism with Nazism much as Mussolini had combined Futurism with Fascism. An especially difficult problem with Nolde was that he was an early member of the Party. He was thoroughly amazed when later on his work was labeled "degenerate."[105]

Periodicals such as *Kunst der Nation* and *Kunstkammer* attempted to lobby for the survival of the expressionists. In 1934, for example, *Kunst der Nation* used a Barlach sculpture as a cover design and featured articles on Beckmann, Rholfs and Emil Nolde. By 1936, however, such art periodicals were supplanted by Rosenberg's ultra-orthodox publication, *Die Kunst im Dritten Reich.*[106]

Die Kunst im Dritten Reich, after 1940, *Die Kunst im Deutschen Reich,* was published monthly in two editions, one of which had a section on architecture called "Die Baukunst." The title of the journal was beautifully lettered in gold on the cover, as was the logo, a combination of images including the head of a helmeted Athena, a torch, and an eagle with a wreathed swastika in its tallons. The journal contained many pictures, most were black and white, but many were in fine color. While most articles propagandized the artistic accomplishments of Third Reich artists and architects, German artists of the past also received attention. The journal included advertisements for galleries, architectural firms and other services and wares of the art world. Scattered throughout the journal, however, were advertisements for such products as cigarettes and waterheaters. No expense was spared to make it visually attractive and impressive.

In order to remove all doubts about what Hitler believed constituted degenerate art, it was decided that all concerned would be taught through an exhibition. On June 30, 1937, Goebbels issued a decree which read:

On the express authority of the Führer, I hereby empower the President of the Reich Chamber of Visual Arts, Professor Ziegler of Munich, to select and secure for an exhibition works of German degenerate art since 1910, both painting and sculpture, which are now in collections owned by the German Reich, by provinces, and by municipalities. You are requested to give Professor Ziegler your full support during his examination and selection of these works. Dr Goebbels.[107]

Ziegler, a painter of nudes, which earned him the nickname "master of German pubic hair," selected a committee of five dedicated Nazis to visit German museums and confiscate practically all German modern art.[108] The committee went beyond the limits of their commission and included works from before 1910 and works by non-German artists in their collection. Among the artists they selected were Alexander Archipenko, Georges Braque, Marc Chagall, Giorgio de Chirico, Robert Delaunay, André Derain, Theo van Doesburg, James Ensor, Paul Gauguin, Vincent van Gogh, Albert Bleizes, Alex Jawlensky, Wassily Kandinsky, Fernand Leger, El Lissitzky, Mondrian, Edvard Munch, Pablo Picasso, Georges Rouault, and Maurice de Vlaminck. This lists serves as a sample of only the best known artists, for an estimated 15,997 works by 1,400 artists were taken from museums all over Germany.[109] From this collection, works by 112 artists were selected and shown in a 1937 "Exhibition of Degenerate Art," in Munich.

The "Exhibition of Degenerate Art," was housed in a few halls located in the old gallery building of the Hofgarten arcades and usually used by the Archaeological Institute for its collection of plaster casts. Efforts were made to present the works in the worst possible setting in order to exaggerate the Party's view of their worthlessness and degeneracy. Paul Ortwin Rave, who attended the exhibit, stated:

...the works were crowded together there in long, narrow rows that were made even more claustrophobic by partitions. The mode of display was deliberately detrimental to the works, lighting was terrible...The paintings were hung helter-skelter, as though fools or children had been in charge. The walls were plastered from floor to ceiling with paintings. There was no semblance of order, and paintings were stuck in wherever they would fit, peering out between sculptures standing on the floor or on pedestals. The works were provided with inflammatory labels, commentaries, and obscene jokes.[110]

The guide for the "Exhibition of Degenerate Art," included an explanation for the establishment of the exhibit. In essence, it reiterated the Party's attack on Jews and Bolshevists who had debased art. It issued a weak apology to Aryan artists among the exhibitors "who, not having followed their former Jewish friends into foreign countries, now honorably struggle and fight for a foundation for a new, healthy creativity," and issued a warning of ostracization to Aryans who had not yet conformed to National Socialist demands.[111] The pressure to reject degenerate art was stressed throughout the guide by the inclusion of excerpts condemning modern art taken from Hitler's speeches. The entire exhibit, therefore, was seen as Hitler's personal condemnation of the artists whose works he saw as degenerate.

The "Exhibition of Degenerate Art" showed works in nine groups. According to the exhibition guide, Group 1 attempted to show the progressive destruction of sensibility for form and color. Group 2 presented depictions of German religiosity. Group 3 attempted to prove the political origins of degenerate art in works of social criticism. Group 4 showed propaganda against military service through such things as mass graves. Group 5 was essentially of supposed prostitutes and pimps. Group 6 included influences of Negroes and South Sea Islanders which they believed were created to remove racial consciousness. Group 7 showed the Negro as the racial ideal along with the cretin and the paralytic. Group 8 was called "Jewish Trash" and Group 9 was called the height of degeneracy, "Abstract and Constructivist Pictures." The latter portion of the guide compared works by these artists with works by the mentally ill and favored the latter.

Occasionally corrections were made in the decisions regarding degenerate artists. For example, Franz Marc's large painting, *The Tower of the Blue Horses*, was marked for exhibition at the show of degenerate art, but it was removed when the League of German Army Officers protested because Marc had been an officer in the Imperial Army and was killed at Verdun, in 1916.[112] Hoffmann visited the Exhibition of Degenerate Art with Hitler and claimed:

...I succeeded in persuading Hitler to instruct Goebbels to withdraw at once a very considerable number of pictures. Among them, I remember, were the *Walchensee* by Lovis Corinth, a Richard Dix, which was a masterpiece of technical execution, in no way degenerate, but with a slight tendency toward pacifism, and some drawings by Lehmbruck and others.[113]

Such accounts, assuming they are correct, serve to indicate how imperfect the system was and how carelessly artists were handled during the early years of the Third Reich.

The plunder of art collections for the Exhibition of Degenerate Art was given *ex post facto* legal sanction on May 31, 1938. The law stated that Hitler ordered such appropriation and had authority over the collected items. The works became the property of the Reich and the former owners received no compensation for their losses.

After the "Exhibition of Degenerate Art" in Munich, a traveling exhibit of these works was taken throughout the Reich. Thereafter, the confiscated works were dispersed in several ways. Goering appropriated some of the least offensive works for his residence at Karinhall. A collection of one hundred and twenty-five were taken for auction by the Swiss art dealer named Fischer in Lucerne, on June 30, 1939. Of these, thirty-six, which did not sell at auction, were sold after the war broke out for 2,900 Swiss francs. The remainder of the collected works were deemed "the dregs of degenerate art" and were finally burned in the courtyard of the Berlin Central Fire Department on March 20, 1939. Of the 4,829 destroyed works, 1,004 were paintings and sculpture and 3,825 were watercolors, drawings and prints.[114]

Numerous art collections throughout the world were enriched by this Nazi auction of works considered to be degenerate. The van Gogh self-portrait which had been in Munich, for example, sold for 175,000 Swiss francs and went to New York, while the Picassos went to Brussels. The Museum of Living Art of New York University received *Composition with Blue* (1926) by Mondrian and *Proun* (1920) by El Lissitzky. The University announced that it would hold the works in trust for the German people.[115]

The Degenerate Art Show was planned to coincide with the opening of the House of German Art, which Hitler and Troost designed. It featured the first exhibition of works by Aryan artists which conformed to Hitler's taste. This premier of official art was celebrated with great pomp on July 18, 1937, one day before the Degenerate Art exhibition opened. Some 2,009,899 visitors went to the Exhibition of Degenerate Art. That was more than three times the 600,000 visitors who saw the exhibition of Aryan art in 1937. This was the first of eight years of exhibitions of approved art, each begun with great celebration. In 1938 there were 460,000 visitors, in 1939, about 400,00 visitors, in 1940, about 600,000 visitors, in 1941, 700,000 visitors and in 1942, over 840,000 visitors.[116]

The opening of the House of German Art was full of spectacle and pageantry. In the great parade to celebrate the opening participants wore historical costumes and fancy dress, and models of German artworks were exhibited. The pageant was divided into sections which celebrated 2,000 years of German culture. The historical section of the parade alone had 3,212 costumed participants. The modern portion included 3,191 marchers, 456 animals—horses, dogs, falcons—and 26 trucks. The final portion of the parade was given over to a military division.[117]

Initially it was thought the House of German Art would be a storehouse of works from the entire history of German art. Hitler decided, however, that it should contain only contemporary art. Adolf Ziegler initiated a competition of works by Aryan artists at home and abroad. Papers for 25,000 works were submitted but only 15,000 works were actually sent in for the first exhibit, and 900 of these were selected to be shown. Hoffmann, Hitler's photographer, was in charge of the exhibition, but Hitler had the final say about selections and reportedly rejected eighty works with the comment, "I won't tolerate unfinished paintings." He also refused to tolerate problematic art, colors which were not true to nature, or abstract forms.[118]

In his speech to open the House of German Art, Hitler leveled his usual attacks on the Parliamentary-Democratic Weimar government. He also credited the Jews, "through control of the Press," with intimidation of those who championed "the normal sound intelligence and instincts of men," and the development of art into "an international experience." He believed the latter resulted in the loss of national identification in art and art works which were not created as eternal monuments but rather, were produced with the motto "Every year something fresh." Art works for the House of German Art, he insisted, must reflect clarity, the central characteristic of the German people, which had inspired painters, sculptors, architects, thinkers, poets, and above all, musicians throughout the ages. He warned those who created works which disregarded realism in form and color that, if they really did see things the way they showed them in their art, and, if their defective vision were deemed hereditary, the Minister for the Interior would see to it that such a defect not be allowed to perpetuate itself. On the other hand, if they did not believe in the reality of their impressions but sought on other grounds to impose such "humbug" upon the nation, they would be taken to criminal court. Art was not to be created for the artist but for the people, Hitler asserted, and the people would henceforth judge art, not art critics. He stated that when people walked through the gallery, they would henceforth judge art, not art critics. He stated that when people walked through the gallery, they would recognize that he was the spokesman and counsellor for the museum.[119]

Hitler also defined acceptability for Aryan artists who wished to work. They had to familiarize themselves with what he believed to be appropriate art. Several sources of information were available to them. Common sense told them they should avoid techniques like the artists being rejected. Hitler and other National Socialists also provided the names of art movements which were not acceptable. Hitler's own works, insofar as they were familiar with them, served as examples. This was recognized in the descriptive catalogue for an exhibition of Hitler's watercolors which was held in Florence, in 1984. It insisted, "Hitler's watercolours are an illuminating and coherent preface to the official paintings of the Third Reich."[120] Hoffmann, Hitler's photographer, published a folio of facsimiles of Hitler's paintings in 1936, which made at least a few of Hitler's works available to artists. Hitler, however, refused to allow his own works to be exhibited.[121] In addition to these sources, the journal *Die Kunst in Dritten Reich* provided examples of acceptable art techniques and subjects.

Hinz suggested that Third Reich artists drew upon past traditions and thus their works represented a continuance or evolution in German art and not a revolution. He further concluded that "the so-called Fuhrer's Project Linz made eminently clear on what traditions these mediators between the National Socialist present and the art of the past drew." This project, also called Special Mission Linz (*Sonderauftrag* Linz), was Hitler's secret project concerned with the collection of art works for his proposed museum in Linz.[122] Charles de Jaeger thoroughly examined this project in his excellent work entitled *The Linz File: Hitler's Plunder of European Art.* De Jaeger's work demonstrated the extreme concern with the acquisition of art by Hitler and other Third Reich officials, which led to the plunder of museums not only in Germany, but in every location which came under their domination during World War II. Works by the artists which Hitler personally preferred were amassed largely from these collections, although he also collected through purchases and received a number of works as gifts. To examine this process in detail would be to reiterate de Jaeger's work. Therefore, attention will be limited to an examination of the works Hitler collected for the proposed Linz Museum as a clue to the taste he imposed upon Third Reich Artists.

A floor plan for the proposed Linz Museum included indications that Hitler planned rooms for works by the nineteenth-century German artists Cornelius, Führich, Bartholdy, Schwind, Böcklin, Uhde, Trübner, Leibl, Feuerback, Marées, Roth Engerth Werner, Menzel, Makart, Piloty, Grützner, and Defregger. It is also generally accepted that he planned to devote rooms to Rudolf von Alt, the master who inspired his own youthful painting, as well as Spitzweg, Lenbach, and Waldmüller.[123] These artists painted representationally, with attention to accurate rendering of forms and colors in nature. Their works are free of the problematic concerns of the expressionists. They are essentially free of the more turbulent aspects of Romanticism, with the exception of a few works by such artists as Böcklin, which reflect interest in the mystical aspects of life. These bourgeois artists were the models that contemporary artists should turn to in order to reassert the continuity of Western painting, a continuity what had been broken by degenerate artists. Hitler's love of these artists was related to that aspect of his Volkish ideology which defined Germans as inherently romantic. As he said:

Our romanticism has its origins in the entense appreciation of nature that is inherent in us Germans. Properly to appreciate such artists as Weber, Ludwig Richter and the other Romantics, one must know Franconian mountains for that is the background which gives birth to romanticism in both music and painting; and, of course, the stories and legends of our folk-lore also make a potent contribution.[124]

Hoffman suggested that in the beginning, Hitler collected in a rather informal way, selecting pictures he simply liked.[125] Later Hitler turned to dealers to procure pictures he wanted. Two art historians were particularly important in this adventure, Hans Posse and Hermann Voss. Posse set the precedent for turning the Linz collection into more than a center for Bavarian painting. As a result, the inventory of works included works by Boucher (7), Pieter Breugel the Elder (2), Canaletto (4), Cranach (5), van Dyck (7), Fragonard (4), Jan van Goyen (9), Goya (3), Frans Hals (7), Leonardo da Vinci (1), Lotto (3), van Ostade (10), Raphael (2), Rembrandt (10), Rubens (19), Ruisdael (18), Jan Steen (9), Teniers (14), Ter Borch (9), Tintoretto (13), Titian (2), Vermeer (2), Watteau (3), and Wouwerman (7).[126]

Hitler's personal collection of paintings included works by many of the German, nineteenth-century artists of the Linz collection. In addition, he gathered works by such artists as Kaulbach, Zügel, von Stuck, Botticelli, Bordone, Grützner, and Pannini. He also purchased works by contemporary artists such as Werner Peiner, Max Zaeper, J.B. Godron, K.F. Olszweski and Willi Kriegel.[127]

As suggested earlier, Hitler's collections exhibit his preference for genre paintings by German artists. Most of these artists dedicated their work to landscapes with people. Several of them also painted portraits. Two artists reflect his taste for folksy humor. Such are the works of Karl Spitzweg and Hans Grützner. Spitzweg, a self-taught Biedermeier painter, favored everyday scenes with touches of mirth about awkward poets, bookworms and prospective suitors. Hans Grützner specialized in scenes of drunken monks and corpulent tavern-keepers. Exceptional examples of Hitler's taste are the sometimes sensuous works of Hans Makart and the often erotic works of Franz von Stuck. Hitler told Hanfstaengl that the two artists who had the greatest impact on his life were Richard Wagner and von Stuck. He seemed particularly taken with von Stuck's works of nude females with huge black snakes entwined around their bodies and between their legs.[128]

Third Reich artists, using Hitler's taste as a directive, set about creating thousands of works in the approved style. Hence, painting under the Third Reich was never strictly concerned with realism but the projection of the substance of National Socialist ideology.

Work was a central subject of Third Reich art. Within the *Gemeinschaft* framework, all work was seen as service to the Reich. Farmers in their fields, weavers at looms, and industrial workers were all German workers for the Reich. A commonly painted triad of workers was the industrial worker, the farmer and the soldier. They were shown as equals in social value. Artists found the triptych of religious painting useful for such works. It brought to their secular subjects a sacred mantle. They also often painted works with a view from below eye level, which was intended to convey superiority.

The role of women in the Third Reich was reflected symbolically in much Third Reich art. Men and women were comrades in work for the Reich. Initially, however, it was never intended that women be a part of the industrial work force, as they became during the late years of the war.

Throughout most of the Third Reich, women essentially followed the edict of Wilhelm II, which declared that three things were possible for women— *Kirche, Kuche, und Kinder* (Church, Kitchen and Children).[129]

In order to serve the Reich, artists often continued to paint the way they were accustomed to working or changed their visual conceptions slightly and gave their paintings titles which suggested the new artistic motifs. This made it possible for genre painting to achieve symbolic significance. Many landscapes, for example, were given titles which reflected fertility and the tie between Germans and the mystic soil of Germany, although there was nothing in the pictures to suggest such qualities. Farm families, equipment, tools and animals were also painted with the idea of promoting the blood and soil thesis. Rural life was the basis of the *Gemeinschaft* spirit with which Hitler wished to permeate the Reich.

It has been estimated that 40 percent of the works in the 1937 exhibition were landscapes, some 15.5 percent concerned "Womenhood and Manhood," 10 percent were animals, 7 percent were farmers and .5 percent were of artisans. An additional 1.5 percent were portraits of National Socialist functionaries and 1.5 percent were of their new public buildings. Later exhibitions gave greater attention to war paintings, allegory and armament. Many of these works and others sent on tours throughout the Reich were deliberately devoted to propaganda for the National Socialist ideology. Such were the exhibits called "Blood and Soil," "Race and Nation," and competitions for pictures which were sponsored by such groups as the Reich Association for Large Families, which offered prizes for "artistically exemplary representations of genetically healthy families with many children."[130]

Hinz called the Great German Art Exhibitions "nothing more than displays of works for sale." An average of 800 to 1,000 works were sold each year, which brought their artists 1.5 to 2 million Reich marks. Many were purchased for display in public buildings by the government itself. Of these, most "were sculptures and large paintings that were high priced and of little interest to the private collector." Hitler, for example, purchased for the Reich Chancellery 123 oil paintings, eight prints, and four sculptures, which cost a total of 367,530 Reich marks.[131]

It is apparent from the above discussion that Hitler successfully imposed his artistic taste upon German art. It is equally true that he imposed his musical tastes upon the Third Reich. His personal involvement in this imposition was considerably less than his concern about the art of the Third Reich, however. He relied heavily upon Goebbels to deplete Jewish and modern elements in music and develop means for using music as an aid to propagandize the party ideology. He saw to it that Hitler's ideas for carrying music to the people were implemented through traveling orchestras and promoted other ventures for providing music for all citizens of the new movement. Hitler concerned himself with his interest in promoting the construction of opera houses and the attendance of performances. From time to time, he became involved in plans for various performances, including providing some sketches for stage designs. In general, however, he indulged himself in his continued association with the Bayreuth performances and showed scant interest in other classical music. As time went on, he developed an increasing taste for lighter music, particularly that of Lehár, attended ballets, and even went to revues.

Hitler once described himself as one of the most musical people in the world. When he then whistled a tune incorrectly and someone pointed it out, he retorted, "It's not I who am whistling it wrong, but the composer who made a blunder here."[132] Hitler had to maintain a self-image and a public image which conformed to his views of the special characteristics of a leader. To Hitler, musical men alone felt the vibrations of the Volkish soul (*Volkseele*), knew the sensitive words that could move men, and could put the correct political action into effect. Political leaders had to be musical. Therefore, in 1925, he deprecated Ludendorff's political abilities as the general had no musical taste. In 1945, he passed the same judgement upon Himmler.[133]

In *Mein Kampf*, Hitler made clear his feelings about the importance of music when he declared it to be, along with architecture, the queen of arts.[134] During the Third Reich, however, his personal attention to the visual arts far outweighed his concerns with music. This imbalance was apparent in his speeches on culture. His few comments on music do show that he wanted a spirit of clarity to prevail. He sought "great masters who shall echo in music the emotions of our soul," and educate the public in the appreciation of opera.[135] Hitler also pointed to the German *lied* (song), as a great contributor to the feeling of *Gemeinschaft* and stressed that singers spoke for the life of the German people.[136]

Hitler's concerns about the purification of German Music through the elimination of modern and Jewish elements, and his insistence upon excellence in the performance of music rooted in traditional compositional practices were monitored by Goebbels' Ministry, and the subdivision of the Chamber of Culture directly responsible for music, the Reich Chamber of Music. Peter Rabbe, who served a term as President of the Reich Chamber of Music, claimed that the chamber:

...was founded to encourage a study of music, to enhance the standing of the musicians, and to provide an agency through which the needs of the musicians shall be recognized, thus carrying out a task which neither individuals nor earlier organizations had been able to accomplish.[137]

In an examination of the progress of the Reich Chamber of Culture during the first five years of the Reich, Goebbels stressed that the initial commission of the Reich Chamber of Music was two-fold. It was to "increase the average production of the German musical profession by suitable encouragement of individual talent," and alleviate, "as far as possible, the unemployment among musicians." He further stated the Chamber of Music saw to it that:

Thousands of so-called 'amateurs' were eliminated thanks to rigorous examinations. No profession contained such a number of 'botchers' and ne'er-do-wells as the musical one, which had served as refuge for all those who were incapable of any useful work whatever.

Hence, a purge had to be undertaken among composers, performers, musical publishers, and music shops. A higher standard was henceforth required of all those who aspired to join the musical profession.[138]

This practice severely disrupted the whole sphere of amateur music in Germany. Amateur bands, for example, were tested for competency, and, if they failed, they were forbidden to compete with professional groups seeking employment for dances and socials. This whole matter of testing for competency was no small feat, for Goebbels declared that in 1938, there were in existence some 8,000 amateur bands comprising 120,000 musicians. They also exerted control over 25,000 mixed-voice choirs and a mixed choir membership of 125,000. Goebbels also boasted he had reduced chronic unemployment among musicians from 24,000 to only 14,000 by 1938. These changes, however, were achieved only through the use of draconian measures designed to purge German music of all persons, composition, and elements defined as Jewish, modern or anti-Nazi. Already in 1933, *Modern Music* reported Bruno Walter had been forbidden to perform in the Leipzig *Gewandhaus* and the Berlin Philharmonic. Horenstein was denied work, as he was a Jew, while Fritz Bush, an Aryan, had been fired because he would not join the Nazi party. Szenkar, Steinberg, Rosenstock, Stiedry, Klemperer and others were given "leaves of absence."[139] To this list must be added the names of many others dismissed for a variety of reasons: Schoenberg, Schrecker, Hindemith, Serkin, Gal, Muck, and Lotte Lehmann. Fritz Zweig, his wife Tilly de Garmo, Lotte Schoene, and Marcel Noe were dismissed from the Berlin State Opera at one fell swoop. The world premier of Schrecker's opera *Christophorus*, scheduled prior to Hitler's accession to power, was promptly canceled.[140]

A commission composed of Wilhelm Furtwäengler, Wilhelm Bachaus, and George Kulenkampf was immediately established to censor the programs of all public concerts. As one result, a scheduled series of Brahms chamber music by Schnabel, Hubermann, Piatigorsky, and Hindemith was canceled. Even music journal editors were not exempted from the purge—Mersmann was removed from the editorship of the journal *Melos*.[141]

The international music community reacted immediately and decisively to these events. On April 1, 1933, with the new Nazi state only two months old, Arturo Toscanini, Walter Damrosch, Frank Damrosch, Serge Koussevitzky, Arthur Bodanzky, Harold Bauer, Ossip Gabrilovitch, Alfred Hertz, Charles Martin Loeffler, Fritz Reiner, and Rubin Goldmark sent a cable to Hitler urging him to stop racial and religious discrimination. It stated:

Chancellor Adolf Hitler, Berlin, Germany. Your Excellency: The undersigned artists who live and execute their art in the United States of America feel the moral obligation to appeal to your Excellency to put a stop to the persecutions of their colleagues in Germany for political or religious reasons. We beg you to consider that the artist all over the world is estimated for his talent alone and not for his national or religious convictions...We are convinced that such persecutions as take place in Germany at present are not based on your instruction, and that it cannot possibly be your desire to damage the high cultural esteem Germany, until now, has been enjoying in the eyes of the whole civilized world. Hoping that our appeal in behalf of our colleagues will not be allowed to pass unheard, we are, Respectfully yours, etc.[142]

On April 4, 1933, the following answer was given to Toscanini and the other musicians:

According to newspaper reports, several conductors and musicians in the United States—Arturo Toscanini, Walter Damrosch, Serge Koussevitzky, Arthur Bodanzky, Harold Bauer, Ossip Gabrilovitch, Alfred Hertz, Charles Loeffler, Fritz Reiner, and Rubin Goldmark—have lodged a complaint with the Chancellor because of the rejection of certain Jewish and Marxist fellow-musicians in Germany...Pending clarification of this matter, I direct that the compositions and records of the afore-mentioned gentlemen shall no longer find a place on the programs of German broadcasters and also that no musical performance in which they in any wise have a part shall be received from concert halls or other senders.[143]

By June 5, 1933, the patron saint of this protest against Hitler's policies, Arturo Toscanini, notified the German government of his refusal to conduct at the Bayreuth Festival in view of discrimination against Jewish musicians in Germany.[144] Toscanini did stay away from Bayreuth, even when Hitler wrote him a personal letter inviting him to conduct.[145] Toscanini was joined in his refusal to participate in the musical life of Nazi Germany by Fritz Kreisler, who stated "Art is international, and I oppose chauvinism in art wherever I encounter it." He further stated he would not perform in Germany until musicians, irrespective of nationality, race or creed, were "actually welcomed" back.[146]

The prominent musical contribution of Jews to the creative life of pre-Nazi Germany presented Hitler with major problems and forced him into contradictory decisions as he attempted to preserve some semblance of quality in German music. Works by Mahler, Mayerbeer, and Mendelssohn were declared "degenerate" because the composers were Jews. German publishing houses, however, continued to publish their music for export-profit.[147] Carl Orff and Wagner-Regeny accepted commissions to create new scores to replace Mendelssohn's incidental music to *A Midsummer Night's Dream*.[148] The statue of Mendelssohn in front of the Leipzig *Gewandhaus* was destroyed.[149] However, Emanuel List, the American Jewish baritone, was deliberately requested to remain with the Berlin State Opera as was the German Leo Blech. Furtwängler invited Vladimir Horowitz and Yehudi Menuhin to perform with the Berlin Philharmonic. The *Opera News* noted in 1972 that a number of Jewish musicians were allowed to remain in their positions in Berlin until 1937—to have systematically removed them would have devastated the opera scene.[150]

The involvement of Jews in the creation of certain operas and operettas presented the régime with problems. Several of Richard Strauss's operas, for example, were based on libretti by Jewish writers, as were operettas by Franz Lehár. While Strauss received considerable rebuke, Lehár was forgiven, essentially because he was a favorite composer of Hitler. *Carmen,* a favorite of German audiences, was composed by Bizet, who had some Jewish blood. This situation was resolved by Bizet being officially Aryanized.[151] Mozart's *Le Nozze di Figaro, Don Giovanni,* and *Cosi Fan Tutti* were stigmatized by their librettist, Lorenzo da Ponte, who was a baptized Jew. These three Mozart operas, plus his *Die Gaertnerin aus Liebe* had been translated into German by Hermann Levi, so they were given new texts by Siegfried Anheisser, an Aryan. Although not by a Jewish librettist, Mozart's *Die Zauberflöte* was condemned as a "vehicle of masonic ideas" until Hitler declared "Only a man lacking in national respect would condemn Mozart's *Magic Flute* because it may sometimes come into conflict with his own ideas."[152]

Handel presented the Nazi's with another kind of situation. They had no problem with Handel himself nor his music. They did dislike the non-Aryan titles and themes of some of his works—chorals such as *Esther, Deborah* and *Judas Maccabeus.* The combination of Nordic music and Old Testament titles and themes was repugnant to them. Eventually, an Aryan author was commissioned to write new texts suitable to the times. Judas Maccabeus thus became *Hero and Work for Peace.* It then described "the distress and resurgence of the German people."[153] Jewish musicians were allowed to perform for fellow Jews until 1938, and, for some, it made it possible for them to survive until they could emigrate.

Jazz was also defined by the Reich as a musically degenerate idiom, which was non-traditional and the product of lesser peoples—Negroes and Jews. Some Aryan citizens and party members, however, found it difficult to give it up. Condemnation of American jazz had appeared in the journal *Zeitschrift für Musik* before the National Socialists came to power. Particularly offensive to the author were the classes in jazz offered by the Hoch Conservatory of Frankfort, whose director was Jewish. The advertisements for these classes ran counter to the Volkish ideology in that they called jazz "a much-needed transfusion of Negro musical blood with German." Operas were also presented in "verjazzte" versions while Hans Sluckenschmidt defined the use of jazz in church. A Negro bar opened in Berlin in 1932, and the *Zeitschrift für Musik* called it "a slap in the face of every German musician" and demanded "the speediest elimination of the black pestilence" for the sake of "unemployed native musicians." The state opera of Austria reacted to the encroachment of jazz music by prohibiting their orchestral players from moonlighting in jazz bands. There was a tendency for the followers of Wilhelm Frick, director of the Ministry of the Interior in Thurengia, in 1930, to ignore the prohibition of jazz in the hope that expulsion of jazz would come "from within the people."[154]

Jazz was not heard over the German radio during the Third Reich because it was officially banned. Jazz bands and swing orchestras were barred from public appearances. Efforts to eliminate recorded jazz and swing were futile, however, as records by Josephine Baker, Guy Lombardo, Victor Young, Benny Goodman, and Leo Reisman, and sheet music by George Gershwin and

Irving Berlin was still purchasable in 1938. The reason for the victory of practice over policy appeared to have been "the lack of an alternative to American jazz except rump-slapping peasant dances and waltzes."[155] As late as 1937, both Goering and Goebbels danced to a foreign jazz band at a Berlin Hotel.[156] Dodd reported that Hitler thought jazz was primitive and depraved, but he permitted two or three places to stay open in Berlin for foreigners.[157] This was perhaps why "in 1937 the official SA paper discerned 'impudent swamp flowers of Negroid pandemonium in German dance-halls regrettably abetted by so-called German dance bands.' " A form of "German jazz" was attempted by Peter Kreuder, Theo Mackeben and Barnabas von Geczay. There were, nevertheless, efforts to rid German bands of the jazz influence through a purge of the saxophone, a "symbol of Negroid lewdness" and excessive use of percussion instruments.[158]

Goebbels' Ministry was also concerned with Hitler's proscription against modernism. As Rockwell pointed out, however, National Socialist policies against modernism did not seem to negatively effect music and opera as much as it did the visual arts. Perhaps this was due in part to the smaller number of modern composers as compared with the number of avant-garde painters and other creators in the visual arts. It may also have been due to the fact that, since the twenties, classical music had become "an increasingly secure preserve of traditionalism."[159] Experimental music, therefore, had a smaller audience to be rebuffed by the purge of modern music.

The key attribute of modern music to arouse Nazi ire was dissonance, of which Severus Ziegler said, "We do not reject dissonance *per se* or the enrichment of rhythm, but dissonance as a principle, and the irruption of alien rhythm."[160] This nebulous definition reflects the difficulty the régime had in delineating the characteristics of the music they found to be degenerate.

Much criticism was directed against the Viennese composer and teacher Arnold Schoenberg, whose compositional techniques in his later works left the traditional realm to which Hitler and his followers were tied. Schoenberg was immediately black listed by the régime, not only for being Jewish, but also for his modernism. He moved to the United States in 1933, became an American citizen in 1940, and taught and composed until his death in 1951. The works of one of his followers, Alban Berg, were heard in Germany at least until 1934.

Paul Hindemith, an Aryan composer of remarkable originality, was treated harshly by the Third Reich government because of his non-traditional techniques. In 1934, for example, the Chamber of Music refused him permission for a performance of his opera *Mathis der Maler*. The rationale for this refusal was a scene in the opera which appeared to criticize the burning of an estimated 20,000 un-German books in Germany, in 1933.[161] He was also criticized for "having written an immoral, comic work (*Neues vom Tag*, 1929) in which the heroine was shown in a bath-tub."[162] The chamber further criticized him for his association with Jewish musicians, but worst of all, they saw him as an Aryan composer who used non-traditional techniques and refused to change. He went into exile, first to Switzerland, and then to the United States, in 1939, where he stayed throughout the war.[163]

Other compositions branded as "degenerate," due to their modern elements, included Stravinsky's *Le Sacre de Printemps*, most of Bartok's works, Krenek's *Johnny spielt auf*, and Kurt Weills' *Threepenny Opera* and *Mahogonny*. Boris Blacher's *Geigenmusik* was dismissed as "cats miaowing" while Richard Mohaupt's almost bitonal *Wirtin von Pinsk* was closed after only one performance.[164]

In 1938, one year after the "Exhibition of Degenerate Art," an "Exhibition of Degenerate Music" was held before the Reich Music Congress in Dusseldorf. It was arranged by Severus Ziegler, manager of the Weimar Theater, who was anxious to play a parallel role in music similar to that of his brother in art. The performance included works by Schoenberg, Kestenberg, Stravinsky, Hindemith, Mahler, Krenek, Milhaud, and Weill. The catalogue described the exhibition as:

...the reflection of a veritable witches' sabbath of the most frivolous spiritual-artistic Bolshevism...of the triumph of subhumanity arrogant Jewish insolence and complete spiritual cretinization. Jewish music and German music are poles apart.[165]

This concert served as a farewell to works by Jewish composers and modern music until Germany's music was revitalized after World War II.

Following the *Anschluss*, Nazi musical regulations were extended to Austria with disastrous results. In August, 1938, the American critic Vincent Sheean attended three performances of the Vienna Opera with the Vienna Philharmonic in the pit. The ejection of twelve Jewish players left a "dispirited body which played raggedly and without tone." One performer blamed it on the lack of resonance from the audience. The audience too had changed. It was full of black and brown shirts, SS and SA men, and people wearing peasant dress (a thing unknown in Vienna before) to show their pure Aryanism.[166]

While many were profoundly disturbed by the devastation of music, theater, and the arts through the loss of many excellent musicians, it must be pointed out that there were several composers and conductors of considerable repute who remained in Germany during the Third Reich. Given the domestic musical tumult and the international musical attack on Nazi policies, Goebbels deemed it important to retain some semblance of musical prestige for Germany. Hence, he worked very hard to protect these musicians.[167] One of the more important ones was Wilhelm Furtwäengler, of the Berlin orchestra. Furtwäengler, however, was difficult to handle. At the time of Toscanini's protest, Furtwäengler published a public protest against Nazi musical anti-semitism. Goebbels carefully answered for the government and was successful in calming Furtwäengler's fears. In October, 1934, Furtwäengler courageously performed a symphonic adaptation of Hindemith's *Mathis der Maler*. When he was severely attacked by the National Socialist Cultural Association, Furtwäengler again issued a public defense of music as art and the same evening received a standing ovation from the audience when he appeared to conduct the Berlin Philharmonic.

Furtwäengler, still under attack from Rosenberg, again chose to protest—this time by resigning on December 4, as vice president of the Reich Chamber of Music, Prussian State Councillor and director of the Berlin State Opera. Goebbels feared Furtwäengler might emigrate and embarrass the government. However, any such possibility was precluded by a campaign against Furtwäengler launched by Toscanini which generated resentment against Furtwäengler abroad. After February, 1935, Frutwäengler refused to meet with Goebbels and continued his antagonism toward the Nazis. While he did agree to conduct at Bayreuth in 1936, he refused to conduct for propaganda tours during the war years. During the bombings of Berlin, he declined the offer of a private bunker from Hitler and continued to provide performances for the Berliners.[168] Furtwäengler strikes one as a naive and tragic figure. He did not understand the nature of the Nazi state until it was too late to leave, and, when he finally did understand, he stayed on out of a sense of duty to the German People.

Richard Strauss, due to his association with National Socialism, became notorious as the most prominent composer to remain in Nazi Germany. He was sixty-nine years old when Hitler came to power. The years before were filled with recognition, essentially for his symphonic poems and operas. In 1933, he accepted the position of President of the Reich Chamber of Music. He also agreed to take the place of the exiled Bruno Walter as guest conductor for the Berlin Philharmonic and deputized for Toscanini, at the Bayreuth Festival. To his discredit, he also sent a telegram of support to Goebbels when the régime took action against the composer Hindemith and the conductor Furtwäengler, and he never made a public protest against the dismissal of talented Jewish musicians in Germany, many of whom were his personal friends.[169] He did, however, write a letter to Stefan Zweig, his librettist for *Die Schweigsame Frau (The Silent Woman)*, who was Jewish, declaring his disgust with the Party's racist policies. The interception of this letter by the Gestapo caused his dismissal from the Presidency of the Chamber of Music. It is generally accepted, however, that he was allowed to retire or retired of his own volition, due particularly to his age and discontent with the disapproval of his collaboration with Zweig and Hugo von Hofmannsthal, librettist for many of his operas including the 1933 work called *Arabella*. Von Hofmannsthal was one-quarter Jewish, which was enough for the régime to declare him impure. In retirement, Strauss continued to produce operas, including *Friedenstaf (Peace Day)* 1938, a one-act opera set in a "beleagured town during the Thirty Years War," which may have been a reflection of the composer's awareness of the inevitable conflict in Germany and a weak effort to call for peace. His later works, with a non-Jewish librettist, include *Daphne* (1938) and *Die Liebe Der Danae*, which was to have premiered in 1944, but a Nazi edict closed the theater due to the plot against Hitler's life.[170] Strauss was cleared of all charges that he had participated in the Nazi movement or benefited from the régime by a di-Nazification court in Munich on June 8, 1948.   He was, however, a composer of the Nazi period and he supported, at least in part, its practices, but he was not a composer of Nazi music.

Not all composers, however, had difficulties with the régime. Hans Pfitzner was a "leading composer of strong nationalistic leaning who essentially subscribed to the Nazi creed." He had a full and productive career before Hitler took power. He had spent years in teaching, conducting, and composing and held positions such as the Directorship of the Conservatory and the Municipal Opera in Dresden (1910-1926). He was a traditional composer and championed romanticism. As such, he "devoted much time and energy to combating the 'modernist' danger." He championed the nationalistic movement in post-World War I Europe and composed *Von Deutscher Seele (On the German Soul)* as a result. He saw himself as an unappreciated genius who was "continuing Wagner's struggle on behalf of German values and culture even into the Nazi period." His goal was "to save the nation through his music and to save music through a revitalized Germany." He supported the National Socialists in their crusade against modernism and the intrusion of such foreign elements as jazz into German music. He also joined in their projects to take music to the people. In 1937, for example, he conducted a concert of his own symphonies in a railway repair shop. His works were admired in Germany, but he had little impact in other countries. His compositions conformed to the Nazi restrictions regarding the avoidance of modern musical techniques and influences such as jazz. This was due more to his own inclination than to restrictions placed upon him by the Reich. His music was an extension of nineteenth-century practices and conformed to his personal Volkish or Nationalistic ideology, which was spiritually like that of Hitler's. However, he was not a composer of Nazi music. He died in Salzburg on May 22, 1949, shortly after his eightieth birthday.[171]

Carl Orff was a more youthful composer who became one of the more successful musicians of the Third Reich. His success came with his *Carmina Burana* of 1936, which, though not well received initially, became one of the staple music compositions of the Third Reich. It drew its text from the thirteenth-century collection of Goliard songs and poems discovered in the Bavarian monastery of Benediktbeuren in 1803. Orff set twenty-four poems that praised nature and love, the tavern and the free life, along with some that contained an undercurrent of protest against those who cannot fit into their society. The melodies are quite folk-like in their simplicity and clear-cut stanzas.[172] For these reasons perhaps, Hitler liked the work.

Orff's success was shared by Werner Egk, a Bavarian. His initial opera, *The Magic Fiddle*, enjoyed a huge success in 1935 because it abounded in melodic passages that avoided any trace of contrapuntalism and abstraction. In 1938, he premiered his work *Peer Gynt*. Based on Ibsen's poetic drama, it had a neo-romantic score that was quite rich in instrumental color and strictly adhered to the rules of tonality. Goebbels ravaged it only to find that Hitler, at a subsequent performance, approvingly invited Egk to his box. Egk was given a 10,000-mark commission, and his *Peer Gynt* was placed on the official repertoire of opera houses all over the Reich.[173]

There were also several other Third Reich composers who were well received by the régime. Paul Graener, for example, continued along conventional lines during the Nazi era, reaching his hundredth opus with *The Prince of Homburg* (1935). Wagner-Regeny gained success with his neo-classical work *The Favorite*, and Josef Haas achieved considerable success with his *Tobias Wunderlich*.[174]

It had become apparent to composers who desired success that the classical and nineteenth-century composers provided the musical vocabulary upon which they should base their works. Wagner, of course, was the strongest source of inspiration. Because Strauss appeared secure musically, he too was copied. In hindsight, it is apparent the Third Reich never produced any distinctive music of its own. It produced a few works in traditional modes, but ultimately, it failed to produce an exciting body of Nazi music. As one result, the régime had to resort to endless programs of Bach, Mozart, Brahms, Schubert and, above all, Wagner.

The Third Reich was more successful in caring for the financial well-being of its Aryan musicians. Goebbels reported that the Chamber of Music had established an old age fund for composers. It also had provided financial assistance to about one-hundred orchestras throughout the Reich, and had established musical counselors in 1,200 towns to develop the musical life, work with official and private organizations, and especially, to help young artists with scheduling public appearances.[175] This aspect of the chamber's role in the musical life of towns all over Germany was the realization of Hitler's youthful dream of taking music to those who did not have the advantage of living in large cities with a full musical life. While still with Kubizek, it may be recalled, he discussed the possibilities of setting up traveling orchestras to accomplish this goal.

The chamber of music also became involved in the financial problems of musicians. By 1936, the Chamber of Music had procured work for about 3,000 bands and guaranteed each musician one free day weekly, monthly salaries instead of daily wages, and monthly instead of daily notices of termination from a position. The Chamber also had set up funds for the purchase of instruments and tuition for deserving students and the publication of musical works. They also extended the copy right of musical compositions from thirty to fifty years. The Reich, to 1936, had provided legal assistance in 43,000 cases and instituted proceedings in 3,000 others, which had obtained 1,800,000 marks for members.[176] On the whole, the régime did improve the quality of life for musicians approved by the régime. This is especially true where it is compared to their situation during the Weimar Republic.

During the early republic, Weimar had subsidized theaters and their productions, and they had generally prospered. Once the depression hit, the government slashed its support of the arts. It then became economically impossible for theaters to promote less-well-attended experimental productions, and they perforce turned to standard favorites of the opera repertoire to retain their audiences. Salaries were limited to $9,000 a year by decree. Guest artists received $150 an evening but could perform no more than six times a month. Increasingly, serious works were replaced by operettas and revues as theaters sought to maximize their paying audiences.[177] Those performers able to do so, emigrated during this period to improve their earning ability. Richard Tauber, for example, left German opera to sing operettas on the London stage for $1,250 a week. The production of musical instruments also suffered a severe decline in this period. Prior to 1914, Germany produced 140,000 pianos annually with one-third destined for export. By 1930, seven newly merged manufacturers agreed to restrict production to 18,000 pianos. In the end, they had difficulty selling the 8,000 they actually produced.[178]

During the years of the depression, musicians suffered in part because of competition from radio, recordings, and sound films. Hundreds of musicians were released from movie-house orchestras, and radio stations used more recorded music. The position of Germany's musicians was further diminished by such unusual practices as the importation of an American to teach German *Lieder* at a Berlin academy and black jazz-bands displacing local salon orchestras.[179]

According to Goebbels, the Reich improved conditions in the theaters so that by 1938, there were 159 theaters owned by the Reich, the provinces, and the municipalities. Operas were performed in over ninety big theaters. New theaters were opened only when granted permission by a special court which judged their financial and artistic conditions. The Reich Theatrical Academy reported private installations and students were given support by *Die Bühne*. Special festival weeks, such as the annual Bayreuth Festival were among their highest achievements. A 1935-1936 census of one-half of the largest theaters found "124 different operettas had been performed (25 of them for the first time)." The number of operas performed exceeded the number of operettas and twelve of these operas were performed for the first time.[180]

Goebbels' Ministry also controlled all radio broadcasts in the Third Reich. The value of this means for spreading the Nazi message was realized early in Hitler's chancellorship. At that time, the "People's receiver" was mass produced and sold for seventy-six marks. Sometime later, the "German mini-receiver," the cheapest radio in the world, was marketed for thirty-five marks. By 1942, sixteen million of the twenty-three million Greater German households had radios.[181]

During the early months of the Third Reich, the air waves were filled with German military marches, overlayed with the thud of goose-stepping. Indeed, the entire Third Reich was permeated with martial music. As Herzstein stated, the Nazi period was:

...a world in which brutal determination appeared in the guise of martial music and pathos laden salutes to the fallen heroes of both world wars...[A]n epoch when music encouraged men to suffer and die, yet offered solace and made men tougher; there was music sad and heroic, 'The Song of the Good Comrade,' 'Raise the Banner,' and famous old Prussian marches taken over by the Nazis because of their symbolic unity with an heroic past—the 'Hohenfriedberger,' and the 'Petersburger,' the 'March from the Time of Frederick the Great.'[182]

After the Anschluss, in 1938, Goebbels called for Austrian marches to be included along with Prussian marches in radio broadcasts. *We're Marching against England* was played *ad nauseam* on the radio between later 1939 and early 1941 as Hitler's hopes for conciliatory relations with England waned. With Hitler's march into the Balkans, on April 6, 1941, the *Prinz Eugen March* was played to evoke the memory of the Austrian military hero of the eighteenth-century Turkish wars.[183]

On June 21, 1941, the eve of Germany's attack on the Soviet Union, Speer was called into Hitler's Berlin salon after dinner. Hitler had a record of Liszt's *Les Préludes* played and said, "You'll hear that often in the near future, because it is going to be our victory fanfare for the Russian campaign. Funk chose it. How do you like it?" Hitler had personally selected a musical fanfare for each of the previous campaigns. They were played before announcements of striking victories.[184]

Throughout the Third Reich, the *Horst Wessel Lied* continued to be a favorite song. In 1938, a commemorative cantata for Horst Wessel was composed by Cesar Bresgen and Heinrich Spitha. It was entitled *The SA Lives For Ever* and had three movements which were called "His song kept time with our marching," "The world belongs to leaders," and "Soldiers are always soldiers."[185]

Several marches and songs performed by Nazi bands and choruses at Nuremberg, Munich, Berlin, and other centers were made available to the American public on two records called *Hitler's Inferno* by Audio Fidelity Incorporated. Selections on the records include the *Horst Wessel Lied, Wir Fuhren Auf das Meer Hinaus, Ade, Polenland, Wenn Wir Fahren Gegen Engeland, Heil Hitler Dir!* and *Wenn Die S.S. Und Die S.A. Aufmarschiert.* The works are performed with fervent enthusiasm. They indicate a preference for a four-four measure signature and a tempo of about 120 beats per minute. Most of the works reflect the party's origins in beer-hall band music with a strongly punctuated bass line. Most of the songs, as well as the speeches on the record, were taken from German radio stations after the war.[186]

Music had indeed played a significant part in party spectacles, especially the annual Nuremberg rallies. Hitler's arrival into the meeting area was made even more dramatic by the playing of the *Badenweiler March*, a work reserved for him alone. It was composed on August 12, 1914, by Georg Fürst, Hitler's *Regimentsmusikmeister.*[187]

The significance the Third Reich placed upon martial music is apparent in a collection of songs for the *Hitlerjugend*. The sixty-nine selections are divided into songs for the "New Times," the farmers, the soldiers, riders and travelers. The texts encourage patriotism and are surprisingly free of exhortations to hatred of Germany's enemies or Jews. Several of the texts were written by the leader of the *Hitlerjugend*, Baldur von Schirach, whose skills in writing poetry influenced Hitler's decision to appoint him as head of the *Hitlerjugend*. He wrote, for example, the text for a marching song called *Vaterland, hör deiner Söhne Schwur (Fatherland, Hear the Oath of Your Sons)*.[188] One of the texts was written by a member of the *Hitlerjugend*, Heinz A. Mumbächer. Most, however, are by a variety of composers it has proved impossible to identify. A few of the songs have texts which praise the SA and SS. Other militant songs include selections such as *Es geht wohl zu der Sommerszeit,,* from the Thirty-Years War, and *Wir find des Geyers schwarze Haufen,* from the Baurenkriege of 1925. There are also several pieces from the sixteenth century which are farmers' songs. Such is the selection called *Wir zogen in das Feld.*[189]

The music for the texts came from a variety of sources. Several of the contemporary composers were well-trained musicians who also composed classical works and music for the theater and films. Some held doctoral degrees and had studied with composers such as Hidenmith and Mahler.[190]

In the collection under examination, the songs are easy arrangements for the piano. While a few have a hymnlike arrangement of parts, most reflect a preference for unison singing by the *Hitlerjugend*. The works are all very short, from two to eight music lines in length. Most have several verses, and a few have as many as ten. The melodies are very easy to sing. Most are in major keys. They were obviously arranged in keys having only a few sharps or flats. Most, for example, are in G or F major. The rhythm patterns of these arrangements are also simple, and the four-four measure signature is almost exclusively used.

Advertisements included in the back of this collection indicate that the songs were also published in arrangements for violin and voice. There are also advertisements for other collections such as *Neues Deutschland, Deutsch Jugend am Klavier, Frei Weg,* for piano, violin and cello, *Allen voran!, Deutsch Heimat,* and *Was Die deutschen Kinder Singen.* All of these collections were published by B. Schott's Söhne, which continues to be a major German music publisher.

In addition to other ceremonies and rallies, Reich services for the dead included favored music selections. Commemorative wreaths were placed on the monument to those who died in the November 9, 1923 abortive putsch, to bands playing such solemn, heroic works as *Raise the Banner.* This was also used in the funeral procession Goebbels planned for Fritz Todt. He also selected "The Funeral March from Wagner's *Götterdammerung,* the *Song of the Good Comrade,* and the national anthem, *Deutschland über Alles.*[191]

In 1934, Goebbels, realizing the need for respite from military music, issued a decree which called for lighter music on the radio for several weeks following intensely emotional experiences such as party rallies. In order for the propagandistic value of radio broadcasts to be realized, Goebbels also accepted that the Reich had to provide programs which would encourage citizens to keep their radios turned on. Between 1932 and 1937, therefore, the amount of air time dedicated to music increased to sixty-nine percent, seven-eights of which was lighter music. These programs included operas by the nineteenth-century masters Weber, Lortzing, Cornelius and Nicolai, and operettas. Johan Strauss, Franx Lehár, Paul Lincke and lesser composers like Eduard Kunecke and Emil Rezenicek were heard repeatedly.[192] Goebbels was aware that not everyone had a comprehension of music sufficient for appreciation of such works as Wagner's operas. He found it necessary that simple forms of music should exist and that creators of those forms should be made to realize that they render a service to the Reich. Then too, Hitler doubtlessly approved of the inclusion of lighter music, for, he was especially fond of operettas.[193]

Many symphonic programs by the Berlin and Vienna Philharmonic Orchestras were broadcast during the Third Reich. They were usually held to an hour's length, but special exceptions were made for such works as Bruckner's lengthy *Seventh Symphony*. Certain instrumental works became monograms for special events and announcements over the radio. The *Meistersinger* overture was played for Goebbels' annual radio celebration of Hitler's birthday, and Beethoven's *Eroica* was played to introduce Hitler's speeches on Heroes' Remembrance Day. Herzstein claimed that in a special effort to keep Germans out of the churches, special attention was given to Sunday broadcasts of the finest classical and church music and poetry readings.[194]

Goebbels also banned the playing of Mozart's *Requiem* over the radio during the war, because it was "world-renouncing and depressing." Beethoven's *Fifth Symphony* was also rejected because it had become an allied victory signal. The war also brought confusion about playing, singing, and listening to music of the enemy. This resulted in a ban on the music of Ravel, Debussy, Chopin, Bizet, and Tchaikovsky. Nevertheless, Borodin's *Prince Igor* was performed at Hamburg during the German campaign in Russia.[194]

Musical compositions were often changed to suit the restrictions of the Third Reich. In Beethoven's *Fidelio*, for example, Leonora's loyalty to Florestan was given emphasis in order to take attention away from the prison scenes, which were too relevant to concentration camps, while Wilhelm Backhus was praised for playing the Schumann concerto with a new German image, which avoided the typical effeminate manner of playing Schumann.[195]

A portion of the Nazi government, surely not comprised of musicologists, saw a serious problem in the respective value of major and minor keys in music. Some argued greater gifts were required to compose in a major key because the composer had to "take upon himself the contradiction and paradox of life." More "inner strength" was needed than in the case of a minor key. Minor keys, on the other hand, were associated with non-Aryan music.[196] The realization that a great number of songs of the movement were not in a major key but had "a marked affinity with an alien system of sound" was quite disturbing to some, such as Rosenberg.[197] However, there was never a resolution of the dispute.

The Nazi leadership, however, did reach some agreement on the music areas each was to dominate. During the Third Reich, for example, Goebbels laid down the guidelines for radio and films while Goering and Schirach provided direction to the operas at Berlin and Vienna. Hitler patronized the music communities in Munich, Wiemar, Bayreuth and Linz. Hitler endowed Linz with a large orchestra called the Bruckner Orchestra. In Munich, as has been seen, he was most concerned with the visual arts. He endowed Weimar with an annual allowance of 60,000 marks, gave advice on staging and casting, and enjoyed contact with the artists. Hitler also contributed substantial sums to the support of Wagner's music in Bayreuth and granted the operation a complete tax exemption.

Bayreuth became Hitler's 'Court Theater' and thrived under his patronage. As will be recalled, before Hitler's attempted coup in 1923, which earned him a term in Landsberg Prison, he had visited Wagner's grave and declared to Winifred Wagner, "Out of *Parsifal* I will make a religion." The full meaning of this remark was clarified by Hitler some thirteen years later. In the spring of 1936, Hitler ordered German troops into the Rhineland, which had been demilitarized since 1918. Not long afterward, Hitler went on a triumphal train tour of the region. Although his trip was punctuated with dramatic speeches and church bells saluting his victory, Hitler realized the retaking of the Rhineland showed more bravura than military strength and was thankful for the pacifity of the Western powers. He said, "Am I glad! Good Lord, am I glad it's gone so smoothly. Sure enough, the world belongs to the brave man. He's the one God helps." As his train continued the noctournal journey through the Ruhr district, it passed glowing blast furnaces, slag heaps, and derricks, and Hitler asked that a record of Wagner's music be played. When the prelude of *Parsifal* began to sound he reiterated his intention to develop a religion out of it as "One can serve God only in the garb of the hero" without any "pretense of humility."[198] Surprisingly, *Parsifal* was dropped from the Third Reich repertoire when the war started, "presumably because its Christian overtones antagonized the neo-paganists surrounding Rosenberg."[199] The habit of dreary resentments did not permit Hitler to enjoy the success of his tour, for as the record continued with the funeral march from *Götterdämmerung*, Hitler recalled:

I first heard it in Vienna. At the Opera. And I still remember as if it were today how madly excited I became on the way home over a few yammering Yids I had to pass. I cannot think of a more incompatible contrast. This glorious mystery of the dying hero and this Jewish crap![200]

Fest believed that the finale of *Götterdämmerung* was the extreme expression of opera to Hitler. During his years of attending opera at the Bayreuth theater, when the stronghold of the gods collapsed in musical climax, he would usually take the hand of Frau Winifred Wagner and emotionally kiss her hand.[201]

Hitler also carried his interest in stage designs for Wagner's works into the years of his Chancellorship. Speer witnessed Hitler's "amazing knowledge of stagecraft, his interest in the diameter of revolving stages, lift mechanisms, and especially different lighting techniques." Speer heard Hitler discuss lighting and scenery for Wagner's music-dramas with Benno von Arent, whom Hitler had made Reich State Designer and Supervisor of opera and operetta decor. He also provided Arent with "neatly executed stage designs, colored with crayons, for all acts of *Tristan and Isolda*" and sketches for all scenes of *Der Ring des Niebelungen,* which he had poured over night after night for three weeks. Later, when von Arent was commissioned to stage *Meistersinger* at the opening performance for the Party Rally, Hitler closely studied lighting for the moonlight scenes and "went into ecstasies over the brilliant colors he wanted for the final scene on the mastersinger's meadow, and over the romantic look of the little gabled houses opposite Hans Sach's cobbler's shop."[202]

Hitler's attitude toward Wagner's works was decidedly conservative. H. H. Stuckenschmitt reported in *Modern Music* in 1933, that Heinz Tietzen and Emil Pretorius, "two representatives of modern ideas in the theatre," gave the *Ring* and *Meistersinger* "novel scenic dress" in contrast to the Bayreuth tradition, and the "Keepers of the Grail" protested against the "cultural-bolshevistic" interpretation of Wagner, but the government was satisfied. Hitler's own conservativism resulted in his request that Arent replace Emil Pretorius, who had long done the sets for the Bayreuth Festival. Winifred Wagner avoided this change by pretending she did not know what Hitler was driving at in their conversations about the conductors.[203] It is generally recognized, however, that during the Third Reich, the performances came closer to approximating Wagner's original Bayreuth concept than they had immediately before the Reich. Indeed, it became increasingly a German event, for fewer and fewer foreigners were seen there.

It was not uncommon for Hitler to intervene in the appointment of musicians to important theatrical posts. Often, he did this to "preserve tradition and keep overbold innovators out of the positions of power." For such reasons, Karl Elmendorff was given directorship of the Dresden City Opera, in 1942. He often showed very strong feelings about conductors in particular. He said Knappertsbusch, for example, was "no better than a military band leader," and he mistrusted Karajan because he conducted without a score and so could not catch blunders on the part of the singers, "which was inconsiderate of the public as well as the singers." Schirach believed Hitler would have "interfered if Karajan had not been a protégé of Goering's, just as Knappertsbusch enjoyed the protection of Eva Braun," who liked the conductor's "manly good looks."[204]

Schaum believed Hitler saw himself as a conductor before crowds. Snyder also argued Hitler's control of his audience showed parallels to that of a conductor. He orchestrated the rhythm of his words, the applause of his audience and, with appropriate gestures, immediately called a halt to the shouts of his listeners.[205]

Hitler also took a keen interest in singers during his years as Chancellor. Jewish singers like List and Kipnis were banned at Bayreuth after 1933. Kirsten Flagstad was ordered not to appear there shortly afterward because of her standing in America. Both Herbert Janssen and Frieda Leider were married to Jews and were likewise banned from Bayreuth appearances some time later. In 1937, on the eve of the Nuremberg Congress, *Time* reported Hitler attended a five-hour, unabridged performance of Wagner's *Die Meistersinger*. *Time* stated "Hitler's favorite tenor, soulful looking Eyvind Lahome (ne plain Victor Johnson of Birmingham, Ala.)" was applauded by Hitler as the ideal interpreter of Walther, and he "awarded him the rare state title of Kämmersanger."[206] One very practical reason for the construction of so many opera theaters in Germany, according to Hitler, was that they could provide plenty of small places for more of Germany's talented voices to "try out" and thus help relieve the critical shortage of Wagnerian tenors.

Hitler believed that one of the hardships which the war had imposed upon him was "his having to forsake this whole world of the performing arts." He continued to relish gossip about his favorite singers which Goebbels, Schaub, and others would share with him. In the later years of the war, Hitler gave up viewing evening films and instead played records.[207] Even though he had an excellent record collection, he would not listen to baroque nor classical music, chamber music nor symphonies. When alone with his coterie, Hitler invariably requested bravura selections from Wagner's operas followed by light operettas. He made a game of guessing the names of the sopranos and was quite pleased when he guessed correctly.[208]

Speer recalled Hitler's attempt to impose his love of Wagnerian opera upon the party leadership. At a performance of *Die Meistersinger*, during the 1933 Nuremberg Rally, Hitler arrived to find the opera house almost empty. He sent patrols to bring in party functionaries from the quarters, beer halls, and cafés. The next year he ordered them to show up. They did, but looked bored or fell asleep. After 1935, the "indifferent party audience was replaced by members of the public, who had to buy their tickets." Once war broke out, "Hitler gave tickets to the festival performances to convalescent soldiers, deserving munitions workers, nurses and others."[209]

Once a year, Hitler invited businessmen, who had particularly given generously to the party, to a gala event at the Chancellery. After the banquet, members of the Berlin opera houses performed. In 1939, several such leading industrialists gave Hitler the original scores of Wagner's *Rienzi*, *Das Reingold*, *Die Walküre* and *Die Gotterdämmerung*. Hitler was particularly excited about the orchestral sketch for the latter. He showed sheet after sheet to his guests and made knowledgeable comments. Borman pointed out to Hitler that the gift had cost nearly a million marks.[210]

During the Third Reich, Hitler's interest in classical music, apart from Wagner's operas, was very limited. Hanfstaengl noted Hitler's lack of interest in Bach's music. He also declared Hitler would listen to Chopin and

Schumann, as well as some of Richard Strauss's operas. Grosshans stated that Hitler was fond of Weber's *Freischütz*, Puccini's *La Bohème* and Verdi's *Aida*. De Jaegger, however, thought Hitler disliked Italian opera except for *Aida*.[211]

Unlike his love of Wagner, Hitler's enthusiasm for Bruckner was low-keyed. His interest in Bruckner's music may not have been as keen as his pride that the composer had lived in Linz. Nevertheless, homage was paid to Bruckner by Hitler's endowment of the Bruckner Orchestra in Linz and the performance of a movement of one of his symphonies before his speeches on culture at the Nuremberg Party Rallies. Hitler also took care that Bruckner's music was fostered at the St. Florian monastery, and his plans for the redesign of Linz included a monument to glorify the composer.[212] Hitler's support of the composer was also reflected in a list of the qualifications which the directors of the Gewandhaus Orchestra, in Leipzig, were given to use in the selection of a replacement for the great Bruno Walter. The New director:

...must love Bruckner. In the realm of late and neo-romantic music he must be able to distinguish between the timeless and the fashionable, between manifestations of the German soul and shallow virtuosity; he must have the clearest judgment as to where, in contemporary music, German humanity struggles for expression and where it does not.[213]

In the end, the Third Reich finally died to the strains of a slow movement from Bruckner's Seventh Symphony, played after the announcement of Hitler's suicide by Radio Berlin.[214]

Hitler also loved operettas, especially the works of Franz Lehár, although Lehár had a Jewish wife and had collaborated with the Jewish librettist Beda Löhner. Hitler, seemingly undisturbed by Lehár's association with Löhner, ranked his opera *Die Lustige Witwe (The Merry Widow)* "as the equal of the finest opera." He also believed his *Die Fledermaus, Die Vogelhandler* and *Die Zigeunerbaron* "were sacred portions of the German cultural heritage." In Berlin, Hitler never missed a production of *Die Fledermaus* and *The Merry Widow* and contributed considerable sums to have them staged in an elaborate style.[215]

Hitler generally spoke on musical questions with the same degree of infallibility and assurance as he displayed as a politician, war-leader, and architect. On April 20, 1943, with German troops fighting for survival in North Africa and Russia, Hitler decided to entertain his birthday guests with a recording of *The Merry Widow*. When Borman asked Hitler whether he wanted to hear the performance by Johannes Heesters in Munich or the Berlin production conducted by Lehár himself, Hitler discussed the merits of each before he asserted the Munich performance was "ten percent better."[216]

Hitler looked with marked repugnance on contemporary male ballet dancers who "displayed themselves in their close-fitting leotards." He told Speer with disgust that when they appeared, "I always have to look away." He also took little interest in modern interpretive ballet. After attending one such performance at the urging of Goebbels, he termed it a "cultural disgrace" as it "had nothing to do with dancing, but looked rather more like so much hopping around punctuated with strenuous leaps into the air."[217] With the exception of his view of male ballet dancers, Hitler loved traditional ballet "as much as he did operetta." He approached it with the same type of pontifical judgment molded by his late nineteenth-century bourgeois concept of the female dancer as a "beautiful picture of a gracious creature gliding weightlessly across the stage with no other purpose than to delight the eye."[218] Hitler considered the Hoeppner sisters, who were dancers with the Berlin Municipal Opera, as the "very essence of beauty." He invited them to his private rooms for tea, sat between them on a sofa, and held "each by the hand like a worshipful teenager." Hitler also enjoyed dance revues that featured nearly nude female dancers. One such American performer who appeared in Munich totally captivated Hitler. He invited her to tea and made it "quite plain" to Speer that "he would lay siege to her if it were not for his accursed official position." Apart from Unity Mitford, she was "the only foreigner ever admitted to his circle." Hitler, according to Speer, particularly enjoyed performances at the Berlin Wintergarten and the Metropol Theater and "would certainly have gone more frequently but for the fact that he was embarrassed to be seen there" because they staged "insipid musicals with plenty of scantily clad girls."[219]

Hitler absolutely refused to take part in ballroom-dancing himself, even at gala affairs when it might be considered appropriate. When Helene Hanfstaengl offered to teach Hitler to waltz, he refused because it was an unworthy act for a stateman. When he was told Washington, Frederick the Great and Napoleon enjoyed dancing, Hitler responded it was:

...a stupid waste of time and these Viennese waltzes are too effeminate for a man to dance. This craze is by no means the least factor in the decline of their Empire. That is what I hate about Vienna.[220]

On another occasion, he stated he found ballroom dancing "the essence of effeminacy." Certain dances, on the other hand, such as the dynamic, pounding German *Schuhplatter*, he thought "worthy of any man."[221] Rudolf Bode, the "chief mystagogue of dancing" in the Third Reich, was allowed to repeatedly make statements similar to the following:

In the dance we relieve the great primal laws of nature. As far as the male partner is concerned, the basic movement attuned to the thrust and the blow, inevitably tends toward the soldierly. In the case of the female the instinctive vibration is of a circular character— a circular character connected with the swastika, the rune of life with its eternally circular motion.[222]

Even though he occasionally attended popular revues, Hitler was unaffected by their music. Hanfstaengl insisted Hitler never hummed or whistled any popular tunes but limited himself to themes from Wagner. The only exception to this habit was Hitler's whistling of the Walt Disney tune "Who's Afraid of the Big Bad Wolf?"[223] This latter tune appealed to him as it was a play on an old German diminutive of "Adolf." Early in his political career, he enjoyed being called "Wolf" by his associates and later, gave variations of the name to his various military headquarters and favored the Alsatian wolfhound as a pet.

Hitler had little interest in other music forms, such as chamber music, although the *Burghof* had an excellent collection of records and state of the art photographic equipment. His musical preferences always remained quite limited—a fact which Hitler made no effort to remedy.

From the foregoing, Hitler's aesthetic concepts and attitudes can be seen to represent little beyond a conservative, bourgeois mentality that rejected all elements of the new artistic scene that were appearing at his birth and during his early youth. This conservative, banal, artistic outlook, he overlaid with nationalistic and racial veneers in his early adulthood. When Hitler became chancellor, his aesthetic values became those of the Third Reich. Either through Hitler's active intervention and imposition or by his passive consent, the art, sculpture, architecture and music of Nazi Germany became conservative, bourgeois, racial and nationalistic. In achieving this state, Hitler did not invent any new Nazi artistic insights. Rather, he utilized pre-existent German work that met with his approval and ruthlessly pruned away all opposing elements. The only new characteristic he added to these officially approved but preexistent elements was his insistence on monumentality in architecture and sculpture. This element, however, was exaggerated to the point where his architecture and sculpture ultimately lost any sense of reality and humanity.

The only artistic field in which Hitler met substantial opposition was music. Musicians, by the very nature of their art, are highly social beings in the execution of their work. Even here, however, he was able finally to impose his will.

Hitler met with success in the imposition of his aesthetic upon the post-war generation precisely because they suffered from the same feelings of trauma and inferiority that he did. He came to power because he, more successfully than any other German politician, offered relief and remedies for their psychic pain and bolstered their heart-felt need to feel superior following their defeat in the war. As Carr noted, his success was due "to the coincidence of his personal pathology" with the needs of a "disturbed" society.[224] His artistic imposition played no small part in his ability to meet their needs. What is necessary next then, is to investigate the origin and nature of Hitler's mental pathology.

Chapter 5
An Adlerian Interpretation of Hitler's Architecture, Art and Music

A wide variety of psychological interpretations have been applied to Hitler. As early as November, 1938, *The New Republic* noted that an American psychiatrist identified Hitler as "a psychopathic paranoid personality" characterized by "algolagnia" or "pleasure in pain." A second psychiatrist described Hitler as an "infantile personality" motivated by sadistic "childhood fixations." A third psychiatrist insisted Hitler was a "compulsive neurotic" with "masochistic inner conflict." The following spring, *The New Republic* returned to the subject with an anonymous article which identified Hitler as a "narcissistic neurotic" who bore a "frightful unconscious rage" against his mother.[1]

This confusion and disagreement has continued to plague subsequent researchers. Langer described Hitler as a "neurotic psychopath" or a "hysterical psychopath." Murray saw Hitler as a paranoid schizophrenic while Erikson called Hitler a "psychopathic paranoid." To Waite, Hitler was a borderline personality teetering between neurosis and psychosis.[2]

A number of problems present themselves at this point. These characterizations are only broad approximations whose definitions continually evolve. Further, taken by themselves, they tell us nothing about the origins of whatever mental disturbances Hitler may have had. Finally, they are based upon suspect evidence, are contradictorily interpreted, and employ essentially Freudian models.

Most psychiatrists have tended to stress the relationship between Hitler and his parents as the starting point for any diagnosis of his mental pathology. Langer and Murray insisted Hitler hated his authoritarian, "castrating" father while developing an oedipal, incestuous desire for his mother.[3] They assumed, without any supportive evidence, that Hitler witnessed his parents in sexual intercourse. Hitler became for them a sexual pervert who throughout his life was possessed by feelings of guilt and inadequacy. It is noteworthy that the only medical observer who witnessed the interaction between Hitler and his mother denied any pathological element in their relationship.[4] Erich Fromm, faced with the same evidence, argued Hitler did not hate his father— neither did he love his mother. Hitler was a narcissistic personality who was never able to love anyone.[5]

116

A variation on the oedipal theme was suggested by Stierlin. Stierlin insisted Hitler was "delegated" by his traumatized mother to reassure her she was a good mother, to absolve her guilt for marrying her uncle, to justify her sacrifices by becoming important, and to avenge her *vis-à-vis* her husband. Hitler was torn between the impossible nature of these tasks and the moral imperative she gave him which conflicted with the natural desire he had for independence. Hitler had to carry her shame and guilt while simultaneously suppressing them to become her proper "delegate."[6]

Binion, in yet another variation of the Freudian approach, argued Hitler had an oral fixation which arrested his psychological growth. His lust for conquest derived from his desire to "recover the breast-fed bliss of a fledgling." Klara's operation for breast-cancer was a trauma which was later recapitulated in Germany's defeat in 1918. Hitler dedicated his life henceforth to reversing the trauma by conquering for Germany a "feeding ground" in Eastern Europe.[7]

Erikson believed Hitler replaced his beloved mother Klara with "super-human mother figures" such as fate, nature, the volk and, above all, Germany. Hence, Hitler struggled continually to fight and please simultaneously these super-mother abstractions which intended to both destroy him and to bless him. Hitler thus remained throughout his life an "unbroken adolescent."[8]

Bromberg and Small asserted Hitler was a "narcissistic personality with paranoid features functioning on a borderline personality level." Hitler's mother, a "wretched" woman overcome with misery, unconsciously projected her "angry feelings, disappointed hopes, and disturbed self-regard" onto her son. Hitler, who was monorchidic, blamed his mother for his condition and sought continually to compensate for his feeling of castration.[9]

Waite described Hitler as a paranoid, borderline personality with "oedipal problems" which were intensified by monorchism and his having observed his parents in sexual intercourse. He ended by being infertile, sexually perverted, and unable to compose a stable sense of identity. Hitler always felt "split" or torn apart and attempted to resolve this split by attributing good qualities to himself and projecting bad ones on all others— especially the Jews.[10]

These interpretations have been drastically summarized and much of their reasoning omitted in order to stress that they apply a Freudian psychoanalytic model to Hitler's mental state. Most combine varying mixtures of conjecture, surmise, argument by analogy and intuition. The situation is even worse when Hitler's sex life is discussed, for there the evidence is all hearsay. Not only was Hitler reticent and discreet about all personal matters, but the material cited actually consists of supposition, slander, and third-hand gossip gleaned from tainted sources. There has been much made of a supposed masochistic streak in Hitler that expressed itself in his need to have females urinate or defecate on him while he masturbated.[11] However, the source of the story was a film director, A. Zeissler, an emigrè understandably prejudiced against Hitler, who gave as the source of his information a disturbed actress, Renate Mueller, who committed suicide and could not verify the incident. It was later repeated by Otto Strasser, a political opponent of Hitler, whose information is suspect at a number of points. While such a perversion is possible, much conjecture about Hitler's sex life is perhaps motivated by the feeling that as Hitler was abnormal, his sexual activities had to be abnormal. At any rate, the evidence is so biased and tenuous that it would be rejected outright if its subject were not Hitler.

A decided advantage in the use of an Adlerian model to examine Hitler is Adler's rejection of the need for a psychosexual history of an individual. While Adler identified the sexual development of every individual as one of the three problems demanding resolution, he rejected the concept of "the omnipotent sexual libido" which Freud and his followers supported. For some nine years, Adler himself was among those who studied with Freud in Vienna. As his personal approach to psychology developed, he withdrew from Freud's aura and developed his own ideas. He called his method Individual Psychology and took pride in the fact that it was "the first school of psychology to break with the assumption of inner forces, such as instincts, drives, unconsciousness, etc., as irrational material," which Freud emphasized.[12]

Adler's approach stressed the uniqueness of each individual in his effort to deal with life. In 1914, he defined Individual Psychology as an attempt to determine the picture of a self-consistent personality from an examination of separate life manifestations and forms of expression. His method presupposed the self-consistency and unity of the individual and demanded that separate traits be compared, reduced to their common denominator and combined into a comprehensive portrait of an individual.[13]

Adler believed every individual has a sense of inferiority, which is manifested early in life. Indeed, dependence upon adults places him initially in an inferior position from which he strives to acquire peace and security. While his success will depend upon many factors, it will be determined in large part by his creative reaction to family peculiarities, those who nurse him and other individuals in his environment.[14] Adler placed great significance on the child's response to conditions of his embryonal stage, the tempo of his organic development, his endocrine system, his muscular build and the quality of his nutrition. He also realized a child's movement toward peace and security was effected by his reaction to conditions of his environment.[15]

Adler recognized that a child cannot be expected to objectively appraise his situation. It is, however, the degree of inferiority one feels, regardless of its veracity, which will determine the way he strives to move away from his feeling of inferiority toward a feeling of superiority. Adler called this movement from the "minus" to the "plus" position an individual's life-style or style of life.[16] An individual begins his struggle before he has ideas or language skills adequate to give it expression. With insufficient emotional skills, little capacity for action and guided by wins and losses which provide subjective and deficient criteria, he forms a goal to be reached in the future. The goal gives direction to all an individual's actions and movements.

Therefore, when an individual's goal is known, it is possible to understand the meaning of his individual acts. Conversely, when individual acts are studied, the meaning of the goal becomes clearer. This relationship between goals and acts is an important premise of Individual Psychology. It emphasized that a person's actions in his movement toward his goal spring as a unit from his personality. Therefore, a person's actions disclose his meaning of life.[17]

The goal, unknown to the individual, determines his approach to the tasks of life. It causes the individual to perceive situations, not as they are in reality, but through the prejudices of his personal schema of apperception. Adler argued this abstract, unconscious goal of rectifying the felt position of inferiority results in a tangible, concrete goal. An individual may wish, for example, to be a teacher for the abstract goal of ruling over inferiors, or desire to be a doctor for the abstract goal of preventing death or living in economic security.[18]

In the establishment of his goal, the child emulates individuals in his environment who represent strength. Adler recognized that, although the child may have the "goal of goals," that is, he may wish to be all powerful like God, he substitutes more concrete models. He may, therefore, emulate a strong father and later, a policeman, a doctor, a teacher and so on. His emulation is observable in his conduct, play, attitudes, imitative gestures, play, wishes, daydreams, favorite stories, and ideas about his future vocation. The child establishes such imaginary goals in order to structure the chaotic, fluid, and intangible elements of life.[19]

Adler believed that a critical aspect of the child's establishment of a life-style and the selection of goals is his development of social interest. Initially, the sociological circle is parent centered or family centered. Later, his social consciousness is tested in the arena of the larger community. Adler stressed that "the individual as a complete being cannot be dragged out of his connection with life—perhaps it would be better to say, with the community."[20] The child must, therefore, be "educated for the community" and "only those are suited to be teachers and educators who themselves have developed social interests."[21] They have the first opportunity to build the child's self-confidence and strength in social experiences.

Adler clearly defines the role of the mother in the proper socialization of the child. Prenatally related to the child physically, she must relate the child to herself psychologically. This attachment allows her to nourish the child's growing awareness of social concepts, of work and of love. When properly handled, she can slowly transform his love for her and his dependance upon her into a responsible, benevolent and confident attitude toward society.[22]

Adler was equally clear in his definition of the role the father must play in the family. He must prove to his wife and child and to society that he is a good fellow man. His worth is reflected in the way he deals with his occupation, his friendships, and with love—the three problems of life. The father's role is equal to the mother's in the care and protection of the family.[23]

An individual must be taught to have social interest not only for the acquisition of his own goals, but also for the general welfare of society. Adler believed an individual cannot be considered apart from his social situation, for all of life's problems merge into the social problems of neighborly love, work and sexual love. The more a child is made ready for cooperation, love and fellowship the more valuable will his accomplishments be in his movement away from his position of inferiority. His actions and feelings will be given over to concerns for the general welfare of mankind. Regardless of his intellectual ability, his contribution to the solution of social concerns will bring him a sense of value which Adler believed to be identical to happiness.[24]

Adler found every individual is unique in his approach to problem solving. His method is not predetermined, and his solution of a problem depends upon how he views himself in relation to a given problem. He is limited not only by innate human limitations but also by self-imposed limitations. His relationship to the outside world is not determined by heredity nor environment. While heredity provides certain abilities and environment affords certain impressions, it is a person's interpretation of experiences which provides him with creative materials for building an attitude toward life which determines his relationship to the world.[25]

Although Adler repeatedly called for every individual to be treated as unique in his approach to the solution of the problems of life, he provided students of Individual Psychology with four general classifications of behavior and attitudes which individuals use in their approach to problem solving. The first type has a more or less dominant or "ruling" attitude in all their relationships. The second type "expects everything from others and leans on others." Adler called this type the "getting" type. The third type "is inclined to feel successful by avoiding the solution of problems." They try to side-step problems in order to avoid defeat. The fourth type "struggles, to a greater or lesser degree, for a solution of these problems in a way which is useful to others."[26]

Adler accepted a limited complex of inferiority and the striving for superiority, as innate and necessary for the advancement of humanity. In extreme form, however, the complex is more like "a disease whose ravages vary under different circumstances." If an individual feels after repeated attempts at resolving his inferior feelings that it is impossible for him to overcome obstacles, "he will try to hypnotize himself or autointoxicate himself into feeling superior." His inferior feelings remain and continue to be provoked by the same situations. They become the permanent undercurrent of his psychic life and can be very destructive.[28]

Adler described the inferiority complex as the individual's belief "that he is not strong enough to solve a given problem in a socially useful way." Adler came to the conclusion that, "the inferiority (symptom) complex, that is, the persistence of the consequences of the feeling of inferiority, and the retention of that feeling, finds its explanation in greater lack of social feeling."

Inherent in the inferiority complex is the superiority complex. Adler declared that "the word complex as attached to inferiority (feeling) and superiority merely represents an exaggerated condition of the sense of inferiority and the striving for superiority." When both children and adults feel weak, they lose their social interest and strive for personal superiority. Their solutions for the problems of life are sought in a way in which they can obtain "personal superiority without any admixture of social interest."[29]

The show-off, for example, is someone with both an inferiority and a superiority complex. He "does not feel strong enough to compete with others on the useful side of life," so he compensates with negative behavior. Adler believed such outward signs of the feeling of inferiority are also found in a person who gesticulates strongly when speaking. He fears his words will not carry weight and uses gestures to guarantee attention to himself. Such an individual "assumes he is superior when he is not and the false success compensates him for the state of inferiority which he cannot bear." Adler declared that a "normal person does not have a superiority complex, he does not even have a sense of superiority." He will strive to be successful, and as long as his striving is expressed in work, it will not lead him to false valuations, the root of mental illness.[30]

Persons with a superiority complex are arrogant, snobbish, boastful and tyrranical. They suffer from inordinate hero-worship, seek the company of prominent persons and depreciate those who are weak or of lesser stature. They display exaggerated emotional states of anger, desire for revenge, grief and loud laughter. They direct conversations and attention towards themselves at every opportunity, and they even credit themselves with remarkable abilities such as telepathic powers and prophetic inspiration.

Adler believed that there are certain other conditions which may so augment a child's natural sense of inferiority that he will develop an inferiority complex which seeks compensation in a superiority complex. This occurs in such cases as children who are born with inferior organs, but also in organically "normal" children who are pampered and become dependent, or suffer from neglect. Childhood illnesses may be an obstacle to proper development of a child's social interests. Some diseases, by their nature, cause physical deformities which result in poor social feeling. Other diseases may show little or no outward deformity, but the anxiety and care of attending adults give the child "a great sense of his own personal worth without his contributing anything himself."[31] The child may persist in demanding inordinate attention after the disease has run its course. Self-love continues and social interest is disrupted.

A child's sense of inferiority may also be augmented by a pampering mother. If a mother is unable to give equal attention to her child, her husband, and her social life, and considers only her relation to her child, she will be unable to avoid pampering and spoiling him. In so doing, she makes it difficult for him to have independence and the "ability to cooperate with others." If she is not interested in the father, it will be extremely difficult for her to turn his interest toward the father. The mother "must turn the child's interest also to the social life around him, to the other children of the family, to friends, relatives, and fellow human beings in general."[32] If she is unwilling or unable to help him extend to others the love and trust she has built between herself and the child, he will be in an inferior position to deal with the problems of life. He will live in the belief that everything should be done for him by others, and, in later life, he will not want to look after his own affairs. The pampered child dominates his pampering parent. Therefore, he will want to dominate other persons throughout his life. When the child finds he cannot do so, he may react in the opposite way and draw back from the world into the family "with all his fantasies— sexual fantasies often included," instead of making necessary adjustments in his social feeling.[33]

Pampering by the mother may also disrupt the child's development of a permanent relationship with his father. This may also happen "when there is imperfect social feeling, or when the child dislikes him."[34] The father may harm his relationship with his child if he attempts to prevent the mother's pampering of the child or tries to force the child to respond to his authority or conform to his principles. While the father may be successful in these efforts, he will never have real cooperation, and the child's social feeling will be harmed. When the father is the one who executes punishment, the child comes to regard men as the final authority and the real power in life. It disturbs the relation of the child with the father and makes him fear him instead of feeling he is a real friend.[35]

When the mother protests against having another child, the only child may be completely enslaved because she fears losing him. He develops a "mother complex," in which he is so extremely attached to his mother that he "wishes to push the father out of the family picture." He wants to be the center of his mother's attention and lives in fear that his mother will have more children. When his position is challenged, he sees it as a great injustice. Many difficulties arise later in life when he is not the center of attention.[36]

The birth of a second child makes the only child feel he has been "dethroned." If the second child is born three or four years after the oldest child, he intrudes upon the life-style which the oldest child has already established. Even a single year, however, between two births can make the oldest feel dethroned. Impulses of hate and death wishes toward the second child occur in especially pampered children. Oldest children are "almost always regarded as the representative of the family and of its conservative tradition." In one way or another, oldest children generally show an interest in the past and are pessimistic about the future. They treasure the time when they were the center of attention. They suffer from a loss of power and in later life want to be in a position where they can "take part in the exercise of authority and exaggerate the importance of rules and laws." They want everything done by rules which should never be changed and stress the preservation of power "in the hands of those entitled to it." This reflects the conservative dimension of dethroned oldest children.[37]

When the socialization of a child is not disrupted by pampering, or some other factor, he begins to feel he is a member with equal right in the home. By becoming a partner, instead of a burden, he develops courage and confidence to deal with the problems of later life.

Adolf Hitler fits totally the Adlerian concepts. Hitler, as seen earlier, was pampered by his mother because he was sickly and she was afraid he would die like the first three children she had borne. For five years, he was the only child of Alois and Klara Hitler, and the bond between mother and son seemed undisturbed by the presence of two children by his father's previous marriage. He dominated Klara's attention, and according to the Adlerian model, he would seek to dominate others throughout his life. When this did not always happen, his response was negative behavior, including sickness, since he was also a sickly pampered child.

Hitler's relationship with his father obviously suffered from the pampering of his mother. Although he claimed in *Mein Kampf* that he loved his father, on other occasions he confessed that he never loved him. Alois's own pathetic youth doubtlessly left him crippled in his parenting skills, for there is at least some evidence that he resorted to brute force in the discipline of his son. There is also some evidence that Alois's drinking caused Adolf considerable consternation, furnished grounds for his own abstinence, and was a destructive influence in their relationship. Klara's inability or unwillingness to help Adolf extend his love to his father and his father's poor parenting responses, however, appear to be the major reasons for the difficult and harmful relationship which existed between Hitler and his father. This critical step in the development of his social interest in humanity was disrupted, and its effects would never be corrected. The proper socialization of the young Hitler was thus stymied at the outset.

Adler thought that many people develop an exclusion complex. It exists in thousands of variations, and essentially may be defined as characterizing people who always want to reduce their sphere of action, who want to "remove all problems." This complex is used "as a crutch by the insecure person," who wants to "reach personal superiority by an easy way."[38] Adler found that "one of the most common influences on a child's mind is the feeling of suppression brought about by a father's or mother's excessive punishment or abuse." The child strives for release and sometimes this is "expressed in an attitude of psychological exclusion."[39] The child will thus tend to exclude people. In extreme cases, the neurotic individual would, if given the power and opportunity, exercise the ultimate form of exclusion—murder.

When Hitler was five years old, his brother Edmund was born, and, in Adlerian terms, Hitler felt dethroned. The very presence of another child was a threat to his well-established life-style. His mother's pampering had made him accustomed to being the center of attention, and he then had to share that position with Edmund. According to the Adlerian model, Hitler, as the oldest child, may even have come to wish for the death of his intrusive brother. If this happened, it may account for the dramatic change in Hitler's personality at the time of his brother's death. While an ordinary interpreter with well-developed social interest might prefer to attribute the change to grief or loneliness, in an Adlerian model it may be seen as Hitler's first experience of his exclusion complex. If his brother was perceived as a problem, and he wished for his death, and Edmund then died, Hitler would have believed his very desire had effected the removal of his problem. If a brother can be so easily dismissed, no one is safe from exclusion once the real power to do so is achieved. This complex explains the seeming ease with which other such problems were handled later in Hitler's life. Roehm and other followers of the early years of the movement, for example, were excluded by death as were the millions of Jews Hitler came to see as Germany's major problems.

Adler believed that when children are born with inferior organs, their painful and weak bodies are burdensome. They have feelings of inferiority and strive to arrive at a goal "in which they forsee and presume a feeling of superiority." Life is extremely difficult for them. Because they are preoccupied with their own persons they are selfish, inconsiderate, and lack social interest. They are not confident and "fear defeat more than they desire success."[40] Children who have a sex organ defect will, at an early age, evade tests of their worth and lose their spontaneity. They are shy, want to be pampered, prefer to do things alone, fear work, or read incessantly. Proof of masculinity becomes an important goal.[41] The implication here is that any physical inferiority has an early and negative impact upon the child. Fuller implications of sex organ inferiority may, however, develop in adolescence.

There is evidence that Hitler suffered from this "organ inferiority" described by Adler. The official Russian autopsy performed on his body, following its discovery in a shell-crater outside his bunker, revealed that Hitler's "left testicle could not be found either in the scrotum or on the spermatic cord inside the inguinal canal nor in the small pelvis."[42] This condition, known as monochism, would not necessarily have impared his sexual performance. It would, however, have been a potent force in his development of a feeling of neurotic inferiority that could be compensated for only by a corresponding sense of superiority.

In *Mein Kampf*, Hitler provided a glimpse of the relationship he had with his father during his adolescent years. Basic to this discussion was their conflict over his selection of a life goal. Alois wanted his son to be a civil servant like he was. Hitler admitted his admiration for the courage with which Alois selected an occupation which permitted him to escape life in the backward Waldviertel region, but he stressed that he had no desire to follow in the same occupation. Being a civil servant would not have fulfilled Hitler's personal needs—it would not have given him the necessary sense of superiority. Indeed, Adler found that, "one of the most frequent strivings is the attempt to excel other members of the family; and especially to go farther than the father or mother."[43] He also found that a child's choice of occupations tells much about his style of life, the direction of his striving and what in life is most valuable to him. Hitler quite early embarked on a quest for an occupation that would provide the necessary compensation for his felt inferiority. It was essential that the choice, whatever it was, provide the required sense of self-worth to Hitler.

Hitler's father was the strongest personality in his environment during his early years. Therefore, there was the greatest possibility for emulation by the young Hitler. But, while he may have emulated him in other ways, he found he could not follow in his father's occupation. In *Mein Kampf*, he shared with his readers other figures he admired as possible role models. He expressed his interest in being an abbot of the school he attended in Lembach. He was drawn to the role, not for the reasons a person with social interest would be, but because he loved the splendor of the church festivals and because he believed his own voice was quite good. He blamed his father for discouragement of this goal because he could not appreciate his oratorical talents. As a pampered child, the role of abbot doubtlessly appealed to him because it placed the celebrant at the center of attention. His statements also make clear how early in life he placed importance upon the power of his voice. This parallels his boastful statement that at this time his "oratorical talent was being developed in the form of more or less violent arguments with my schoolmates."[44]

There were other role models of his early years who played a part in the development of Hitler's establishment of goals later in life. He became fascinated with real and imaginary soldiers and wars. He found heroic figures to emulate in history books, adventures by Karl May, and Wagner's operas. He practiced his battle skills in play with his younger friends and bragged about being "a little ringleader." In so doing, Hitler conformed to Adler's model that children who want to feel superior "exclude stronger children and play with weaker children whom they can rule and dominate."[45] Adler believed there is much to be learned from a child's play about his preparation for the future. He considered games as educational aids and stimuli for the spirit, for fantasy, and for life-techniques of a child. He stated that a child's choice of games, the way he approaches it, and the importance he gives it, tell much about his relationship to his environment and his fellow man. In his play, he shows how friendly he is and "particularly whether he has the tendency to be a ruler." Indeed, his whole attitude toward life is observable.[46] Hitler thus gave early evidence of a leadership complex, which would not find full expression until his rise to power. Persons who have this complex "feel badly in any other role," and spend "day and night attempting to be at the head." They "do not like to be losers in a game, or to be the horse rather than the coachman." Adler found that this complex may be due to a child's position among his siblings, that "all geniuses have this complex," but so do others who have the ability, training, and opportunity for leadership.[47]

In *Mein Kampf*, Hitler declared that he decided on the concrete goal of being an artist at the age of twelve. It is not known whether he realized the full significance of this selection or whether he simply chose an area which gave him pleasure and for which he apparently had some talent. From his comments, it is clear that he could not have chosen any goal which placed limitations upon his liberty and removed him from being able to follow his own time schedule. In Adlerian terms, Hitler decided to be an artist because he perceived this as a goal which would move him away from his position of inferiority and to one of stability and respectability. Hitler and Adler both came from Austria, and Hitler shared Adler's thesis that to poets and artists we attribute "the greatest dignity."[48] Once made, this decision to become an artist remained Hitler's goal all through his adolescence.

The records from Hitler's early school years indicate little problem with his studies. In *Mein Kampf*, he wrote of his later decision to prove to his father the sincerity of his desire to become an artist by failing in his studies in *Realschule*. Evidently due to his mother's insistence, he continued his studies after his father's death. At that point, however, his grades show a pitiful succession of failures, which were in stark contrast to his earlier grades and the mental acumen so obvious in his later life. In order to put an end to his studies, he resorted to an illness, presumably a lung condition which persuaded his mother that he must quit *Realschule*. Once more the pampered, sickly Adolf dominated his mother. According to the Adlerian model, Hitler's educational failures were predictable once his decision to be an artist was made. The *Realschule* afforded little opportunity for him to achieve his goal, and, as Adler stressed, educational influences are "likely to be accepted only when they seem to hold a promise of success for the individual's life-style."[49]

In *Mein Kampf* Hitler wrote of other experiences and discoveries he made during his *Realschule* years which profoundly influenced the selection of his goals in the future. He declared that he became a nationalist and so learned to grasp the meaning of history. As students of Dr. Leopold Poetsch, Hitler and his "fellow ruffians" were acquainted with the Pan-Germanism of Ritter George von Schoenerer. Poetsch disciplined his students by an appeal to national honor. Hitler declared that he thereupon became a fanatical German Nationalist.[50]

The teachings of Poetsch did much to nullify the possibility for school to correct Hitler's inadequate social interest. He nurtured in Hitler and his fellow students the view that they were members of an elite portion of humanity beyond which their social interest must not extend. As Adler stressed, there are those whose feelings of inferiority seek a purely personal compensation in the conviction of the worthlessness of everyone else. They misuse the occasional uncertainties which people have regarding social interest in order to encourage socially harmful ideas and ways of life "in the name of salvation" for the present or future society.[51] Adler believed that such conditions prevented children from entering into the community and called for all concerned to work "against poorly understood nationalism if it harms the community of men."[52]

Hitler's social interest, to the extent that it existed at all, thus became exclusively centered upon the Germanic people. Non-Germans would thus have no value for him and could be totally excluded from his definition of humanity. They would have no meaning for him except as an explanation for the misfortunes he thought were inflicted upon the Germanic people. In his neurotic condition, based on the exclusion principle of Adler, they would have to be removed—if necessary, by murder. While this murderous intent was not fully developed at this time, the psychological seed had been planted.

While still in Linz, Hitler decided to study music. During his early years in Vienna, he experimented with the writing of an opera. He also wrote poetry and a play. At times, he even registered with the police as a writer and not as a painter. All of these creative efforts reflected his fascination with fantasy, his love of the arts, and his desire to follow an occupation which would bring him respectability and remove his feeling of inferiority. Wagner served as a role model for Hitler at this time. To Hitler, Wagner epitomized the ideal of the nationalistic, complete artist with whom he could identify. Like Wagner, he could achieve the superior status accorded to the artist of genius. Like Wagner, he could extol the superiority of Germanic blood and denigrate non-Germanic peoples like the "alien" Jew. Wagner provided the heroic models with whom Hitler wished to identify—a Rienzi or Siegfried. In short, Wagner was all that the youthful Hitler desired to be.

Hitler's applications to the Vienna Academy of Fine Arts were positive efforts to achieve his concrete goal of being an artist. In Adlerian terms, he was attempting to resolve one of the three problems everyone must face, that of having an occupation. With his second failure to gain admission, however, Hitler was devastated and fell into a period of despair which most scholars describe but generally fail to explain. As will be recalled, Hitler took to living on park benches, eventually found his way to a *dosshouse*, and depended upon churches and other organizations for food. There also exists some evidence that he resorted to begging during this difficult time. The most inexplicable aspect of his situation was his failure to use the 25 kronen-per-month orphan's pension to which he was entitled. Payne attempted to explain Hitler as a victim of the dull euphoria that comes with extreme poverty. Hitler's condition during this time approximates Adler's description of a nervous breakdown. Adler measured the extent of a breakdown by the degree which a person is found unable to participate in the demands and benefits of society. Neurotic individuals who are aloof from society have a "false attitude toward all life problems, the social, the vocational and the sexual problems." They see such problems as private affairs without general relationships, and they lose courage easily when confronted with problems. Their psychological tolerance depends in large part upon the degree of their social ties. When one's tolerance is exceeded, a person's attitude toward the demands of life is low. On the other hand, encouragement strengthens his tolerance and defers the outbreak of neurosis.[53]

Hitler was thus plunged into a slough of despair. His effort to compensate for his sense of inferiority by becoming an artist was thwarted. The failure of his compensatory mechanism was devastating. Life became a burden that offered no hope of the success he dreamed about and which had given his existence meaning.

Hitler found sanctuary in a *Mannerheim* after his period of living first on the streets of Vienna and then in a *dosshouse*. For several years, he lived essentially cut off from the outside world. He conformed to Adler's view of the neurotic with a tendency toward exclusion. In order to protect his view of the world, the neurotic with the exclusion tendency builds a wall against the demands of the community life he is in. He pushes aside all problems of life and gives himself over to concern with his personal feelings and observation of his symptoms. The symptoms are the result of his reactions to being in a situation in which he is too weak to arrive at the goal he set for himself, "when he feels too weak to play a pre-eminent role commensurate with that which should be his according to his picture of the world."[54]

Critical to Hitler's survival at this point was the reestablishment of progress toward his goal of being a painter. This was due in large part to the help of Reinhold Hanisch. As will be recalled, Hitler painted pictures and Hanish sold them for a percentage of the sale until Hitler accused Hanish in a court case of having cheated him out of a small amount.

Hitler's painting during this period remained conservative, stilted, and tenuous. He painted hundreds of city scenes and landscapes in the style of the nineteenth-century artists whom he admired and whose works he believed represented a tradition of respectability which must be preserved. His works also often reflected his extreme interest in architectural structures which represented power and authority. That his works sold well enough for him to sustain himself did much to confirm his belief that his tastes were shared by many others. He was unable, however, to correct his inability to draw or paint people—which the academy had stressed as his greatest artistic weakness. This lack of interest in the inclusion of a reasonable number of human forms in his works, doubtlessly reflected his lack of genuine social interest. He also never became a part of the community of modern artists who were active during his stay in Vienna and who might have done much to develop his skills. His paintings reveal a personality that could play only one note and that, not very well. Although his paintings during the war revealed a spontaneity of style never before seen in his work, they continued to reflect his lack of interest in humanity.

There is some evidence that Hitler continued to pursue his goal of being an artist after the war. There is even stronger evidence that he increasingly came to see himself as a student of architecture. This goal had been suggested to him by the director of the academy who had found his skills in painting inadequate but recognized Hitler's strong interest in architecture. Hitler himself, still earlier, had realized his interest in architecture, during his first visit to Vienna. It was then that he wrote to Kubizek that he had more interest in the museum's architecture than its contents. In later years, Hitler stated that during his years in Vienna, after his failure to be accepted at the art academy, he painted to make a living and studied architecture. Although he studied on his own, he developed considerable skills. This was recognized by Speer during his association with Hitler. His desire to be an architect found no results, other than his sketches, until his rise to power. This goal of being the architect of magnificent structures could not be realized until other goals had been reached. At this time, it was only a fantasy of which he could daydream and maintain his mental compensations.

During his years in Vienna, Hitler claimed to have expanded his social interest. He built, however, on the foundation of nationalistic views which Dr. Poetsch had laid down during his *Realschule* years. He gravitated to organizations, individuals, and journals which nourished his growing conviction that the German people must be saved from the hated non-German elements, including the Jews. Hitler's social interest was not filled with the desire to help suffering humanity, but was tainted by excessive self-interest and hatred. When all other efforts at mental compensation failed him, Hitler could still define himself as a member of the superior Germanic people.

Hitler used the reading room of the *Mannerheim* as a studio and a forum. There, he declaimed his nationalistic and racial views, as he had done earlier with his fellow students in *Realschule* and his friend Kubizek. He became known for his powers of argumentation as he tested his political and cultural ideas. Hitler was always ready to answer a challenge of his opinions. Throughout his life he would continue to exhibit what Adler called a "proof complex." People with this complex need to prove that they are without faults and that they have a right to exist. They fear being wrong, consider actions as tests of whether they receive recognition as being perfect, and assume that everyone in their environment is interested in their efforts.[55] The way of life Hitler followed in Vienna was transported to Munich in 1913. He painted well enough to maintain himself, but not well enough to receive any recognition. His feeling of inferiority thus continued and no adequate compensatory device presented itself to him until 1914.

With the outbreak of World War I, Hitler found a new way to compensate for his feeling of inferiority. This compensation was built upon his youthful interest in war and soldiering and allowed him to play the role of a Wagnerian hero. It may have relieved him of the shame he had carried since his youth, when he realized his father and all of Austria had failed to fight as one Germany in the Franco-Prussian War. As if relieved of a great pain, he volunteered to fight in a German regiment. If fate would not let him be a great painter, he believed it would let him be a great soldier. With joy, therefore, he embraced the opportunity to remove his sense of inferiority in a great cause for the Fatherland.

By all accounts, Hitler was an excellent soldier. He was thoroughly dedicated to a cause, which meant tremendous suffering through four years of brutal trench warfare. He received medals for his bravery and was generally respected for his dedication. This was the first goal which Hitler had embraced with complete abandon. His total dedication to fighting for his adopted Fatherland did much to ensure his personal devastation when the war was lost. Germany was defeated and he could no longer play the role of a Wagnerian hero fighting for his country.

During World War I, Adler served as a physician in the Austrian army. His experiences led to the writing of several articles dealing with war. His reflections include comments on war as an abuse of social interest, the motivations for war, the attitudes of participants, and the resulting psychological effects of war.[56] Although Hitler had joined the German army and not the Austrian army in World War I, Adler's explanations are equally applicable to Hitler.

Adler believed that, in the evolution of humanity, the "common people seem always to have been on the track to social interest." Although communal life has repeatedly asserted itself, it has fallen as often in the face of power-craving social classes in their thirst for dominance. Writing in 1918, Adler stressed that the power principle prevails in our culture. It is not adhered to openly but through the exploitation of social interest. The method of exploitation is not direct violence, since it is unpopular, but an appeal to justice, custom, freedom, and the welfare of the oppressed in the name of culture.[57]

Adler saw a correlation between a person's social interest and his attitude toward war. He found that the individual who is more socially adjusted is at a disadvantage in the social struggle. His sense of being right lets him sleep quietly. On the other hand, an unsocial or antisocial person is restless and is always planning attacks on the community. A third type, the lazy and undecided person, is easy prey to an active antisocial person or group. The needs of communal life are thus distorted by those who cultivate the power principle, and social interest "is transformed from an end into a means and is pressed into the service of nationalism and imperialism."[58]

Adler believed that the response of an individual in service to the Austrian government during World War I, depended in large part upon the way he came into the service. The draftees generally rejected war service. They only varied in their methods of refutation. He also found a smaller group, whom he called adventurers, "who in their ignorance had counted on a very short and gay war and had volunteered for the front." The majority, he believed, chose the service to escape "the unpleasantnesses of their home, their job, and other urgent problems." He believed that some of these men actually went to the front as a way of committing suicide. Other, high-minded individuals refused time for their wounds to heal because they were concerned about returning to their friends and comrades at the front.[59]

Adler found that most of the volunteers for service in World War I who retained their enthusiasm were "victims of a false pride." They could not be judged by their behavior at the beginning of the war, when they cheered, bragged, sang songs and blindly accepted the call to die. There was no way out, so they made a virtue of necessity. Initially they had answered the call to arms of their superiors. Later, they came to believe they themselves "had uttered the call," and found a psychological means for dealing with their situation. They were transformed into "heroes and defenders of the Fatherland and of their own honor." They went into the "holy battle" defending their country "in the intoxication of their regained self-esteem." They had not been able to see themselves as "victims of the power urges of others," so they turned to dreams of "self-willed and self-sought deeds of heroism." They could not bear the feeling of lowliness which was demanded by an admission that they had been manipulated by those above them, so they found some solace in accepting the falsehood that they had proclaimed the war.[60]

Hitler was in Pasewalk Hospital recovering from exposure to poisonous gas when he received word that the war was lost. He was traumatized by the extreme sense of inferiority in which his loss placed him and all of Germany. He could no longer see himself as the invincible Wagnerian hero whose victory was guaranteed by virtue of being a member of a superior race. Once again, similar to the period when he had been rejected by the art academy, Hitler was plunged into despair and suffered all the symptoms of a nervous breakdown. Hitler could think of nothing better to do than remain in the reduced Weimar army and surrender himself to the bare demands of existence.

One calamitous result was the reinforcement of his antisocial feelings, particularly toward the Jews and, what was the same to his mind, the Communists. Unable to accept the reality that Germany had been defeated on the field of battle and that the sacrifices of four years of war had all been in vain, he adopted the "stab-in-the-back" explanation for the defeat. To Hitler, as to countless other Germans, the defeat was explicable only as the result of the various revolutions that erupted on the home-front led, in many instances, by Jews such as Karl Liebknecht and Rosa Luxemburg— who were also communists. Hitler, who had already developed an exclusion principle as a way of life, would henceforth attribute to the Jews and Communists a diabolical determination to destroy the German Volk. For this, they deserved the ultimate exclusion—death.

It seems clear that the war also led Hitler to adopt a rude, brutal attitude that supported and intensified his antisocial, exclusionary mental construct. This provided a veneer of intellectual respectability for the attitudes he had formed to overcome his sense of inferiority and its corollary, a sense of superiority.

Hitler's goal of political involvement became possible with his contact with a political group which he molded to conform to his ideology—the National Socialist German Worker's Party. His leadership complex made it impossible for him simply to remain a member of the organization, so, by 1921, he demanded and received dictatorial power.

Hitler brought to the party an already well-formed *Weltanschauung*. Under the influence of Dietrich Eckart, however, his nationalistic attitudes were transformed into a Volkish ideology which identified Aryans as the standardbearers of all culture. Eckart also hardened Hitler's already well-pronounced anti-Semitism, and encouraged in him the view that Jews be handled by exclusion, a problem-solving complex which became increasingly marked in Hitler in later years.

The depth of Eckart's influence upon Hitler went beyond that of a casual political association. Eckart was a father figure Hitler could emulate, as he could not emulate his natural father. Eckart gave him support and approval of his goals, which Alois was never able to give. Hitler mourned his death and made Eckart a patrons saint of the movement. Pictures and busts of Eckart were enshrined in party sanctuaries as the movement grew. Eckart must be given responsibility for nourishing in Hitler the most profoundly negative dimension of his psyche.

During the period of the Partei-Kampf, Hitler initially saw himself as the drummer for a yet unidentified savior of the German people. Gradually, with the increased support of his ideology, he came to see himself as the redeemer. Adler found that the redeemer complex characterizes people who assert a sense of superiority in solving the problems of others. In extreme cases, such an individual believes he was sent by God to heal the evils of humanity.[61]

The prototype for his role as a redeemer was Hitler's youthful response to the character Rienzi in Wagner's opera by that name. Kubizek was witness to Hitler's vision of a great mission which paralleled that of Rienzi. This was reinforced with Hitler's continued obsession with the heroic figures in Wagner's operas, especially Parsifal, out of whose experiences he claimed to have made a religion.

Hitler also found compensation for his sense of inferiority in the belief that he was predestined for greatness due to his narrow escapes from death. He was, after all, the only surviving son of six children born to his parents. He also had narrow brushes with death during World War I, and he escaped death when sixteen of his followers were killed around him during the attempted coup of November, 1923. His sense of invincibility was later reinforced by his survival of several assassination attempts.

Adler stated that a person with such views has a predestination complex. His attitude toward life reflects his belief that nothing can happen to him. Such a complex gives the person "great support and self-assurance." Especially interesting for the present study is Adler's statement that this complex is very dangerous for society when a person in public life believes he can accomplish unusual achievements and that nothing can happen to him. Adler believed that persons with his complex had a pampered life style in their youth, and they grew accustomed to their mother getting them out of difficulties. The possibilities for success exist for such persons, but when setbacks come, the "pampered will overlook them or answer them with a breakdown (possibly schizophrenia, cyclothymia, melancholia, crime)."[62]

With his rise to power, Hitler set about the full imposition of the compensations upon Germany that he had developed for himself. He demanded that a sense of *Gemeinschaft* be reestablished. As he had grown to feel superior as a member of the greater German community, he believed they too would sense their strength as a single community bound by blood to the German soil. He told Germans to replace their shame for having lost World War I with hatred of the Jews. He led them to believe that their superiority could once more be established, if they returned to the traditional values in all of the arts and excluded the degenerate influence of the Jews and modernists. A visible sign of their superiority would be the tremendous public buildings he would design and construct for them.

With his rise to power, Hitler had given considerable attention to architecture. His sketchbook of 1925 indicated that the goal of being an architect had not been abandoned. With his first access to funds and other support, Hitler began the fulfillment of his dream of being an architect. Early structures were quite modest and in keeping with the limitations of his resources. With his consolidation of power, Hitler began to build works of monumental scale. Several of his architectural projects were of such enormous proportions that they can only be described as the works of a megalomaniac. Adler believed that the megalomaniacal person plays his role in life in a socially useless way. His early feelings of inferiority were compensated for in a worthless way by the development of a superiority complex. Hitler's grand-scale architectural projects can thus be explained as his compensation for an inferiority complex. His failure to become an artist and the postponement of his opportunity to be a practicing architect were without doubt the contributing factors to the over-compensation that led him to construct the surrealistic fantasies in stone he envisioned for the Third Reich. In all of these constructions, a central position was designed and situated to call attention to Hitler. Each project thus asserted the centrality of his person and authority. They demonstrated his over-compensation and demand for superiority to the point where they became totally unrealistic.

In art, Hitler exercised his compensatory domination and power through the establishment of the various *Reichskammers*, his use of Heinrich Hoffmann as curator of the annual House of German Art exhibitions, the use of commissions, and the journal, *Die Kunst im Dritten Reich*. He insisted that all elements of Jewish and modern art be eliminated in the Third Reich, and, as the Third Reich expanded, the territories that came to be included within it. The very nature of the art that was approved reflected his own compensation devices. As one who came from an unstable family, he stressed the theme of the family in Nazi art. As part of this effort to meet his neurotic needs, he particularly wanted paintings of the German peasantry to justify the peasant background of his own family. This also met his overt political efforts at propaganda to create the *Gemeinschaft*. Another theme stressed in the art of the Third Reich was the affirmation of motherhood, which met Hitler's compulsion to glorify indirectly his own mother. Hitler also fostered erotic elements in Nazi art, possibly as a compensation for his own lack of sexual strength. Nazi artists clothed eroticism in classical forms and themes, which made it acceptable to the bourgeois mind of Hitler and his followers. This use of classicism also allowed Hitler to stress his myth that the Aryans were racially derived from the Doric Greeks.

Throughout the range of Nazi art, Hitler eliminated the element of subjectivity inherent in modern art. He was never able to outgrow the realism expressed in his own adolescent watercolors and oils. In order to meet his neurotic needs, he imposed this limitation on the artists of the Third Reich. This doubtlessly contributed to the shallowness of the Third Reich art, which Hitler attempted to mask through the elimination of all art criticism.

Hitler's interest in music was, for all his sincerity, more of a pose to meet his neurotic need for compensation than a general interest in music as an end in itself. Hitler was, for example, interested in Wagner because this obsession allowed him to identify with Wagnerian heroes. It further afforded him a neurotic means of asserting a focus for his *Gemeinschaft* mythology. Ultimately, it provided him with an opportunity to emulate Wagner himself as a role model. Apart from his obsession with Wagner's operas, Hitler had little interest in music other than an ambivalent appreciation of ballet and a well-defined love of frothy operettas. Outside of these specific forms, music was the servant of propaganda techniques for supporting his rise to power, his position as chancellor, and his later image as a warlord.

In music, as in architecture and art, Hitler imposed his demand for the elimination of all Jewish elements. He also insisted on the purification of German music through its purge of all Jazz and other modern elements. He promoted the support of Aryan music and musicians through commissions, traveling orchestras, and the erection of opera houses. Except for the promotion of an interest in opera, Hitler was not as directly involved in the imposition of his compensations on music as he was in the fields of architecture and art. Rather, having laid out the general principles and guidelines, he left the imposition to Goebbels.

Given Hitler's restrictions, the music of the Third Reich was limited in its ability to evolve new music forms and techniques. It could only endlessly repeat the non-Jewish, traditional corpus of music. No major serious musical work was ever composed during the period of the Third Reich which can truly be called "Nazi music." If the Third Reich had lasted for a thousand years, as Hitler proposed, German music would have remained frozen in time.

Two final compensations of Adolf Hitler need to be mentioned. No sooner had Hitler become chancellor of Germany, than he embarked on a program to overthrow the Treaty of Versailles and reverse Germany's defeat of 1918. He re-militarized Germany, exploited the weaknesses of the western democracies, and directed the German economy toward a war footing. By

1937, he regained the Saar, re-militarized the Rhineland and demoralized the leaders of England and France. By 1938, he had annexed Austria and the Sudentenland and become the arbiter of the fate of Europe. After absorbing Czechslovakia in the spring of 1939, he moved toward war with Poland and, in September, 1939, ignited World War II in Europe. By the early spring of 1941, Hitler had become the great warlord whose armies dominated the European continent. With each victory, diplomatic or military, his megalomania increased until in 1941, he added both the Soviet Union and the United States to the list of his opponents and was striving for world domination.

At the same time, Hitler directed a second war against the Jewish people. Beginning in 1933, he moved from their exclusion from his *Gemeinschaft* Volkish state to their murder. Projecting on to these helpless, innocent people all of his own nihilism, he transformed them into the ultimate victims of his hatred, neurotic exclusionism and lack of socialization. In 1941, he adopted a deliberate policy of mass-murder of all those Jews he could reach in Europe. In this murderous compensation for his own neurotic condition, he became forever identified with the greatest mass murder program in history. Ironically, this murderous assault led to the creation of the modern state of Israel in 1948.

The full elucidation of Hitler's compensatory devices as military leader and mass-executioner must be left to further study by others. They are mentioned here as they reveal, as in the case of his other compensations, that they carried within them the seeds of their own destruction. At the end of April, 1945, Hitler realized he had failed to achieve his goals. Germany lay in ruins while his vaunted Third Reich consisted of only the few city-blocks as yet unconquered by the advancing Russian army. As on earlier occasions when his ambitions were thwarted and his compensatory devices failed, Hitler turned to the thought of suicide as he had at the time of the putsch and Geli's suicide—a move completely explicable according to the Adlerian model.

Individual Psychology, by its very nature, demands that each individual's life-style be examined in terms of his preparation for the handling of external problems. When there is sufficient lack of social interest, suicide presents itself as one possible resolution of these difficulties. Adler thus believed that "suicide is a solution only for one who in the face of an urgent problem has arrived at the end of his limited social interest."[63] Adler also found, through studies of the childhoods of persons who committed suicide, that they had similar traits. They were problem children, pampered by at least one parent, complacent and oversensitive. They showed hurt feelings easily and were poor losers. Such persons seldom directly attacked others but tried to influence them through complaining, sadness and suffering. Difficult life situations often caused psychological collapse, as well as increased ambition, vanity and awareness of their value of others. They often grieved deeply over small matters and expressed a desire for sickness or death in the face of humiliation. They showed their emotions through tantrums and self-injury. Their pampered background caused them to treat others as if it were their duty to fulfill their every wish, and occasionally, they were self-critical or abusive in order to elicit sympathy from others.[64] All of these characteristics were present in Hitler's personality and behavior to a marked degree throughout his life.

Adler believed, in essence, that "the life-style of the potential suicide is characterized by the fact that he hurts others by dreaming himself into injuries or by administering them to himself." His attack is leveled against whoever is hurt the most by his suicide. The person who commits suicide thinks too much of himself and too little of others. He is not able "to play, function, live and die with others." He exaggerates his own worth and "expects with great tension results which are always favorable to him." His idea of suicide comes "in the face of an urgent confronting exogenous problem for which the individual in question has an insufficient social interest."[65]

In resorting to suicide, Adolf Hitler performed the ultimate deletion described by Adler. On April 30, 1945, in the company of his wife, Eva Braun Hitler, Adolf Hitler committed suicide. With his death, the Third Reich died and the German people were free, for the first time in twelve years, to develop their own destiny apart from that of Hitler.

Chapter 6
Conclusions

Who was the man Adolf Hitler? The history of his career as a military leader and Chancellor of the Third Reich has been documented in great detail. The effect of his destruction upon the world in general, and upon the Jews in particular, has been amply documented. Yet, the character of Adolf Hitler has remained illusive. To Marxists, he was simply the public creature of a capitalism in its death throws. Others have seen him as a magnificant hater, a consumate orator, or a mass hypnotist. Still others have regarded him as a diabolical being animated by an unbridled desire for personal power. To the man on the street, it is enough to merely dismiss Hitler as a madman. These descriptions may say much, but they fail at several key points. They do not inform us of the origins of his neuroticism. They also fail to illuminate the evolution of his mind and ultimately fall short of the real purpose—understanding. They fail to tell us how the son of a petit-bureaucrat from rural Austria, of limited education, who in his adolescence was a shiftless, unemployed neurotic living from day to day in the *dosshouses* of Vienna, could appear in Germany, be accepted by millions of Germans as a savior, and construct from the ruins of Weimar a nation that in six short years came to dominate Europe. To the rational person, there must be an explanation of the mind of Adolf Hitler and the neuroticisms, tensions, and conflicts that raged within him.

Why is so little known of the inner workings of Adolf Hitler's mind? Part of the answer lies in the repulsion that any decent human must feel when examining Adolf Hitler. His mind was narrow, bigoted, brutal, and in its own view, infallible. One searches in vain for any attractive feature in it. Another part of the problem rests in the material presented by those closest to him. To excuse themselves, they often resorted to descriptions of him as a seducer of their will power or a hypocrite who used and deceived them. Only in such a manner could they excuse their own involvement in the greatest mass murder in history. Still another part of the answer lies in the fact that those few efforts which have been made to understand his mind have *a priori* assumed that they must employ a Freudian model even though the prerequisite psycho-sexual material is not available. As a result, they were often reduced to use of unsubstantiated gossip, arguments from analogous case studies, and outright invention.

137

This study, however, has demonstrated that the mind of Adolf Hitler may best be understood through the use of the psychological understandings developed by Alfred Adler. The primary virtue of the use of his model lies in its insistence that one must both begin and end with the observed behavior of an individual. Unlike the Freudian model, it allows one to argue from that which is known rather than from that which in all probability will remain a fog of mystery.

The Adlerian model, when applied to Adolf Hitler, showed that he was a pampered neurotic child, who suffered from a gigantic sense of inferiority. As an adolescent, Hitler compensated for this inferiority through the construction of the fantasy that he would one day receive recognition as a great artist. Concurrently, he began to develop the myth that he was a member of a superior racial type. His interest in Wagner at this stage provided him with a role model, which supported his racial mythology, identified him with a musical genius, and nourished his fantasies of himself as a Wagnerian hero.

With his failure to pass the entrance examination to the Vienna Academy of Fine Arts, his compensatory goal of being a great artist turned to ashes and Hitler drifted into an aimless existence in first Vienna and then Munich. Only through the production of numerous landscapes and city scenes was he able to survive on a mere subsistence income. These works revealed his conservative identity with nineteenth-century artists of realistic techniques, his profound interest in architecture which represented authority and power, his complete rejection of subjective elements in art, and, due to his inability to represent human figures, a lack of social interest as defined by Adler.

The outbreak of war in 1914 provided Hitler with the opportunity to institute a new set of compensations for his inferiority. By joining the German army, he acted out his long fantasized role as a Wagnerian hero. He saw himself as participating in a struggle to save the Fatherland of the Aryan race. His dedication to this cause was strengthened by his being twice awarded the iron cross for his heroism. His success in the role of a soldier made Germany's loss of the war all the more devastating for Hitler. The armistice threw him into a period of lassitude and mental depression. His participation in the war had provided him only temporary relief from his feelings of inferiority.

Hitler's recovery from his mental breakdown came with his decision to enter politics. His discovery of the embryonic Nazi party again opened up a path for compensation for his inferior feelings. He began to see himself as a redeemer of the master race. With the determination of a Rienzi, he took upon himself the task of elevating the German people from their position of degradation following the war. He found an explanation for the defeat of the master race through the invention of the myth of a Jewish-Communist conspiracy that had stabbed Germany in the back and betrayed the heroic soldiers of her army. By 1923 he was so confident of his new position as a politician-savior, that he attempted a *putsch* which was unsuccessful and brought him a prison sentence. Once more Hitler was unable to deal with the destruction of his methods for compensating for his inferiority. This time, as he would do on several later occasions, he attempted suicide.

Hitler emerged from prison with the realization that he could not achieve power over Germany by force. He then became determined to compensate for his inferior position through the creation of a social revolution. As undisputed Fuehrer, he pushed the party toward the creation of an Aryan *Gemeinschaft* which would become the cultural, political, and military master of Europe. He increasingly insisted that the projected *Gemeinschaft* could be achieved only through the vigorous elimination of all Jewish, modern and subjective elements. His lack of normal socialization allowed him to envision the brutal, murderous, deletion, and exclusion of these elements from the artistic life of Germany. His vision of a *Gemeinschaft* of racially pure Aryans struck a responsive chord in the millions of Germans who also suffered from an inferiority complex arising out of their defeat in World War I and their subsequent degradation. Hitler had come to believe that his personal compensations were those suited to become the compensatory devices of the German people. Indeed, his followers generally embraced Hitler's compensations as their own. Upon becoming Chancellor of Germany, Hitler dogmatically and brutally imposed his neurotic compensations upon all Germans without let or hindrance.

Hitler's intention of establishing an Aryan *Gemeinschaft* in Germany contained a major flaw, however. Given the technological and industrial development of Germany, it could only be achieved through methods intrinsic to the *Gesellschaft*. The more Hitler attempted to use the *Gesellschaft* and its impersonal methods of control, the quicker he in actuality undercut the *Gemeinschaft*. The dream of establishing a *Gemeinschaft* was, therefore, an anachronism that could exist only in Hitler's own neurotic mind. The *Gemeinschaft*, by its very nature, was organic. What Hitler attempted to do was to so limit, define, and prune the *Gemeinschaft* that it would have lost all of its power of adaptation. By deletion and exclusion, applied without a well-developed social interest, Hitler precluded any creative development within his proposed *Gemeinschaft*. Although Hitler has been called a Social Darwinist, he was not such in the usual sense of the word. Whereas Social Darwinism stressed struggle, change, the survival of the strongest, and a ceaseless battle of competition, Hitler, through the use of modern industrial technology and impersonal bureaucratic methods ended all competition by the ruthless suppression of all opponents. His was, therefore, a distortion of the concept of *Gemeinschaft* so eloquently described by Tonnies.

Hitler saw himself as the redeemer of the culture of the *Gemeinschaft*. As such, he established the organizational mechanism for purging the arts of all "degenerate" elements. He also demanded that the Reich support Aryan architects, artists, and musicians who conformed to the standards he saw as proper for the German people for the next thousand years. In art, he took a personal interest during the early years of the Third Reich, but gradually turned the responsibility for maintenance of his demands over to such followers as Goebbels and Hoffmann. In music, he showed initial concern that degenerate elements be eliminated, promoted the concept of traveling Reich orchestras, promoted the construction of opera houses, but generally showed less concern about the development of a body of music which could be called products of the Nazi movement. He continued to enjoy the friendship of the Wagner family and his infatuation with Richard Wagner's music. He also developed an interest in lighter music, such as the operettas of Lehár. It was in architecture that Hitler showed his primary artistic interest during the Third Reich. Here, Hitler's mental strivings for compensation to alleviate his inferiority became surrealistic. He found it necessary that the buildings he constructed be larger than those of any other people. His final building projects became so megalomaniacal that they could only be described as creations of a disturbed mind.

This same surrealistic frame of mind led him to attempt to conquer and dominate Europe through the establishment of a Reich that would endure for a thousand years. By April of 1945, however, when it was apparent that none of his goals could or would be achieved, and with his compensatory drives in tatters, Adolf Hitler committed suicide.

Bibliography

Primary Sources

Adler, Alfred. *Social Interest: A Challenge to Mankind.* Trans. John Linton and Richard Vaughan. London: Faber and Faber, Ltd., 1983.

———. *Superiority and Social Interest: A Collection of Later Writings.* Eds. Heinz L. and Rowena R. Ansbacher. Evanston, IL: Northwestern University Press, 1964.

———. *The Individual Psychology of Alfred Adler.* Eds. Heinz L. Ansbacher and Rowena R. Ansbacher. New York: Basic Books, Inc., 1956.

———. *The Neurotic Constitution.* Trans. H. Ansbacher. New York: Dodd and Company, 1930.

———. *The Practice and Theory of Individual Psychology.* Trans. P. Radin. New York: Harcourt, Brace, and Company, 1932.

———. *The Science of Living.* Ed. Heinz L. Ansbacher. New York: Doubleday and Company, Inc., 1969.

———. *Understanding Human Nature.* Trans. Walter B. Wolfe. London: George Allen and Unwin, Ltd., 1968.

———. *What Life Should Mean To You.* Ed. Alan Porter. New York: Perigee Books, 1980.

A Nation Builds: Contemporary German Architecture. New York: German Library of Information, 1940.

Bardi, Amilcore, ed. *The Water Colours of Hitler, Recovered Art Works.* Florence: Fratelli Alinari Editirice, 1984.

Die Kunst im Dritten Reich. After 1940 *Die Kunst im Deutschen Reich.* Munich: Zentralverlag Franz Eber.

Entartete Kunst: Ausstellungsführer. N.p.: n.p., n.d.

Goering, Herman, et al. *Adolf Hitler.* English edition Jonathan R. Manning. Phoenix: C.O.L. Publishing, Inc., 1973.

Hitler, Adolf. *Mein Kampf.* Trans. Ralph Manheim. Boston: Houghton Mifflin Company, 1971.

———. *Hitler's Secret Conversations, 1941-1944.* New York: Farrar Strauss and Young, 1953.

Hoffmann, Heinrich. *Sieben Aquarelle.* Munich: Franz Eber Verlag, 1983.

Lane, Barbara M., and Rupp, Leila J., eds. and trans. *Nazi Ideology Before 1933.* Austin, TX: University of Texas Press, 1978.

Organizationsbuch der NSDAP. Ed. Der Reichsorganistionsleiter der NSDAP. Munich: N.p., 1936.

Price, Billy F. *Adolf Hitler: The Unknown Artist.* Houston: Billy F. Price Publishing Company, 1983.

Snyder, Louis L., ed. *Hitler's Third Reich: A Documentary History.* Chicago: Nelson-Hall, 1981.

The Hitler Trial Before the People's Court in Munich. Trans. H. Francis Freniens, Lucie Karcic, Philip Fandek. New York: Universal Publications of America, Inc., 1976.

The Speeches of Adolf Hitler. Ed. Norman H. Baynes. London: Oxford University Press, 1942.

Waite, Robert G., ed. *Hitler and Nazi Germany*. New York: Holt, Rinehart and Winston, 1965.

Secondary Sources

Allen, William S. *The Nazi Seizure of Power: The Experience of a Single German Town, 1922-1945*. Rev. ed. New York: Franklin Watts, 1984.

The Authentic Librettos of the Wagner Operas. New York: Crown Publishers, 1983.

Ayçoberry, Pierre. *The Nazi Question*. Trans. Robert Hurley. New York: Paneheon Books, 1981.

Baedaker, Karl. *London and Its Environs*. Leipzig: K. Baedaker Verlag, 1884.

────── *Paris and Its Environs*. Leipzig: K. Baedaker Verlag, 1884.

Barnes, James J., and Patricia P. *Hitler's 'Mein Kampf' in Britain and America*. New York: Cambridge Press, 1980.

Bayles, William D. *Caesars in Goose Step*. New York: Harper and Brothers, 1940.

Bezymenski, Lev. *The Death of Adolf Hitler*. New York: Harcourt Brace Jovanovich, Inc., 1978.

Binion, Rudolph. *Hitler Among the Germans*. De Kalb, IL: Northern Illinois University Press, 1984.

Bramsted, Ernst K. *Goebbels and National Socialist Propaganda, 1925-1945*. Yipsilanti: Michigan State University Press, 1965.

Brombert, Norbert, and Small, Verna Volz. *Hitler's Psychopathology* New York: International Universities Press, 1983.

Bullock, Alan. *Hitler: A Study in Tyranny*. New York: Harper and Row, Publishers, 1964.

Burden, Hamilton T. *The Nuremberg Party Rallies, 1923-1939*. London: Pall Mall Press, 1967.

Carr, William. *Hitler, A Study in Personality and Politics*. New York: St. Martin's Press, 1979.

Craig, Gordon A. *Germany, 1866-1945*. New York: Oxford University Press, 1978.

Davidson, Eugene. *The Making of Adolf Hitler*. New York: Macmillan and Company. 1977.

────── *The Trial of the Germans*. New York: Macmillan Company, 1966.

Deuel, Wallace B. *People Under Hitler*. New York: Harcourt, Brace and Company, 1942.

Dietrich, Otto. *Zwölf Jahre mit Hitler*. Munich: Isar Verlag, 1955.

Dodd, Martha. *Through Embassy Eyes*. New York: Garden City Publishing Company, 1939.

Eckart, Dietrich. *Der Bolshevismus von Moses bis Lenin: Zwiegespäch zeweischen Adolf Hitler und Mir* . Munich: F. Eber Nachf., 1924.

Eggebrecht, Hans H. *Meyers Taschen-Lexikon Musik*. Mannheim: Meyers Lexikonverlag, 1984.

Ellis, Donald W. "Music in the Third Reich: National Socialist Aesthetic Theory as Governmental Policy." Diss. University of Kansas, 1970.

Erikson, Erik H. *Childhood and Society*. New York: W.W. Norton and Company, 1950.

Fest, Joachim C. *Hitler*. Trans. Richard and Clara Winston. New York: Harcourt Brace Jovanovich, Inc., 1973.

────── *The Face of the Third Reich*. Trans. Michael Bullock. New York: Pantheon Books, 1970.

Flanner, Janet. *An American in Paris*. New York: Simon and Schuster, 1940.

Fleming, Gerald. *Hitler and the Final Solution*. Berkeley: University of California Press, 1984.

Frank, Hans. *Im Angesicht*. Munich: Alfred Beck Verlag, 1953.

Friedlander, Saul. *Reflections on Nazism*, Trans. Thomas Weyr. New York: Avon Books, 1982.

Frischauer, Willi. *The Rise and Fall of Herman Goering*. Boston: Houghton Mifflin Company, 1951.

Fromm, Erich. *Escape From Freedom*. New York: Holt, Rinehart and Winston, 1941.

_____ *The Anatomy of Human Destructiveness*. New York: N.p., 1973.

_____ *The Heart of Man*. New York: Harper and Row, Publishers, 1964.

Geissler, Paul. "Symbol des grossdeutschen Reiches." Ed. Albert Speer. *Die neue Reichskranzlei*. Berlin: N.p., n.d.

Gilbert, G. M. *Nuremberg Diary*. New York: Farrar and Strauss, 1947.

_____ *The Psychology of Dictatorship*. New York: Farrar and Strauss, 1950.

Gisevious, Hans B. *Adolf Hitler: Versuch einer Deutung*. Munich: Rütten und Leoning Verlag, 1963.

Gordon, Harold J., Jr. *History of the Beer-Hall Putsch*. Princeton: Princeton University Press, 1972.

Gremschitz, Bruno. *Austrian Painting from Bedermeier to Modern Times*. Trans. Friedrich Jasper. Vienna: Kunstverlag Wolfrum, 1963.

Grosshans, Henry. *Hitler and the Artists*. New York: Holmes and Meier, 1983.

Grunberger, Richard. *The 12-Year Reich*. New York: Holt, Rinehart and Winston, 1971.

Gutman, Robert W. *Richard Wagner*. New York: Harcourt, Brace and World, Inc., 1968.

Hanfstaengl, Ernst. *The Missing Years*. London: Eyre and Spottiswoode, 1957.

Harris, Robert. *Selling Hitler*. New York: Pantheon Books, 1986.

Heiber, Helmut. *Goebbels*. Trans. John K. Dickinson. New York: Hawthorn Books, 1972.

Heiden, Konrad. *Der Fuehrer*. New York: Lexington Press, 1944.

Heilbut, Anthony. *Exiled in Paradise*. Boston: Beacon Press, 1983.

Helmer, Stephen D. *Hitler's Berlin*. Ann Arbor: V.M.I. Reserch Press, 1985.

Henderson, Sir Neville. *Failure of a Mission*. New York: G.P. Putnam's Sons, 1940.

Herzstein, Robert E. *Adolf Hitler and the German Trauma, 1913-1945*. New York: G.P. Putnam's Sons, 1974.

_____ , ed. *World War II: The Nazis*. Alexandria, VA: Time-Life Books, Inc., 1980.

Hinz, Berthold. *Art in the Third Reich*. Trans. Robert and Rita Kimber. New York: Pantheon Books, 1979.

_____ *Die Malerei im deutschen Faschismus Kunst und Konterrevolution*. Munich: Carl Hanser Verlag, 1974.

Hirschmann, I.A. "The Degradation of Culture." In *Nazism: An Assault on Civilization*. Eds. Pierre van Paasen and James W. Wise. New York: Harrison Smith and Robert Haas, 1934.

Hitler's Third Reich: A Documentary History. Ed. Louis L. Snyder. Chicago: Nelson-Hall, 1981.

Hoffman, Heinrich. *Hitler Was My Friend*. London: Burke, 1955.

Höhne, Heinz. *The Order of the Death's Head*. Trans. Richard Barry. New York: Ballantine Books, 1969.

Jackman, Jarrell C., and Bordon, Carla M., eds. *The Muses Flee Hitler*. Washington, D.C.: Smithsonian Institution Press, 1983.

Jaeger, Charles de. *The Linz File*. Exeter, England: Webb and Bower, 1981.

Jarman, T.L. *The Rise and Fall of Nazi Germany*. 4th ed. New York: New York University Press, 1970.

Jenks, William A. *Vienna and the Young Hitler*. New York: Columbia University Press, 1960.

Jetzinger, Franz. *Hitler's Youth.* Trans. Lawrence Wilson. Westport, CT: Greenwood Press, 1976.

Keitel, Wilhelm. *In the Service of the Reich.* Trans. David Irving. New York: Stein and Day, 1979.

Kobbe's Complete Opera Book. Ed. Earl of Harwood. London: Putnam, 1966.

Koehl, Robert L. *The Black Corps.* Madison: University of Wisconsin Press, 1983.

Kubizek, August. *The Young Hitler.* Trans. E.J. Anderson. New York: Houghton Mifflin Company, 1955.

Kurtz, Harold. *The Second Reich.* New York: American Heritage Press, 1970.

Lane, Barbara M. *Architecture and Politics in Germany, 1918-1945.* Cambridge: Harvard University Press, 1968.

Langer, Walter C. *The Mind of Adolf Hitler.* New York: New American Library, 1972.

Lehmann-Haupt, Hellmut. *Art Under a Dictatorship.* New York: Oxford University Press, 1954.

Lotz, Wilhelm. "Die Innenräume der neuen Reichskanzlei." Ed. Albert Speer. *Die Neue Reichskanzlei.* Berlin: N.p., n.d.

Machlis, Joseph. *Introduction To Contemporary Music.* New York: W. W. Norton and Company, Inc., 1961.

Maltitz, Horst von. *The Evolution of Hitler's Germany.* New York: McGraw-Hill Company, 1973.

Maser, Werner. *Adolf Hitler: Legende, Mythos, Wirklichkeit.* Munich: Bechtle Verlag, 1971.
_____. *Hitler's Mein Kampf.* Munich: Bechtle Verlag, 1966.

Meyer, Michael. "Assumptions and Implementation of Nazi Policy Toward Music." Diss. University of California, Los Angeles, 1971.

Mitchell, Otis C. *Hitler Over Germany.* Philadelphia: Institute for the Study of Human Issues, 1983.

Moser, Hans J. *Musik Lexicon.* Hamburg: Musikverlag Hans Sikorski, 1951.

Mosse, George L. *The Crisis of German Ideology.* New York: Schocken Books, 1964.
_____. *The Nationalization of the Masses.* New York: The New American Library, Inc., 1975.

Neumann, Franz. *Behemoth: The Structure and Practice of National Socialism, 1933-1944.* New York: Oxford University Press, 1944.

Orlow, Dietrich. *The History of the Nazi Party, 1919-1923.* Pittsburg: University of Pittsburg Press, 1969.

Otto, Christian F. "American Skyscrapers and Weimar Modern: Transactions between Face and Ideas." in *The Muses Flee Hitler.* Eds. Jarrell C. Jackman and Carla Bordon. Washington, D.C.: Smithsonian Institution Press, 1983.

Overy, R.J. *Goering, The 'Iron Man'.* London: Routledge and Kegan Paul, 1984.

Paxton, Robert O. *Europe in the Twentieth Century.* New York: Harcourt, Brace, Jovanovich Publishers, 1975.

Payne, Robert. *The Life and Death of Adolf Hitler.* New York: Popular Library, 1973.

Pool, James and Suzanne. *Who Financed Hitler.* New York: The Dial Press, 1978.

Rauschning, Hermann. *Men of Chaos.* New York: G.P. Putnam's Sons, 1942.

Reed, Douglas. *Nemesis.* Boston: Houghton Mifflin Company, 1940.

Reimann, Viktor. *Goebbels.* Trans. Stephan Wendt. New York: Doubleday and Company, Inc., 1976.

Roxan, David, and Wonstall, Ken. *The Rape of Art.* New York: Coward-McCann, Inc., 1965.

Sackett, Robert Eban. *Popular Entertainment, Class, and Politics in Munich, 1900-1923.* Cambridge: Harvard University Press, 1982.

Santoro, Cesare. *Hitler Germany as Seen by a Foreigner*. Berlin: Internationaler Verlag, 1939.

Schorske, Carl E. *Fin-De-Siècle Vienna*. New York: Vintage Books, 1981.

Schramm, Percy E. *Hitler: The Man and the Military Leader*. Trans. Donald S. Detweiter. Chicago: Quadrangle Books, 1971.

Schuman, Frederick L. *The Nazi Dictatorship*. New York: Alfred A. Knopf, 1963.

Schwarz, Boris. "The Music World in Migration." In *The Muses Flee Hitler*. Eds. Jarrell C. Jackman and Carla Bordon. Washington, DC: Smithsonian Institution Press, 1983.

Schwarz, Edwin, ed. *Hitler Jugend Singt*. Mainz: B. Schott's Sons, 1933.

Shirer, William L. *The Nightmare Years, 1930-1940*. Boston: Little, Brown and Company, 1984.

Slonimsky, Nicolaus. *Music Since 1900*. New York: Scribners Sons, 1971.

Smith, Bradley F. *Adolf Hitler: His Family, Childhood and Youth*. Stanford: The Hoover Institute, 1967.

Speer, Albert. *Inside the Third Reich*. Trans. Richard Clara Winston. New York: Macmillan and Company, 1970.

_____ *Spandau: The Secret Diaries*. Trans. Richard and Clara Winston. New York: Macmillan Publishing Company, Inc., 1976.

Stein, George H., ed. *Hitler*. Englewood Cliffs, NJ: Prentice-Hall, Inc., 1968.

Stierlin, Helm. *Adolf Hitler: A Family Perspective*. New York: The Psychohistory Press, 1976.

Strasser, Otto. *Hitler and I*. London: Cape Publishers, 1940.

Taylor, Robert R. *The Word in Stone*. Berkeley: University of California Press, 1974.

Toland, John. *Adolf Hitler*. New York: Doubleday and Company, 1976.

Tönnies, Ferdinand. *Community and Society*. Trans. Charles P. Loomis. New York: Harper and Row, 1957.

_____ *On Sociology* Ed. Werner J. Cahman and Rudolf Heberle. Chicago: The University of Chicago Press, 1971.

Waite, Robert G. *The Psychopathic God: Adolf Hitler*. New York: Basic Books, Inc., 1977.

Walter, Bruno. *Gustav Mahler*. Trans. James Galston. New York: Greystone Press, 1941.

Walther, Herbert. *Der Fuehrer*. Secaucus, NJ: Chartwell Books, 1978.

Wistrich, Robert. *Who's Who in Nazi Germany*. New York: Macmillan and Company, Inc., 1982.

Wolters, Rudolf. *Albert Speer*. Oldenburg: Gerhard Stalling Verlag, 1943.

_____ "Werk und Schöpfer." In *Die Neue Reichskanzlei*. Ed. Albert Speer. Berlin: N.p., n.d.

Wulf, Joseph, ed. *Die Bildenden Künste im Dritten Reich: Ein Dokumentation*. Gütersloch: Sigbert Mohn Verlag, 1963.

_____ *Musik im Dritten Reich: Eine Dokumentation*. Guetersloh: Sigbert Mohn Verlag, 1963.

Zeman, A.B. *Nazi Propaganda*. 2nd ed. London: Oxford University Press, 1973.

Periodicals

"A Psychiatrist Looks at Hitler," *The New Republic*, 26 April 1939.

The Art Digest, 1 August 1934.

"The Arts Under Hitlerism" *The New Republic*, 7 April 1933.

Bloch, Eduard. "My Patient Adolf Hitler." *Colliers*, 15 and 22 March, 1941.

Ederfield, John. "Total and Totalitarian Art" *Studio International*, April 1970.

"German Music in Decay." *Living Age*, December 1930.

Gerry, Phillipa. "German Painting." *American Magazine of Modern Art*, December 1937.

Hanisch, Reinhold. "I Was Hitler's Buddy." *The New Republic*, 5 April 1939.

———— "I Was Hitler's Buddy." II. *The New Republic*, 12 April 1939.

———— "I Was Hitler's Buddy." III. *The New Republic*, 19 April 1939.

Heiden, Konrad. "Portrait of the Artist as a Young Man." *The Saturday Review of Literature*, 4 December 1943.

"Invisible Government in Germany." *The American Review of Reviews*, 19 July 1924.

"Is Hitler Crazy?" *The New Republic*, 9 November 1938.

"Jew Baiting in Art." *The Art Digest*, 1 October 1935.

Karetnikova, Inga, and Golomstock, Igor. "The Encounter in Paris." *The National Review*, 9 May 1986.

Kershaw, Ian. "The Hitler Myth." *History Today*, November 1985.

Lengyel, Emil. "German Culture in Exile." *The Nation*, 31 May 1933.

"A Million 'Heils.' " *Time*, 20 September 1937.

"Nazi System." *Time*, 30 May 1938.

Nelson, Robert B. "Hitler's Propaganda Machine." *Current History*, April-September 1933.

"Purged Art for N.Y.U." *The Art Digest*, 1 December 1936.

Rockwell, John. "Music Under Hitler." *Opera News*, 15 January 1972.

Sacks, Joel. "Some Aspects of Musical Politics in Pre-Nazi Germany." *Perspectives on New Music*, Fall 1970.

Sheean, Vincent. "Good-bye Vienna." *The New Republic*, 3 August 1938.

Stuckenschmitt, H.H. "Under the Swastika."*Modern Music*, November-December, 1933.

Will, George F. "Our Fascination With Hitler." *Newsweek*, 9 May 1983.

X.T. "Kultur-Terror." *Modern Music*, May-June 1933.

Film

Riefenstahl, Leni. *Triumph of the Will*. Indianapolis: Kartes Video Communications, Inc., n.d.

Recording

Hitler's Inferno. Vols. I and II. New York: Audio Fidelity, 1961.

Notes

Chapter 1

[1]Helm Stierlin, *Adolf Hitler: A Family Perspective* (New York: The Psychohistory Press, 1976), p. 15; William Carr, *Hitler, A Study in Personality and Politics* (New York: St. Martin's Press, 1979), p. vii; Robert Harris, *Selling Hitler* (New York: Pantheon Books, 1986), p. 19.

[2]Pierre Ayçoberry, *The Nazi Question*, trans. Robert Hurley (New York: Pantheon Books, 1981), p. vii.

[3]George F. Will, "Our Fascination with Hitler," *Newsweek* 9 May 1983, p. 92.

[4]See, for example, August Kubizek, *The Young Hitler I Knew*, trans. E.V. Anderson (New York: Houghton Mifflin Company, 1955).

[5]Otto Strasser, *Hitler and I* (London: Cape Publishers, 1940); Ernst ('Putzi') Hanfstaengl, *The Missing Years* (London: Eyre and Spottiswoode, 1957).

[6]Heinrich Hoffman, *Hitler Was My Friend* (London: Burke, 1955).

[7]Saul Friedländer, *Reflections of Nazism*, trans. Thomas Weyr (New York: Avon Books, 1982), p. ix.

[8]Will, "Our Fascination with Hitler," p. 92.

[9]George L. Mosse, *The Crisis of German Ideology* (New York: Shocken Books, 1981), p. 8.

[10]Franz Neumann, *Behemoth: The Structure and Practice of National Socialism, 1933-1944* (New York: Oxford University Press, 1944).

[11]Billy Price, *Adolf Hitler: The Unknown Artist* (Houston: Billy F. Price Publishing Company, 1983), pp 6-7.

[12]Robert G.L. Waite, *The Psychopathic God: Adolf Hitler* (New York: Basic Books, Inc., 1977), p. 64; Stierlin, *Adolf Hitler* p. 73.

[13]George H. Stein, ed., *Hitler* (Englewood Cliffs, NJ: Prentice-Hall, Inc., 1968), p. 134.

[14]Carr, *Hitler*, p. 123; Horst von Maltitz, *The Evolution of Hitler's Germany* (New York: McGraw-Hill Book Company, 1973), p. 338, protested the "evidence" usually sited is "all hearsay" and there are "hopeless confusions" and "contradictions" regarding Hitler's sexual life; Carr, *Hitler* pp. 123, 151.

[15]Eric Fromm, *Escape From Freedom* (New York: Holt, Rinehart and Winston, 1941), p. 221, diagnosed Hitler as the possessor of "simultaneous" sadistic and masochistic drives because he did not love his mother; Eric Fromm, *The Heart of Man* (New York: Harper and Row, 1964), p. 108. defined Hitler as "necrophilous, narcissistic and incestuous" due to a mother fixation; Maltitz, *The Evolution of Hitler's Germany*, p. 360. Accepted Fromm's first interpretation as solid but called Fromm's second interpretation "overly dramatic"; Carr, *Hitler*, p. 153, however, insisted Fromm's second interpretation was "much more convincing."

[16]Carr, *Hitler*, p. 150.

[17]Waite, *The Psychopathic God*, pp. xiii-xv.

Chapter 2

[1]Werner Maser, *Adolf Hitler: Legende, Mythos, Wirklichkeit* Munich: Bechtle Verlag, 1971), pp. 18-19.

[2]Joachim C. Fest, *Hitler*, trans. Richard and Clara Winston (New York: Harcourt Brace Jovanovich, Inc., 1973), p. 13.

[3]Maser, *Adolf Hitler*, p. 17.

[4]So stated Hans Frank, Hitler's lawyer, who was assigned by Hitler to ascertain Hitler's ancestry: Fest, *Hitler*, p. 15; Eugene Davidson, *The Making of Adolf Hitler* (New York: Macmillan and Company, 1977), pp. 5-6, argued the Frankenberger family was Roman Catholic and that their name was not Jewish.

[5]Robert Payne, *The Life and Death of Adolf Hitler* (New York: Popular Library, 1973), p. 7.

[6]Fest, *Hitler*, p. 15; Waite, *The Psychopathic God*, pp. 127-28.

[7]Maser, *Adolf Hitler*, p. 16; cf. Bradley F. Smith, *Adolf Hitler: His Family, Childhood and Youth* (Stanford: The Hoover Institute, 1967), p. 159.

[8]Smith, *Adolf Hitler*, p. 20.

[9]Payne, *The Life and Death*, pp. 3-4, pointed out that in the Waldviertel "the name is spelled in a bewildering variety of ways: Hiedler, Hietler, Huetler, Huedler, Hittler and once in 1701, Hitler."; F. Jetzinger, *Hitler's Youth*, trans. Lawrence Wilson (Westport, CT: Greenwood Press, 1976) p. 32, believed it a "strong probability" that "Hiedler" derived from the Czech "Hidlar" or "Hidlarek"; Otis C. Mitchell, *Hitler Over Germany* (Philadelphia: Institute for the Study of Human Issues, 1983), p. 2, suggested it evolved from the "common" West Slovak "Hidlar."

[10]Maser, *Adolf Hitler*, pp. 36-37; John Toland, *Adolf Hitler* (New York: Doubleday and Company, 1976), p. 5, argued the change was made so that Alois could inherit money from Johann Nepomuk Huttler; Jetzinger, *Hitler's Youth*, p. 30 argued Alois's name was changed so he could pass as a Gentile; Fest, *Hitler*, p. 16, insisted it was done simply to remove any doubts about Alois's "legitimacy" for the Austrian Civil Servant System.

[11]Smith, *Adolf Hitler*, p. 159.

[12]Maser, *Adolf Hitler*, p. 37; Jetzinger, *Hitler's Youth*, p. 40, argued that since Alois was not Hüttler's child, Alois and Klara were not related in any manner.

[13]Smith, *Adolf Hitler*, p. 43.

[14]Payne, *The Life and Death*, p. 17; Waite, *The Psychopathic God*, p. 223.

[15]Adolf Hitler, *Mein Kampf*, trans. Ralph Manheim (Boston: Houghton Mifflin Company, 1971 ed.), p. 38; Jetzinger, *Hitler's Youth*, pp. 78-79, however, demonstrated Alois had a larger pension than a school headmaster's salary and so, "lived in material conditions corresponding to those of the middle class"; Smith, *Adolf Hitler*, p. 47, concurred.

[16]Maser, *Adolf Hitler*, p. 53.

[17]Payne, *The Life and Death*, pp. 44-45.

[18]Jetzinger, *Hitler's Youth* p. 79. Jetzinger has made the definitive study of the income of the Hitler family, including young Adolf's as an orphan.

[19]Maser, *Hitler*, pp. 56-57.

[20]Hitler had a "good natural voice" and was given singing lessons by Father Bernhard Grüner: Jetzinger, *Hitler's Youth*, p. 58; Payne quoted Alois's obituary to the effect that Alois was also a singer: Payne, *The Life and Death*, p. 29.

[21]Payne, *The Life and Death*, p. 21, believed von Hagan's swastika was "probably the ancestor of the Nazi Hakenkreuz." Jetzinger, *Hitler's Youth*, p. 59, said this explanation is "quite untrue" but gave no explanation for his judgment; Smith, *Adolf Hitler*, p. 61, stated this swastika "played no part in Hitler's development,"

but again without his rationale for the statement; Heinz A. Heinz *Germany's Hitler* (London: Hurst and Blackett, 1934), p. 18, apparently first called attention to this swastika; Price, *The Unknown Artist*, p. 201, no. 489, for this swastik.

[22]Hitler, *Mein Kampf*, p. 6; Jetzinger, *Hitler's Youth*, p. 58, saw no reason to doubt these statements by Hitler.

[23]Payne, *The Life and Death*, p. 22; Konrad Heiden, *Der Fuehrer* (New York: Lexington Press, 1944), p. 49, for Hitler's school report at this point.

[24]For a full development of this thesis, see: Erik H. Erikson, *Childhood and Society* (New York: W.W. Norton and Company, 1950).

[25]Hitler, *Mein Kampf*, p. 6; Smith, *Adolf Hitler*, p. 64, argued the conflict developed with the death of Edmund, for it meant his father delegated to Adolf responsibility for the "upward march of the family."

[26]Payne, *The Life and Death*, p. 26.

[27]Hitler, *Mein Kampf*, p. 10; Adolf Hitler, *Hitler's Secret Conversations, 1941-1944* (New York: Farrar, Strauss and Young, 1953), p. 181, attributed the grade decline to his passionate reading of May; Heiden, *Der Fuehrer*, p. 46, stated the artists Makart and Lenback were "more impressive rulers than the true princes, giving laws to society and form to human lives" at this period of Hitler's life; Jetzinger, *Hitler's Youth*, p. 324, denied this conflict but without supporting evidence.

[28]Hans Frank, *Im Angesicht Deutung Hitler's und seiner Zeit auf Grund eigner Erlebnisse und Erkenntnisse* (Munich: Alfred Beck Verglag, 1953), pp. 330-31; Jetzinger, *Hitler's Youth*, p. 60, denied Alois was a heavy drinker, but without adequate documentation.

[29]Jetzinger, *Hitler's Youth*, p. 61, discounted this story; Waite, *The Psychopathic God*, p. 134, placed great reliance on the story although it is secondhand at best.

[30]Waite, *The Psychopathic God*, p.137.

[31]Stierlin, *Adolf Hitler*, p. 24.

[32]Smith, *Adolf Hitler*, p. 63; Jetzinger, *Hitler's Youth*, p. 51.

[33]Hitler, *Mein Kampf*, pp. 16-17.

[34]Jetzinger, *Hitler's Youth*, pp. 85-86.

[35]Price, *The Unknown Artist*, p. 14.

[36]Price: *The Unknown Artist*, p. 14 and p. 146, no. 250, entitled *New Vienna City Hall*. Cf. *The Water Colours of Hitler, Recovered Art Works*, ed. Amilcare Bardi (Florence: Fratelli Alinari Editrice, 1984), pl. 3, *Vienna, Neues Rathaus* and p. 74. Hermann Weiss, in an essay "Water Colours Attributed to Hitler" included in Bardi's work, p. 74, was critical of Price's inclusion of "dubious paintings" although Price shared his doubts about this work and even though the Florence exhibit also included it. Price's purpose was simply to print as many of the works attributed to Hitler as possible as a spur to subsequent research and authentication—and this task Price has admirably performed: Billy F. Price, oral interview by this writer, July, 1985.

[37]Price, *The Unknown Artist*, p. 14. Price was aware of the doubtfulness of the collection he identified as "D-1 Stuttgart" on p. 94, but was consistent in his intention to include all the works attributed to Hitler he could obtain permission to print and allow subsequent researchers to differentiate between them: Billy F. Price, oral interview by this writer, July, 1985. Harris, *Selling Hitler*, pp. 115-116, identified this source as that of Fritz Stiefel, who purchased a large number of forgeries from Konrad Kujau. Price did not identify the owners of the collections by name as many were afraid of public exposure of their interest in Hitler's paintings would subject them to attack both privately and publicly: Billy F. Price, oral interview by this writer, July, 1985. None of the D-1 items are used by this writer for this work.

[38]Price has gone to great expense and trouble to take legal depositions on video

tape by H. Hoffmann, Jr., Henrietta Hoffmann, August Priesack, and others. He graciously allowed this writer to view the tapes in his Houston office, July, 1985. Hoffman acted as Hitler's official art representative; Priesack was the NSDAP archivist for Hitler's works.

[39]Price, *The Unknown Artist*, nos. 3, 7, 9, 15, pp. 95-97. Price noted the drawing of Tilly has often been mistakenly identified as Wallenstein; for an example of such identification, see Toland, *Adolf Hitler*, p. 13, Toland declared it "indicates a budding talent as an artist."

[40]Price, *The Unknown Artist*, nos. 6, 10, 11, 14, pp. 95-96.

[41]Price, *The Unknown Artist,*, no. 8, p. 96, carried the note it was a "Theater Scene (?).''; Price, *The Unknown Artist*, no. 12, p. 97.

[42]Price, *The Unknown Artist* no. 13, p. 97; Waite, *The Psychopathic God*, p. 157.

[43]Price, *The Unknown Artist*, no. 17, and 17A, p. 98.

[44]Price, *The Unknown Artist*, no. 22, p. 99.

[45]Price, *The Unknown Artist*, nos. 18-20, p. 98.

[46]Fest, *Hitler*, pp. 18-19.

[47]Smith, *Adolf Hitler*, p. 9.

[48]Hitler, *Mein Kampf*, p. 18; Heiden, *Der Fuehrer*, pp. 50-51. Jetzinger, *Hitler's Youth*, pp. 89-90, as usual with him, discounted the story but was effectively refuted by Smith, *Adolf Hitler*, p. 97.

[49]Maser, *Adolf Hitler*, p. 72; Smith, *Adolf Hitler,*, p. 97.

[50]Smith, *Adolf Hitler*, p. 98; Smith, *Adolf Hitler*, p. 109; Jetzinger, *Hitler's Youth*, p. 89; Hitler, *Mein Kampf*, p. 20, stated he received no high school diploma.

[51]Hitler, *Secret Conversations*, p. 566.

[52]Jetzinger *Hitler's Youth*, p. 84; Payne, *The Life and Death*, p. 43.

[53]Kubizek, *The Young Hitler*, p. 8; Smith, *Adolf Hitler*, p. 101, stated Kubizek agreed to "play Sancho Panza for young Adolf."

[54]Payne, *The Life and Death*, p. 48; Jetzinger, *Hitler's Youth*, pp. 167-74; Smith, *Adolf Hitler*, p. 101, note 30.

[55]Smith, *Adolf Hitler*, pp. 101-19 passim; Jetzinger, *Hitler's Youth*, pp. 167-74. Most of Jetzinger's criticism concerned dates and places and not statements about music, art, and Hitler's personality.

[56]Toland, *Adolf Hitler*, p. 928.

[57]Payne, *The Life and Death*, p. 48; Jetzinger, *Hitler's Youth*, mentioned this material; for examples of such Kubizek material, see Price, *The Unknown Artist*, nos. 28 and 29, p. 100.

[58]Kubizek, *The Young Hitler*, p. 4; Kubizek intended to pursue a musical career and was a trained musician.

[59]Kubizek, *The Young Hitler*, p.14.

[60]Kubizek, *The Young Hitler*, p. 98; Rienzi is an opera in five acts by Richard Wagner with text by the composer from Bulwar Lytton's novel, *Rienzi*. It was first performed at the Hofoper in Dresden in 1842. Rienzi enjoys the support of the people in Rome until it is revealed he is allied with the German Emperor. This leads to his death at the hands of the Roman populace: *Kobbé's Complete Opera Book*, ed. and revised by the Earl of Harwood (London: Putnam, 1966), pp. 158-61.

[61]Kubizek, *The Young Hitler* p. 100; Kubizek called this incident "the most impressive hour I ever lived through with my friend."

[62]Waite, *The Psychopathic God*, p. 178; cf. musical introduction to the 1934 party film by Leni Riefenstahl, *Triumph of the Will* (Indianapolis: Kartes Video Communications, Inc., n.d.)

[63]Kubizek, *The Young Hitler*, pp. 62-66.

[64]Kubizek, *The Young Hitler*, p. 69.

[65]Jetzinger, *Hitler's Youth*, pp. 105-08; Smith, *Adolf Hitler*, p. 104.

[66]Maser, *Adolf Hitler*, p. 306; Waite, *The Psychopathic God*, p. 180, stated Hitler used Stephanie as a "defense against feeling sexual inadequacy." Maser, *Adolf Hitler*, p. 306, argued too much has been made of the "Stephanie Episode" as it was typical behavior for Austrian adolescents of the late nineteenth century.

[67]Hitler, *Mein Kampf*, p. 19; Kubizek, *The Young Hitler*, p. 105; Smith, *Adolf Hitler*, p. 104, was able to specifically confirm Kubizek by dating the trip to May 7-June 6, 1906.

[68]Kubizek, *The Young Hitler*, p. 111.

[69]Hitler, *Secret Conversations*, p. 261.

[70]Maser, *Adolf Hitler*, p. 73; Smith, *Adolf Hitler*, p. 105; in the 1930s Prevatsky-Wendt changed his name to simply Wendt.

[71]Jetzinger, *Hitler's Youth*,, p. 94; Maser, *Adolf Hitler*, p. 73; Smith, *Adolf Hitler*, p. 105.

[72]Jetzinger, *Hitler's Youth*, p. 94, oral interview with Kubizek; Smith, *Adolf Hitler*, p. 105, note 40, cited a statement by Wendt to this effect in the NSDAP archives.

[73]Payne, *The Life and Death*, p. 56; Kubizek, *The Young Hitler*, p. 119; Smith, *Adolf Hitler*, p. 105; Maser, *Adolf Hitler*, p. 74.

[74]Price, *The Unknown Artist* p. 7; Maser, *Adolf Hitler*, p. 76, provided the most comprehensive list of subjects.

[75]Walter C. Langer, *The Mind of Adolf Hitler* (New York: New American Library, 1972), p. 184; Price, *The Unknown Artist*, p. 7; Maser, *Adolf Hitler*, pp. 76-77.

[76]Price, *The Unknown Artist*, pp. 103-104, nos. 40-46 and p. 23.

[77]Price, *The Unknown Artist*, p.8., provided a facimile of the judges' verdict on Hitler's tests; Maser, *Adolf Hitler*, p. 40.

[78]Maser, *Adolf Hitler*, p. 40; Jetzinger, *Hitler's Youth*, p. 80.

[79]Charles de Jaeger, *The Linz File* (Exeter, England: Webb and Bower, 1981), p. 15: de Jaeger examined these watercolors which are owned by the Marquess of Bath and are stored at Longleat House in Wiltshire.

[80]de Jaeger, *The Linz File*, p. 15; Maser, *Adolf Hitler*, p. 77; Smith, *Adolf Hitler*, p. 204.

[81]Hitler, *Mein Kampf*, p. 20.

[82]Eduard Bloch, "My Patient Adolf Hitler," *Collier's*, 15 and 22 March 1941; cf. Payne, *The Life and Death*, p. 59.

[83]Rudolph Binion, *Hitler Among the Germans* (De Kalb, IL: Northern Illinois University Press Reprint, 1984), p. 18.

[84]Binion, *Hitler Among the Germans*, p. 18.

[85]Waite, *The Psychopathic God*, p. 189, note.

[86]Jetzinger, *Hitler's Youth*, p. 113.

[87]Langer, *Mind of Adolf Hitler*, p. 185.

[88]Jetzinger, *Hitler's Youth* p. 114, oral interview with Kubizek.

[89]Price, *The Unknown Artist*, p. 100, nos. 28 and 29; Kubizek, *The Young Hitler*,, p. 126 ff.

[90]Payne, *The Life and Death*, p. 66.

[91]Payne, *The Life and Death*, p. 66; Hoffman, *Hitler Was My Friend*, p. 190, asserted Hitler refused to listen to Tchaikowsky's music when Chancellor.

[92]Kubizek, *The Young Hitler*, pp. 191-92.

[93]Kubizek, *The Young Hitler*, pp. 154, 190-195.

[94]Payne, *The Life and Death*, p. 69.

[95]Kubizek, *The Young Hitler*, pp. 201, 213.

[96]Kubizek, *The Young Hitler*, p. 213.

[97]Kubizek, *The Young Hitler*, pp. 205, 213.

[98]Kubizek, *The Young Hitler*, p. 213.

[99]Kubizek, *The Young Hitler*, p. 87.

[100]Jetzinger, *Hitler's Youth*, p. 128

[101]Price, *The Unknown Artist*, p. 107, nos. 57 and 58. For an extended discussion of Hitler's architectural plans, see following chapter.

[102]Maser, *Adolf Hitler*, p. 85; Heiden, *Der Feuhrer*, p. 53, and Konrad Heiden, "Portrait of the Artist as a Young Man," *The Saturday Review of Literature*, 4 December 1943, pp. 6-9, mistakenly asserts Hitler was not admitted to even the first test.

[103]Maser, *Adolf Hitler*, pp. 85-86.

[104]Maser, *Adolf Hitler*, p. 86.

[105]Alan Bullock, *Hitler: A Study in Tyranny* (New York: Harper and Row, 1964), p. 7; William A. Jenks, *Vienna and the Young Hitler* (New York: Columbia University Press, 1960), p. 2; Jetzinger, *Hitler's Youth*, p. 109, called this period "the most important" of Hitler's youth.

[106]Hitler, *Mein Kampf*, p. 15

[107]Hitler, *Mein Kampf*, p. 10; Smith, *Adolf Hitler*, pp. 83-84; Jenks, *Vienna*, pp. 71 ff.

[108]Hitler, *Mein Kampf*, p. 52.

[109]Kubizek, *The Young Hitler*, p. 79.

[110]Hitler, *Mein Kampf*, p. 16; Hitler, *Secret Conversations*, pp. 191-92.

[111]Bruno Walter, *Gustav Mahler*, trans. James Galston (New York: Greystone Press, 1941), p. 197.

[112]Kubizek, *The Young Hitler*, p. 153.

[113]Kubizek, *The Young Hitler*, pp. 160 ff.

[114]Hitler, *Mein Kampf*, p. 55.

[115]Hitler, *Mein Kampf*, p. 57; Hitler, *Secret Conversations*, p. 120.

[116]Jetzinger, *Hitler's Youth*, p. 121, oral interview with Kubizek.

[117]Kubizek, *The Young Hitler*, p. 186; Hitler, *Mein Kampf*, p. 21.

[118]Jetzinger, *Hitler's Youth*, p. 131; Payne, *The Life and Death*, p. 78; Fest, *Hitler*, p. 45.

[119]Payne, *The Life and Death*, p. 80.

[120]Heiden, *Der Fuehrer*, p. 55.

[121]Jenks, *Vienna*, p. 31.

[122]Jenks, *Vienna*, p. 31.

[123]Hitler, *Mein Kampf*, p. 21.

[124]Payne, *The Life and Death*, p. 82. Cf. Reinhold Hanisch, "I was Hitler's Buddy," I, *The New Republic*, 5 April 1939, pp. 239-40.

[125]Payne, *The Life and Death*, p. 83.

[126]Hanisch, "I was Hitler's Buddy," I, p. 240.

[127]Smith, *Adolf Hitler*, p. 133; Payne, *The Life and Death*, p. 84.

[128]Price, *The Unknown Artist*, no. 325, p. 163.

[129]Payne, *The Life and Death*, p. 85.

[130]Maser, *Adolf Hitler*, p. 86; Price, *The Unknown Artist*, nos. 318-20, p. 161.

[131]Price, *The Unknown Artist*, p. 15.

132Hitler, *Secret Conversations*, p. 301.

133Price, *The Unknown Artist*, p. 8.

134Price, *The Unknown Artist*, p. 8.

135Hitler, *Mein Kampf*, pp. 34-35.

136Price, *The Unknown Artist*, p. 8

137Carl E. Schorske, *Fin-De-Siecle Vienna: Politics and Culture* (New York: Vintage Books, 1981), p. 24.

138Price, *The Unknown Artist*, p. 8.

139Price, *The Unknown Artist*, no. 272, p. 151; no. 252, p. 147; no. 245, p. 145; no. 193, p. 135.

140Price, *The Unknown Artist*, no. 96; p. 114; nos. 128-29, p. 120.

141Hanisch, "I was Hitler's Buddy," I, pp. 240-41.

142Norbert Bromberg and Vera Volz Small, *Hitler's Psychopathology* (New York: International Universities Press, Inc., 1983), pp. 63, 73; Hanisch took the name Fritz Walter.

143Smith, *Adolf Hitler*, p. 140.

144Reinhold, Hanisch, "I was Hitler's Buddy", I, pp. 239 ff.; "I Was Hitler's Buddy", II, *The New Republic*, 12 April 1939, pp. 270 ff.; "I Was Hitler's Buddy," III, *The New Republic*, 19 April 1939, pp. 297 ff.

145Smith, *Adolf Hitler*, p. 163.

146Maser, *Adolf Hitler*, p. 89; Smith, *Adolf Hitler*, p. 164; Fest, *Hitler*, p. 46.

147Hitler, *Mein Kampf*, p. 34.

148Smith, *Adolf Hitler*, p. 137; Fest, *Hitler*, p. 52.

149Smith, *Adolf Hitler*, p. 138; Fest, *Hitler*, p. 48.

150Smith, *Adolf Hitler*, p. 139.

151Hanisch, "I Was Hitler's Buddy," I, p. 241.

152Heiden claimed Neumann was also an old-clothes dealer and stated, "By a hair's-breadth history escaped the drama of Hitler making his entry into Germany by the side of a Hungarian-Jewish old-clothes dealer": Heiden, *Der Fuehrer*, p. 61.

153Maser, *Adolf Hitler*, pp. 88, 138.

154Price, *The Unknown Artist*, pp. 14-15; Payne, *The Life and Death*, p. 88.

155Price, *The Unknown Artist*, pp. 15, 153.

156Price, *The Unknown Artist*, nos. 98-110, pp. 155-17; nos. N98.1-N98.4, p. 252.

157Price, *The Unknown Artist*, p. 15; no. 167, p. 129; nos. 237-38, p. 144. See, for example, no. 167, p. 129, which is still in the original frame of the dealer Morgenstern.

158Price, *The Unknown Artist*, nos. 173, p. 130, with note "sold by the Viennese frame dealer Morgenstern"; no. 180, p. 131, framed by Morgenstern; no. 268, p. 150.

159Jetzinger, *Hitler's Youth*, p. 138.

160Smith, *Adolf Hitler*, p. 140, note 24: Smith derived this information and that which follows from the archives of the NSDAP.

161Smith, *Adolf Hitler*, p. 145, notes 35-36.

162Payne, *The Life and Death*, p. 91.

163Hitler, *Mein Kampf*, p. 163.

164Fest, *Hitler*, p. 58.

165Hitler, *Mein Kampf*, pp. 126-27.

166Maser, *Adolf Hitler*, pp. 120-23; this information Maser gathered from oral interviews made by the Popps to the NSDAP archivists.

167Payne, *The Life and Death*, p. 98.

168Maser, *Adolf Hitler*, p. 93; Price, *The Unknown Artist*, nos. 342-44, p. 166, see caption: until 1938, when the NSDAP began its research, these were the only three known Hitler oils—the NSDAP subsequently unearthed a number of others; Waite, *The Psychopathic God*, p. 199.

[169]Price, *The Unknown Artist*, p. 9 and no. 396, p. 180; this is the only work in Price's collection which is still owned by its original purchaser.

[170]Price, *The Unknown Artist*, p. 67 and no. 311, p. 159; it was commissioned by Dr. Ernst von Doebner, a Munich judge.

[171]Price, *The Unknown Artist*, p. 81 and no. 387, p. 178; no. 396, p. 180; p. 83 and nos. 384-86, p. 178; no. N386.1, p. 254; p. 80 and no. 380, p. 177.

[172]Maser, *Adolf Hitler*, pp. 122-23.

[173]Jetzinger, *Hitler's Youth*, p. 177.

[174]Hitler, *Mein Kampf*, p. 163.

[175]Hoffmann, *Hitler Was My Friend*, caption on upper photograph opposite p. 17. The photograph was made by Hoffmann; Maser, *Adolf Hitler*, p. 126.

[176]Hitler, *Mein Kampf*, p. 163; Maser, *Adolf Hitler*, p. 127.

[177]Payne, *The Life and Death*, p. 108.

[178]Price, *The Unknown Artist*, nos. 359-359A, p. 171; p. 80 and nos. 421-26, p. 187.

[179]Price, *The Unknown Artist*, p. 90 and no. 441, p. 191. The bike was Hitler's— he served as a messenger in the war: July, 1985, oral interview with Price, who was given the information by Priesack.

[180]Price, *The Unknown Artist*, p. 9; no. 411, p. 184.

[181]Cf. Price, *The Unknown Artist*, p. 24 and no. 83, p. 112.

[182]Payne, *The Life and Death*, p. 112; Toland, *Hitler*, p. 63; Fest, *Hitler*, p. 68.

[183]Maser, *Adolf Hitler*, pp. 134-36, for a detailed chronology of Hitler's military service.

[184]Binion, *Hitler Among the Germans*, pp. 5-11; no documents relating to the incident have been found.

[185]Binion, *Hitler Among the Germans*, p. 35.

[186]Maser, *Adolf Hitler*, p. 149; Payne, *The Life and Death*, p. 121.

[187]Hitler, *Mein Kampf*, pp. 203-04.

[188]Toland, *Hitler*, p. xix.

[189]Hitler, *Mein Kampf*, p. 206.

[190]Toland, *Hitler*, p. xx.

[191]Fest, *Hitler*, p. 78.

[192]Fest, *Hitler* p. 50.

[193]Hitler, *Mein Kampf*, p. 293.

Chapter 3

[1]Maser, *Adolf Hitler*, pp. 108-09.

[2]Price, *The Unknown Artist*, p. 189 and nos. 479 and 480; Maser, *Adolf Hitler*, p. 108.

[3]Ernst Duerlein, ed., *Der Austeig der NSDAP in Augenzeugenberichten* (Munich: Karl Rausch Verlag, 1968), p. 83.

[4]The lectures stressed German history since the Reformation, the political history of the war, Socialism in theory and practice, and the relation between domestic and diplomatic policies; Maser, *Adolf Hitler*, p. 161; Fest, *Hitler*, p. 113.

[5]Werner Maser, *Hitler's Mein Kampf* (Munich: Bechtle Verlag, 1966), p. 73; Maser alleged the concept of "Blood and Soil" provided for Hitler a complete legitimation

for both war and racial murder, p. 174.

[6]Barbara M. Lane and Leila J. Rupp, editors and translators, *Nazi Ideology Before 1933* (Austin, TX: University of Texas Press, 1978), pp. 27-30; Toland, *Adolf Hitler*, p. 83.

[7]Joachim C. Fest, *The Face of the Third Reich*, trans. Michael Bullock (New York: Pantheon Books, 1970), p. 16.

[8]Dietrich Orlow, *The History of the Nazi Party, 1919-1923* (Pittsburg: University of Pittsburg Press, 1969), pp. 11-13.

[9]Frederick L. Schuman, *The Nazi Dictatorship* (New York: Alfred A. Knopf, 1936), p. 19; cf. Hitler, *Mein Kampf*, p. 373.

[10]Hitler, *Mein Kampf*, p. 370.

[11]Land and Rupp, *Nazi Ideology Before 1933*, p.10.

[12]Hitler, *Mein Kampf*, p. 370.

[13]Hanfstaengl, *The Missing Years*, p. 47.

[14]Henry Grosshans, *Hitler and the Artists* (New York: Holmes and Meier, 1983), p. 56.

[15]Grosshans, *Hitler and the Artists*, p. 52.

[16]Toland, *Adolf Hitler*, p. 99.

[17]James and Suzanne Pool, *Who Financed Hitler* (New York: The Dial Press, 1978), p. 33; Hanfstaengl, *The Missing Years*, p. 53.

[18]Hoffman, *Hitler Was My Friend*, p. 63.

[19]Schuman, *The Nazi Dictatorship*, p. 83.

[20]A.B. Zeman, *Nazi Propaganda*, 2nd ed. (London: Oxford University Press, 1973), p. 83.

[21]George L. Mosse, *The Nationalization of the Masses* (New York: The New American Library, Inc., 1975), p. 296; Dietrich Eckart, *Der Bolshewismus von Moses bis Lenin: Zweigespräch zweischen Adolf Hitler und Mir* (Munich: F. Eber Hachf., 1924).

[22]Robert W. Gutman, *Richard Wagner* (New York: Harcourt Brace and World, Inc., 1968), p. 422.

[23]Fest, *Hitler*, p. 172.

[24]Robert Wistrich, *Who's Who in Nazi Germany* (New York: Macmillan Publishing Co., Inc., 1982), p. 25.

[25]Hermann Rauschning, *Men of Chaos* (New York: G.P. Putnam's Sons, 1942), p. 192; William D. Bayles, *Caesars in Goose Step* (New York: Harper and Brothers, 1940), p. 199, called Rosenberg "Hitler's Mystagogue"; G.M. Gilbert, *Nuremberg Diary* (New York: Farrar and Strauss, 1947), pp. 269-270. Rosenberg was sentenced to death at Nuremberg: Eugene Davidson, *The Trial of the Germans* (New York: The Macmillan Company, 1966), p. 143.

[26]Willi Frischauer, *The Rise and Fall of Herman Goering* (Boston: Houghton Mifflin Company, 1951), pp. 14 f.; Wistrich, *Who's Who in Nazi Germany*, p. 102; cf. Fest, *The Face of the Third Reich*, p. 72; R.J. Overy, *Goering, The 'Iron Man'* (London: Routhledge and Kegan Paul, 1984), p. 2, argued, to the contrary, Goering was a "completely committed Nazi and was no mere political opportunist."

[27]Davidson, *The Trial of the Germans*, p. 96; Albert Speer, *Spandau: The Secret Diaries*, trans. Richard and Clara Winston (New York: Macmillan Publishing Company, Inc., 1976), pp. 60-62.

[28]Hanfstaengl, *The Missing Years*, p. 28.

[29]Hanfstaengl, *The Missing Years*, p. 61; Martha Dodd, daughter of the American Ambassador in Berlin, William Dodd, wrote that Hanfstaengl played so vigorously

that the piano "was left crumpled and exhausted" and that "the rooms of the Embassy reverberated with sound for days" after he had played there: Martha Dodd, *Through Embassy Eyes* (New York: Garden City Publishing Company, 1939), p. 44. Fearing for his life, Hanfstaengl fled Germany in 1937: Hanfstaengl, *The Missing Years*, pp. 282-83.

[30]Hoffmann, *Hitler Was My Friend*, caption on photograph of Hitler following p. 71; For over 200 of Hoffmann's photographs of Hitler, including those most commonly utilized in works on Hitler, see: Hermann Goering et al., *Adolf Hitler*, English edition by Jonathan R. Manning (Phoenix: C.O.L. Publishing, Inc., 1973).

[31]Fest, *Hitler*, p. 135; cf. Hoffmann, *Hitler Was My Friend*, p. 50; Heiden, *Der Fuehrer*, p. 151.

[32]Robert E. Herzstein, *Adolf Hitler and the German Trauma, 1913-1945* (New York: G.P. Putnam's Sons, 1974), p. 39; Hanfstaengl, *The Missing Years*, p. 43.

[33]Stierlin, *Adolf Hitler*, p. 74.

[34]Payne, *The Life and Death*, p. 146.

[35]Strasser, *Hitler and I*, p. 19.

[36]Waite, *The Psychopathic God*, p. 122 note; Hitler, *Mein Kampf*, p. 42.

[37]Payne, *The Life and Death*, p. 512; Hanfstaengl, *The Missing Years*, p. 35, stated Hitler reminded him of a skilled violinist playing on a theme; Hoffmann, *Hitler Was My Friend*, photo note following p. 71, asserted Hitler had Hoffmann take photos of Hitler speaking so he could critique his gestures at leisure; Joseph Goebbels, "The Führer Hitler as an Orator," Goering et al., *Adolf Hitler*, p. 31, attributed Hitler's oratorical gifts to his ability to speak to the repressed desires of his audience.

[38]Maltitz, *The Evolution of Hitler's Germany*, p. 193; Dodd, *Through Embassy Eyes*, pp. 66-67, argued a German could be judged by his musical tastes; Hamiltion T. Burden, *The Nuremberg Party Rallies, 1923-1939* (London: Pall Mall Press, 1967), p. 19.

[39]Michael Meyer, "Assumptions and Implementation of Nazi Policy Toward Music," dissertation (Los Angeles: University of California, 1971), p. 163; Janet Flanner, *An American in Paris*, (New York: Simon and Schuster, 1940), pp. 414-415.

[40]Hanfstaengl, *The Missing Years*, pp. 87, 68; Speer, *Inside the Third Reich* p. 19, asserted Hitler's oratory "physically" bore the audience with him as he spoke with "hypnotic persuasiveness"; William L. Shirer, *The Nightmare Years, 1930-1940* (Boston: Little Brown and Company, 1984), p. 127 asserted it was "not so much what he said but how he said it" that moved his audiences.

[41]Fest, *Hitler*, p. 128; Payne, *The Life and Death*, p. 52.

[42]Robert Edwin Herzenstein and the Editors of Time-Life Books, *World War II: The Nazis* (Alexandria, VA: Time-Life Books, Inc., 1980), p. 28.

[43]Hitler, *Mein Kampf*, pp. 495-97.

[44]Hanfstaengl, *The Missing Years*, p. 145.

[45]Stephen D. Helmer, *Hitler's Berlin* (Ann Arbor: U.M.I. Research Press, 1985), p. 77; Stern, *Hitler*, pp. 35-36, takes this view but stresses Hitler gave them an emotive content not present in Fascism.

[46]Hoffmann, *Hitler Was My Friend*, p. 52. Each new standard was "consecrated" by touching it to the "Blood Flag" carried in the 1923 putsch: Herbert Walther, *Der Führer* (Secaucus, NJ: Chartwell Books, 1978), p. 40.

[47]Fest, *Hitler*, p. 107.

[48]Waite, *The Psychopathetic God*, p. 122; Höhne. *Order of the Death's Head*,

pp. 20-21; Price *The Unknown Artist* p. 201, no. 486; Hoffmann, *Hitler Was My Friend*, p. 53.

[49]Price, *The Unknown Artist*, pp. 201-205, nos. 488-95 and 497-506.

[50]William S. Allen, *The Nazi Seizure of Power: The Experience of a Single German Town, 1922-1945*, rev. ed. (New York: Franklin Watts, 1984), p. 37.

[51]Schuman, *The Nazi Dictatorship*, p. 32.

[52]Payne, *The Life and Death*, p. 169.

[53]Helmer, *Hitler's Berlin*, p. 77; Robert L. Koehl, *The Black Corps* (Madison: University of Wisconsin Press, 1983), pp. 9-12.

[54]Koehl, *The Black Corps*, p. 50; Price, *The Unknown Artist*, p. 225, nos. 602 and 602A.

[55]Waite, *The Psychopathetic God*, p. 123.

[56]Burden, *The Nuremberg Party Rallies*, p. 3.

[57]The best account of the putsch is: Harold J. Gordon, Jr., *History of the Beer-Hall Putsch* (Princeton: Princeton University Press, 1972).

[58]Hanfstaengl, *The Missing Years*, pp. 106-107.

[59]Hanfstaengl, *The Missing Years*, p. 108.

[60]Hanfstaengl, *The Missing Years*, p. 112.

[61]Payne, *The Life and Death*, p. 184.

[62]Hanfstaenl, *The Missing Years*, p. 148; Gordon, *Hitler and the Beer-Hall Putsch*, p. 465, noted that Hanfstaengl's sister, Erna, asserted Hitler was not depressed, but Gordon discounted her evidence.

[63]Toland, *Adolf Hitler*, p. 184.

[64]Hanfstaengl, *The Missing Years*, pp. 60, 65.

[65]Hanfstaengl, *The Missing Years*, p. 63.

[66]Payne, *The Life and Death*, p. 171.

[67]Grosshans, *Hitler and the Artists*, p. 20.

[68]No editor, *The Authentic Librettos of the Wagner Operas* (New York: Crown Publishers, 1938), p. 429 ff. for the complete libretto of *Parsifal* cf. Earl of Hartwood, *Koebbé's*, p. 290 ff. for discussion of *Parsifal*.

[69]Gutman, *Richard Wagner*, pp. 428-32.

[70]"Invisible Government in Germany, The American Monthly Review of Reviews", 19 July 1924, pp. 94-95.

[71]*The Hitler Trial Before the People's Court in Munich*, trans. H. Francis Frenien, Lucie Karcic and Philip Fandek (New York: Universal Publications of America, Inc., 1976), V. 1, p. 46 ff.

[72]Waite, *The Psychopathic God*, p. 72. For a history of the controversy over the abridged English translation of 1933 and the complete translation of 1939, see: James J. and Patricia P. Barnes, *Hitler's 'Mein Kampf' in Britain and America* (New York: Cambridge Press, 1980).

[73]Waite, *The Psychopathic God*, pp. 172-73.

[74]Maser, *Hitler's Mein Kampf*, pp. 50-51, for a discussion of Hitler's grammatical errors.

[75]Fest, *Face of the Third Reich*, p. 29; Maser, *Hitler's Mein Kampf*, p. 83, also cites Malthus, Mendel, Chamberlain and Haeckel as sources of Hitler's thought.

[76]Hitler, *Mein Kampf*, pp. 259-62.

[77]Hitler, *Mein Kampf*, pp. 258-59, 261.

[78]Price, *The Unknown Artist*, pp. 206-07, nos. 511-512, and p. 207, no. 516.

[79]Payne, *The Life and Death*, p. 205.

[80]Hanfstaengl, *The Missing Years*, p. 119.

[81]Toland, *Adolf Hitler*, p. 209.

[82]Speer, *Inside the Third Reich*, p. 95.

[83]Price, *The Unknown Artist*, pp. 208-11, nos. 521-34. The designs of the Arch of Triumph and the Great Hall are discussed below in the following chapter.

[84]Herzstein, *Adolf Hitler*, p. 62; Viktor Reimann, *Goebbels*, trans. Stephan Wendt (New York: Doubleday and Company, Inc., 1976), p. 37, denied Goebbels opposed Hitler and attributed the words to the Gauleiter of Hanover, Bernhard Rust; Helmut Heiber, *Goebbels*, trans. John K. Dickinson (New York: Hawthorn Books, 1972), p. 40, believed Goebbels did say "something along this line." The statement seemed to have originated in a dubious remark by Otto Strasser: Douglas Reed, *Nemesis* (Boston: Houghton Mifflin Company, 1940), p. 85.

[85]Wistrich, *Who's Who in Nazi Germany*, p. 96.

[86]Goebbels is generally regarded as the creator of the finished "Hitler Myth" in the Third Reich: Reimann, *Goebbels*, p. 1, argued Goebbels transformed Hitler "into a *Lohengrin* figure" Goebbels himself claimed the creation of this "Hitler Myth" was his greatest propaganda achievement: Ian Kershaw, "The Hitler Myth," *History Today* (November, 1985), p. 27.

[87]Barbara M. Lane, *Architecture and Politics in Germany, 1918-1945* (Cambridge: Harvard University Press, 1968), pp. 149-51; Grosshans, *Hitler and the Artists*, p. 9.

[88]Lane, *Architecture and Politics*, p. 151.

[89]Robert B. Nelson, "Hitler's Propaganda Machine," *Current History* (April-September, 1933), p. 289.

[90]Hinz, *Art in the Third Reich*, p. 25.

[91]Hinz, *Art in the Third Reich*, p. 25.

[92]Lane, *Architecture and Politics in Germany*, p. 158.

[93]Lane, *Architecture and Politics in Germany*, p. 161.

[94]Toland, *Adolf Hitler*, p. 238, makes a good case that Wessel was not a procurer and regards the charge as simple slander.

[95]Hanfstaengl, *The Missing Years*, p. 149.

[96]Riemann, *Goebbels*, p. 116.

[97]The *Horst Wessel Lied* was considered too sacred to be played at a dinner party given by Martha Dodd at the American Embassy: Dodd, *Through Embassy Eyes*, pp. 66-67; it was not even included in the song book for the Hitler Youth: Erwin Schwarz, editor, *Hitler Jugend Singt* (Mainz: B. Schott's Sons, 1933).

[98]Hanfstaengl, *The Missing Years*, pp. 180-81.

[99]Hoffmann, *Hitler Was My Friend*, p. 62.

[100]Speer, *Inside the Third Reich*, p. 50.

[101]Fest, *Hitler*, p. 265; Price, *The Unknown Artist*, p. 232, nos, 632-36.

[102]Binion, *Hitler Among the Germans*, p. 67.

[103]Price, *The Unknown Artist*, p. 221, no. 582.

[104]Hoffmann, *Hitler Was My Friend*, pp. 169-70; Price, *The Unknown Artist*, p. 9.

[105]Hoffman, *Hitler Was My Friend*, p. 150.

[106]Waite, *The Psychopathic God*, p. 226; cf. Hoffmann, *Hitler Was My Friend*, p. 149, Fest, *Hitler*, p. 322.

[107]Fest, *Hitler*, p. 322; Hanfstaengl, *The Missing Years*, p. 167, stated Hitler had made pornographic sketches of Geli, but the evidence is third-hand and extremely dubious; Price, *The Unknown Artist*, p. 222, nos. 588 and 589 are from the DI source and therefore suspect as forgeries.

[108]Hoffmann, *Hitler Was My Friend*, pp. 157-59.

[109]Fest, *Hitler*, p. 323.

[110]Waite, *The Psychopathic God*, p. 227.

[111]Fest, *Hitler*, p. 323.

[112]Waite, *The Psychopathic God*, p. 227.

[113]Hanfstaengl, *The Missing Years*, p. 168; Hanfstaengl's evidence is third-hand and, moreover, is colored by the fact that he regarded Geli, contrary to all other accounts, as "an empty-headed little slut": Hanfstaengl, *The Missing Years*, p. 162.

[114]Fest, *Hitler*, p. 323; cf. Payne, *The Life and Death*, p. 228.

[115]Waite, *The Psychopathic God*, p. 228.

[116]Payne, *The Life and Death*, p. 230.

[117]Mosse, *The Crisis*, p. 13.

[118]Gordon A. Craig, *Germany, 1866-1945* (New York: Oxford University Press, 1978), p. 214; Mosse, *The Crisis* p. 14.

[119]Mosse, *The Crisis*, p. 15.

[120]Mosse, *The Crisis*, p. 16; Maltitz, *The Evolution of Hitler's Germany*, pp. 182 ff., asserted there was a clear "Cult of the Germanic" for two generations before the Third Reich.

[121]Mosse, *The Crisis*, p. 22.

[122]Cf. Hitler's speech to the Rhineland Industrialists, January 27, 1932, in: *Hitler's Third Reich: A Documentary History* ed. Louis L. Snyder (Chicago Nelson-Hall, 1981), pp. 60-69.

[123]Mosse, *The Crisis*, p. 27.

[124]Mosse, *The Crisis*, p. 294.

[125]Hitler, *Mein Kampf*, p. 679.

[126]Mosse, *The Crisis*, p. 295.

[127]G.M. Gilbert, *The Psychology of Dictatorship*, (New York: n.p., 1950), p. 48, cited Hans Frank as noting these statements of Hitler.

[128]Waite, *The Psychopathic God*, p. 109.

[129]Fest, *Hitler*, p. 56.

[130]Ferdinand Tönnies, *Community and Society*, trans. and edited by Charles P. Loomis (New York: Harper and Row, 1957).

[131]Tönnies, *Community and Society*, pp. 62-63

[132]Tönnies, *Community and Society*, p. 92.

[133]Ferdinand Tönnies, *On Sociology: Pure, Applied, and Empirical*, ed. Werner J. Cahman and Rudolf Heberle (Chicago: The University of Chicago Press, 1971), pp. 64-65.

[134]Hitler, *Mein Kampf*, pp. 295-96.

[135]Hitler, *Mein Kampf*, p. 297.

[136]Hitler, *Mein Kampf*, p. 449.

[137]Schuman, *The Nazi Dictatorship*, pp. 514-516.

[138]Hitler, "Proclamation to the German People," February 1, 1933: Snyder, *Hitler's Third Reich*, p. 88.

[139] *Organizationsbuch der NSDAP*, ed. Der Reichsorganistionsleiter der NSDAP (Munich: n.p., 1936), pp. 465 f.

[140]Toland, *Adolf Hitler*, p. 290.

Chapter 4

[1]*The Speeches of Adolf Hitler, April 1922-August 1939*, ed. Norman H. Baynes (London: Oxford University Press, 1942),I, p. 568.

[2]Berthold Hinz, *Die Maleriei im Deutschen Faschismus: Kunst und*

Konterrevolution (Munich: Carl Hanser Verlag, 1974), pp. 25-26.

[3]Berthold Hinz, *Art in the Third Reich* trans. Robert and Beta Kimber. (New York: Pantheon Books, 1979), pp. 27-28.

[4]Snyder, *Hitler's Third Reich*, p. 121

[5]Snyder, *Hitler's Third Reich*, p. 129.

[6]Reimann, *Goebbels*, pp. 166-67, argued Goebbels was artistically "a liberal" who "was not particularly interested in art, with the exception of films." However, Hitler obliged Goebbels "to capitulate to his views." Goering was also a "liberal" who privately and without fanfare collected works not strictly acceptable to Hitler.

[7]Cesare Santoro, *Hitler's Germany as Seen by a Foreigner* (Berlin: Internationaler Verlag, 1939), p. 351.

[8]Santoro, *Hitler's Germany*, p. 351.

[9]*The Art Digest*, 1 August 1934, p. 9.

[10]"Jew Baiting in Art," *The Art Digest*, 1 October 1935, p. 3.

[11]Mosse, *Nazi Culture*, p. 137.

[12]Hitler, *Secret Conversations*, pp. 581-82.

[13]Ernst K. Bramsted, *Goebbels and National Socialist Propaganda, 1925-1945* (Yipsilanti: Michigan State University Press, 1965), p. 83.

[14]Lane, *Architecture and Politics*, p. 147.

[15]*The Speeches of Adolf Hitler*, pp. 572-73.

[16]For the impact on American architecture of those who emigrated to the United States, see: Christian F. Otto, "American Skyscrapers and Weimar Modern: Transactions between Face and Idea," *The Muses Flee Hitler*, pp. 151-63.

[17]Lane, *Architecture and Politics*, p. 180; Reimann, *Goebbels*, p. 168.

[18]Deuel, *People Under Hitler*, p. 130; Fest, *The Face of the Third Reich*, p. 167, notes Rosenberg's progressive loss of influence and so calls him "the Forgotten Disciple."

[19]Lane, *Architecture and Politics*, p. 183.

[20]Lane, *Architecture and Politics*, p. 184

[21]Anthony Heilbut, *Exiled in Paradise* (Boston: Beacon Press, 1983), p. 143.

[22]Robert R. Taylor, *The Word in Stone: The Role of Architecture in the National Socialist Ideology* (Berkeley: University of California Press, 1974), p. 12; *A Nation Builds: Contemporary German Architecture* (New York: German Library of Information, 1940), pp. 57, 104.

[23]Taylor, *The Word in Stone*, p. 121; Goebbels did not exercise any substantive influence on architecture according to Reimann—even in Berlin where he was Gauleiter; Reimann, *Goebbels*, p. 168.

[24]Speer, *Inside the Third Reich*, pp.50, 115.

[25]Hanfstaengl, *The Missing Years*,p.270.

[26]Price, *The Unknown Artist*, p. 245, no. 688; Speer, *Inside the Third Reich*, p. 49.

[27]Speer, *Spandau*, p. 112. Taylor argued the Prussian style was "primitive and manly," a "soldier style": Taylor, *The Word in Stone*, p. 37.

[28]Taylor, *The Word in Stone*, p. 39.

[29]Carr, *Hitler*, p. 138.

[30]Helmer, *Hitler's Berlin*, p. 5.

[31]Speer, *Spandau*, p. 127; Carr, *Hitler*, p.138, agreed there was an "element of political calculation" in this monumentality as Hitler wanted to restore "political self-respect" to the Germans, to consolidate the regime, and to express "national

values" to the future; Lane, *Architecture and Politics*, p. 187.

[32]Fest, *Hitler*, p. 526; Speer, *Inside the Third Reich*, p. 280, reported that this obsession was also demonstrated in Hitler's demand for super-heavy tanks that were failures on the battlefield due to their size.

[33]Taylor, *The Word in Stone*, p.92.

[34]Percy Ernst Schramm, *Hitler: the Man and the Military Leader*, trans. Donald S. Detwiter (Chicago: Quandrangle Books, 1971, p. 62).

[35]Speer, *Spandau*, p. 15; Speer, *Inside the Third Reich*, p. 49.

[36]Speer, *Spandau*,p. 92.

[37]Speer, *Inside the Third Reich*, p. 50.

[38]Lane, *Architecture and Politics*, p. 190. Speer, *Inside the Third Reich*, p. 51, argued there was no "Fuehrer Style" but only neo-classicism carried to the point of "ludicrousness." Anonymous, *A Nation Builds*, p. 14.

[39]Inga Karetnikova and Igor Golomstock, "The Encounter in Paris," *The National Review*, 9 May 1986, pp. 42-45.

[40]Hinz, *Art in the Third Reich*, pp.6-7.

[41]Hinz, *Art in the Third Reich*, p.7

[42]Speer, *Inside the Third Reich*, p.94.

[43]Speer, *Inside the Third Reich*,p.65.

[44]Speer, *Spandau*, p.141.

[45]Speer, *Inside the Third Reich*, p.66.

[46]Lane, *Architecture and Politics*, for example, omits any discussion of the Chancellary building in her discussion of Nazi architecture; cf. Werner Rittich, *New German Architecture* (Berlin: Terromare Office, 1940).

[47]Speer, *Inside the Third Reich*, photo after p. 167 and p. 69, called the result "the first luminescent architecture of this type" and his "most beautiful architectural concept"; Sir Neville Henderson, the British ambassador to Berlin, described the effect as "both solemn and beautiful," a "cathedral of ice": Sir Neville Henderson, *Failure of a Mission* (New York: G.P. Putnam's Sons, 1940), p. 72. John Elderfield, "Total and Totalitarian Art," *Studio International*, April 1970, p. 154, argued Speer actually derived the concept from earlier light festivals of Germans such as Naum Gabo.

[48]Speer, *Inside the Third Reich*, p. 79; see Helmer, *Berlin*, fig. 141, for a model of the Nuremberg Party Rally Grounds and Burden, *The Nuremberg Party Rallies*, p. 2, which provides the only available map this author was able to locate.

[49]The overall dimensions are given in detail by Burden, *The Nuremberg Party Rallies*, p. 60; Taylor, *The Word in Stone*, p. 169, note 52, expressed the size of the field in graphic terms by noting that in 1968 it contained "a parking lot, a cinder track, a baseball diamond, and a soccer field"; Trafalger Square is approximately 489 by 405 feet: K. Baedaker, *London and Environs* (Leipzig: Karl Baedaker Verlag, 1884), p. 147.

[50]Cited in Taylor, *The Word in Stone*, p. 170; for excellent photos of the field, see: Wolters, *Albert Speer*, pp. 18-26; *A Nation Builds*, pp. 62-63.

[51]Speer, *Inside the Third Reich*, pp. 79-80; the American Army used explosives to demolish these towers after the war: Taylor, *The Word in Stone*, p. 170, note 60; the size of the Place de la Concorde is given by Karl Baedaker, *Paris and Its Environs* (Leipzig: Karl Baedaker Verlag, 1884), p. 68.

[52]Speer, *Inside the Third Reich*, pp. 80-81.

[53]Rudolf Wolters, *Albert Speer* (Oldenburg: Gerhard Stalling Verlag, 1943), p. 32.

[54]The Mosaic Room was deliberately designed in a Roman fashion: Rudolf Wolters, "Werk und Schöpfer," Albert Speed, ed., *Die neue Reichskanzlei* (Berlin: n.p., n.d.), p. 52. Its mosaics were executed by Hermann Kaspar of the Munich Art Academy: Taylor, *The Word in Stone*, p. 135; The Round Hall was 14.25 meters in diameter: Albert Speer, *Die neue Reichskanzlei*, pp. 55ff.

[55]Hitler, *Secret Conversations*, p. 575.

[56]Wilhelm Lotz, "Die Innenräume der neuen Reichskanzlei," Speer *Die neue Reichskanzlei*, p. 90.

[57]Paul Geissler, "Symbol des grossdeutschen Reiches," Speer, *Die neue Reichskanzlei*, p. 10; Wolters, *Albert Speer*, p. 33.

[58]Hitler, *Secret Conversations*, p. 543.

[59]Speer, *Inside the Third Reich*, p. 87, noted that Lippert's attitude led Hitler to call the old party member "an incompetent, an idiot, a failure, a zero"; Helmer, *Berlin*, pp. 14, 17 and 105.

[60]Price, *The Unknown Artist*, p. 209, nos. 523, 525, with note they were given to Speer by Hitler; Price, *The Unknown Artist*, p. 237, nos. 656-59.

[61]Speer, *Inside the Third Reich*, p. 88.

[62]Speer, *Inside the Third Reich*, p.182-86.

[63]Speer, *Inside the Third Reich*, p. 182-83; Price, *The Unknown Artist*, p. 210, nos. 533, 534; Speer, *Inside the Third Reich*, pp. 161 and 626, proudly noted the Arc de Triomphe was only 160 feet high by contrast.

[64]Price, *The Unknown Artist*, p. 236, nos. 653, 654.

[65]Speer, *Inside the Third Reich*, p. 161, noted Hitler intended visitors to be "overwhelmed, or rather stunned," by the vista they saw on coming out of the southern railway station; *Die Kunst im Dritten Reich*, July 1939, pp. 217 and 327, provide the size of the boulevard; the Champs Elysèes is approximately two miles long: Baedaker, *Paris and Its Environs*, map R scale.

[66]Price, *The Unknown Artist*, p. 239, no. 667, p. 244, no. 685, p. 240, no. 670, from the Speer Collection.

[67]Speer, *Inside the Third Reich*, pp. 207, 213, 217.

[68]Speer, *Inside the Third Reich*, p. 185; Helmer, *Berlin*, p. 63.

[69]Speer, *Spandau*, photo opposite, p. 197.

[70]David Roxan and Ken Wanstall, *The Rape of Art* (New York: Coward-McCann, Inc., 1965), photo following, p. 52.

[71]Price, *The Unknown Artist*, p. 241, nos. 674, 675; and p. 242, nos. 679-81.

[72]Speer, *Inside the Third Reich*, p. 117.

[73]Speer, *Inside the Third Reich*, p. 171.

[74]Price, *The Unknown Artist*, p. 211, no. 537; p. 245, no. 689, p. 102, nos. 690-92.

[75]Hitler, *Secret Conversations*, p. 262.

[76]Speer, *Inside the Third Reich*, p. 355.

[77]de Jaeger, *The Linz File*, p. 168; Speer, *Spandau*, pp. 170-71.

[78]Speer, *Spandau*, p. 97.

[79]Speer, *Spandau*, p. 94; Price, *The Unknown Artist*, p. 235, nos. 648-649.

[80]Speer, *Spandau*,, pp. 15-16.

[81]Speer, *Spandau*, p. 16.

[82]Speer, *Spandau*, p. 93

[83]Speer, *Spandau*, p. 80.

[84]Speer, *Spandau*, p. 95.

[85]Hitler, *Secret Conversations*, p. 572.

[86]Hellmut Lehmann-Haupt, *Art Under a Dictatorship* (New York: Oxford University Press, 1954), p. 96.

[87]Baynes, *The Speeches of Adolf Hitler*, p. 598; Speech of 6 September 1937.

[88]Speer, *Spandau*, p. 97; de Jaeger, *The Linz File*, p. 113, for a photo of a plaster model of this statue.

[89]Grosshans, *Hitler and the Artists*, p. 90. For a contemporary biographical sketch of Breker, see: Joseph Wulf, ed., *Die Bildenden Künste im Dritten Reich: Eine Dokumentation* (Gütersloh: Sigberg Mohn Verlag, 1963), pp. 252-53; for a more recent biographical sketch, see: Wistrich, *Who's Who in Nazi Germany*, p. 31. There exists no recent, competent study of Nazi sculpture similar to Hinz's *Art in the Third Reich*.

[90]Speer, *Spandau*, p. 261.

[91]"The Arts Under Hitlerism," *The New Republic*, 7 April 1933, p. 268.

[92]Baynes, *The Speeches of Adolf Hitler*, p. 578; Speech of 11 September 1935.

[93]Harold Kurtz, *The Second Reich: Kaiser Wilhelm II and His Germany* (New York: American Heritage Press, 1970), p. 74.

[94]Richard Grunberger, *The 12-Year Reich* (New York: Holt, Rinehart and Winston, 1971), p. 421.

[95]Grunberger, *The 12-Year Reich*, p. 421.

[96]Hinz, *Art in the Third Reich*, p. 28.

[97]Price, *The Unknown Artist*, p. 10, noted Hitler set aside an entire room for the exhibition of Marées' work in his projected museum for Linz.

[98]Hinz, *Art in the Third Reich*, p. 29.

[99]Lehmann-Haupt, *Art Under a Dictatorship*, pp. 74-75.

[100]Hinz, *Art in the Third Reich*, p. 25.

[101]Reimann, *Goebbels*, p. 169.

[102]Phillipa Gerry, "German Painting," *American Magazine of Modern Art*, December 1937, pp. 802-05.

[103]Reimann, *Goebbels*, p. 169.

[104]Lehmann-Haupt, *Art Under a Dictatorship*, p. 72.

[105]Lehmann-Haupt, *Art Under a Dictatorship*, p. 72-73; Wistrich, *Who's Who in Nazi Germany*, pp. 221-22, noted he joined the Nazi party in 1922 and was highly anti-Semitic in his writings.

[106]*Die Kunst im Dritten Reich*, after 1940 *Die Kunst im Deutschen Reich* (Munich: Zentralverlag Franz Eher). The Art Library of the University of Louisville, Kentucky, has an extensive but incomplete set of the journal. The Library of Congress has a complete set.

[107]Hinz, *Art in the Third Reich*, p. 38.

[108]Wistrich, *Who's Who in Nazi Germany*, p. 347.

[110]Cited by Hinz, *Art in the Third Reich*, p. 40.

[111]*Entartete Kunst: Ausstellungsführer*; no authorship or place of publication is provided by the catalogue; an original of the guide is in the Art Library, University of Louisville, Kentucky.

[112]Hinz, *Art in the Third Reich*, p. 31.

[113]Hoffmann, *Hitler Was My Friend*, p. 174.

[114]Hinz, *Art in the Third Reich*, p. 43.

[115]"Purged Art for N.Y.U.," *The Art Digest*, 1 December 1936, p. 6.

[116]Hinz, *Art in the Third Reich*, pp. 1-2.

[117]*Die Kunst im Dritten Reich*, pp. 243-48.

[118]Hinz, *Art in the Third Reich*, p. 9; however, Hoffmann, *Hitler Was My Friend*, p. 171, asserted 8,000 were submitted and 1,700 were chosen for this first exhibition.

[119]Baynes, *The Speeches of Adolf Hitler*, pp. 585-91; Hoffmann, *Hitler Was My Friend*, p. 171, asserted Hitler had the final word on the works exhibited.

[120]Bardi, *The Water Colors of Hitler*, p. 5.

[121]Heinrich Hoffmann, *Sieben Aquarelle* (Munich: Franz Eher, 1938). Lehmann-Haupt, *Art Under a Dictatorship*, p. 253, noted Hitler instructed Goebbels to prohibit exhibitions of his work; cf. de Jaeger, *The Linz File*, p. 41.

[122]Hinz, *Art in the Third Reich*, pp. 20-21.

[123]Price, *The Unknown Artist*, pp. 10-11; Hoffmann, *Hitler Was My Friend*, p. 183, noted Hitler intended to provide the museum with "some ten thousand pictures."

[124]Hitler, *Secret Conversations*, p. 241.

[125]Hoffmann, *Hitler Was My Friend*, p. 168.

[126]Hinz, *Art in the Third Reich*, p. 20.

[127]de Jaeger, *The Linz File*, pp. 96-97.

[128]Waite, *The Psychopathic God*, p. 68 and photo after p. 68.

[129]Emil Lengyel, "German Culture in Exhile, *The Nation*, 31 May 1933, p. 607.

[130]Hinz, *Art in the Third Reich*, pp. 17-18.

[131]Hinz, *Art in the Third Reich*, p. 45.

[132]Fest, *The Face of the Third Reich*, p. 45.

[133]Waite, *The Psychopathic God*, pp. 64 and 443, note 21.

[134]Hitler, *Mein Kampf*, p. 34.

[135]Baynes, *The Speeches of Adolf Hitler*, pp. 572-73; Speech of 11 September 1935.

[136]Baynes, *The Speeches of Adolf Hitler*, pp. 609-10; Speech of 1 August 1937.

[137]Bramsted, *Goebbels and National Socialist Propaganda*, pp. 310-11.

[138]Santoro, *Hitler Germany*, p. 363.

[139]X.T., "Kultur-Terror," *Modern Music*, May-June, 1933, p. 210.

[140]I.A. Hirschmann, "The Degradation of Culture," eds. Pierre van Paasen and James Waterman Wise, *Nazism: An Assault on Civilization* (New York: Harrison Smith and Robert Haas, 1934, pp. 97-102.

[141]Hirschmann, "The Degradation of Culture," p. 99.

[142]"Nazi System," *Time*, 30 May 1938, p. 24.

[143]Slonimsky, *Music Since 1900* (New York: Scribners Sons, 1971), pp. 359-60.

[144]Slonimsky, *Music Since 1900*, p. 364.

[145]Grunberger, *The 12-Year Reich*, p. 412.

[146]Hirschmann, "The Degradation of Culture,", p. 100.

[147]"Nazi System," *Time*, 30 May 1938, p. 24.

[148]Grunberger, *The 12-Year Reich*, p. 408.

[149]Deuel, *People Under Hitler*, p. 280.

[150]John Rockwell, "Music Under Hitler," *Opera News*, 15 January 1972, p. 8.

[151]"Nazi System," *Time*, 30 May 1938, p. 24.

[152]Grunberger, *The 12-Year Reich*, p. 408.

[153]Deuel, *People Under Hitler*, pp. 278-80; Grunberger, *The 12-Year Reich*, p. 409, calls it Wilhelm von Nassau.

[154]Joel Sachs, "Some Aspects of Musical Politics in Pre-Nazi Germany," *Perspectives on New Music*, Fall, 1970, pp. 90-91.

[155]Nazi System," *Time*, 30 May 1938, p. 24.

[156]Rockwell, "Music Under Hitler," p. 8.

[157]Dodd, *Through Embassy Eyes*, p. 291.

[158]Grunberger, *The 12-Year Reich*, pp. 418-419.

[159]Rockwell, "Music Under Hitler," p. 10; Robert Eban Sackett, *Popular Entertainment, Class, and Politics in Munich, 1900-1923* (Cambridge: Harvard University Press, 1982), p. 153.

[160]Grunberger, *The 12-Year Reich*, p. 410.

[161]Grunberger, *The 12-Year Reich*, p. 307.

[162]Craig, *Germany*, p. 651.

[163]Schwarz, "The Music World in Migration" pp. 140-41; Schoenberg, who earlier had converted to Christianity, resumed his Jewish faith in 1933.

[164]Grunberger, *The 12-Year Reich*, p. 410.

[165]Craig, *Germany*, p. 651; Wulf, *Musik im Dritten Reich*, pp. 414-415.

[166]Vincent Sheean, "Good-bye Vienns", *The New Republic*, 3 August 1938, p. 98.

[167]Riemann, *Goebbels*, p. 170, argued Goebbels wanted to be tolerant in the area of music but had to protect his position with Hitler; Heiber, *Goebbels*, p. 169, argued Goebbels had "a minimum of prejudice" musically.

[168]Reimann, *Goebbels*, pp. 171-74; Joseph Wulf, ed., *Musik im Dritten Reich: Eine Dokumentation* (Gueterslok: Sigbert Mohn Verlag, 1963), pp. 337-41.

[169]Wistrich, *Who's Who in the Third Reich*, p. 305.

[170]Wulf, *Musik im Dritten Reich*, pp. 180-184; Reimann, *Goebbels*, pp. 177-79.

[171]Wulf, *Musik im Dritten Reich*, pp. 308-10; Wistrich, *Who's Who in the Third Reich*, 233-34.

[172]Grunberger, *The 12-Year Reich*, p. 410; Joseph Machlis, *Introduction to Contemporary Music* (New York: W.W.Norton and Company, Inc., 1961), pp. 321-22.

[173]Heiber, *Goebbels*, p. 170; Grunberger, *The 12-Year Reich*, pp. 412-13; Wulf, *Musik im Dritten Reich*, pp. 216-17.

[174]Grunberger, *The 12-Year Reich*, p. 414.

[175]Santoro, *Hitler Germany*, p. 364.

[176]Santoro, *Hitler Germany*, p. 364.

[177]Hans Heinsheimer, "German Music on the Bread Line," *Modern Music*, September 1932, pp. 115 f.

[178]Joel Sachs, "Some Aspects of Musical Politics in Pre-Nazi Germany," *Perspectives of New Music*, Fall 1970, p. 94.

[180]Santoro, *Hitler Germany*, pp. 357-58.

[181]Grunberger, *The 12-Year Reich*, p. 401.

[182]Herzstein, *The War That Hitler Won*, p. 21.

[183]Herzstein, *The War That Hitler Won*, p. 180.

[184]Speer, *Inside the Third Reich*, p. 216; Herzstein, *The War That Hitler Won*, p. 179.

[185]Grunberger, *The 12-Year Reich*, p. 416.

[186]*Hitler's Inferno*, vols. I and II (New York: Audio Fidelity, 1961).

[187]Hans Heinrich Eggebrecht, *Meyers Taschen-Lexikon Musik* (Mannheim: Meyers Lexikonverlag, 1984), p. 79; this author was unable to locate a recording or a score for this work.

[188]*H.J. Singt*, ed. Edwin Schwarz (Mainz: B. Schott's Sons, 1933), p. 6.

[189]Schwarz, *H.J. Singt*, passim.

[190]Hans J. Moser, *Musik Lexicon* (Hamburg: Musikverlag Hans Sikorski, 1951), p. 727, on Alfred Morgenroth; p. 122, on Hans Otto Borgmann; p. 113, on George Blumenstaat; p. 134, on Karl Weigl: Weigl moved to the Eastman School of Music

in Rochester in 1946.

[191]Herzstein, *The War That Hitler Won*, pp. 254-55.

[192]Grunberger, *The 12-Year Reich*, pp. 402-03.

[193]Santoro, *Hitler Germany*, p. 23; Speer, *Spandau*, p. 106, noted Hitler saw Lehár as one of the greatest composers in history and felt *The Merry Widow* was the equal of the finest operas; Speer, *Inside the Third Reich*, p. 156, noted Hitler never missed a new production of *The Merry Widow*.

[194]Herzstein, *The War That Hitler Won*, p. 181; Grunberger, *The 12-Year Reich*, p. 415.

[195]Grunberger,*The 12-Year Reich*, pp. 408-09.

[196]Grunberger, *The 12-Year Reich*, p. 409.

[197]Grunberger, *The 12-Year Reich*, p. 409.

[198]Fest, *Hitler*, p. 499.

[199]Grunberger, *The 12-Year Reich*, p. 412.

[200]Fest, *Hitler*, p. 499.

[201]Fest, *Hitler*, p. 520.

[202]Speer, *Spandau*, pp. 102-03.

[203]H.H. Stuckenschmitt, "Under the Swastika," *Modern Music*, November-December 1933, p. 52; Speer, *Spandau*, p. 103.

[204]Speer, *Spandau*, pp. 102-03.

[205]Schaum, *The Nazi Dictatorship*, p. 22; Snyder, *Hitler's Third Reich*, p. 51.

[206]"A Million 'Heils' ", *Time*, 20 September 1937, p. 18.

[207]Speer, *Spandau*, p. 104.

[208]Speer, *Inside the Third Reich*, p. 109.

[209]Speer, *Inside the Third Reich*, pp. 71-72; Grunberger,*The 12-Year Reich*, p. 412.

[210]Speer, *Spandau*, p. 105.

[211]Hanfstaengl, *The Missing Years*, p. 50; Grosshans, *Hitler and the Artists*, pp. 21-22; de Jaeger, *The Linz File*, p. 16.

[212]Speer, *Inside the Third Reich*, p. 156.

[213]Speer, *Inside the Third Reich*, p. 118.

[214]Grunberger, *The 12-Year Reich*, p. 406.

[215]Speer, *Inside the Third Reich*, p. 156; Santoro, *Hitler Germany*, p. 358, noted that in the 1935-1936 season, 124 different operettas were sponsored in state theaters, twenty-five of them for the first time.

[216]Speer, *Spandau*, p. 59.

[217]Speer, *Spandau*, p. 106.

[218]Schramm, Percy E., *Hitler: The Man and the Military Leader*, trans. Donald S. Detweiter, (Chicago: Quadrangle Books, 1971), p. 69.

[219]Speer, *Spandau*, p. 106; Speer, *Inside the Third Reich*, p. 156.

[220]Hanfstaengl, *The Missing Years*, p. 129.

[221]Hitler, *Secret Conversations*, p. 559.

[222]Grunberger, *The 12-Year Reich*, p. 409.

[223]Hanfstaengl, *The Missing Years*, p. 65.

[224]Carr, *Hitler*, p. 165.

Chapter 5

[1]"Is Hitler Crazy,?" *The New Republic*, 9 November 1938, pp. 2-3; "A Psychiatrist Looks at Hitler," *The New Republic*, 26 April 1939, pp. 326-27.

[2]Langer, *The Mind of Adolf Hitler*, pp. 162, 219; Henry A. Murray, *Analysis*

of the Personality of Adolf Hitler, unpublished manuscript, F.D. Roosevelt Library, quoted by Maltitz, *Evolution of Hitler's Germany,* p. 325; Erikson, *Childhood and Society,* pp. 329-330; Waite, *The Psychopathic God,* p. 357.

[3]Langer, *The Mind of Adolf Hitler,* pp. 162-63; Maltitz, *The Evolution of Hitler's Germany,* p. 329.

[4]E. Bloch, "My Patient Hitler," *Colliers,* 15 March 1941, p. 39.

[5]Erich Fromm, *The Anatomy of Human Destructiveness* (New York: n.p., 1973), p. 126, consistently used the Freudian definition of narcissism.

[6]Stierlin, *Adolf Hitler,* pp. 99-100.

[7]Binion, *Hitler,* pp. 57-58.

[8]Erikson, *Childhood and Society,* p. 340.

[9]Bromberg and Small, *Hitler's Psychopathology,* pp. 208-09, 223.

[10]Waite, *The Psychopathic God,* p. 357.

[11]Langer, *The Mind of Adolf Hitler,* p. 192; Brombert and Small, *Hitler's Psychopathology,* p. 246; Waite, *The Psychopathic God,* pp. 237-39, argued the evidence was insufficient and unconvincing.

[12]Alfred Adler, *Superiority and Social Interest: A Collection of Later Writings,* eds. H.L. and R.R. Ansbacher (Evanston, IL: Northwestern University Press, 1964), p. 24.

[13]Alfred Adler, *The Individual Psychology of Alfred Adler,* eds. H.L. and R.R. Ansbacher (New York: Basic Books, Inc., 1956), p. 10.

[14]Alfred Adler, *Understanding Human Nature,* trans. Walter B. Wolfe (London: George Allen and Unwin, Ltd., 1968), p. 70.

[15]Alfred Adler, *Social Interest: A Challenge to Mankind,* trans. John Linton and Richard Vaughan (London: Faber and Faber, Ltd., 1938), p. 220.

[16]Alfred Adler, *The Practice and Theory of Individual Psychology,* trans. P. Radin (New York: Harcourt, Brace and Company, 1932), p. 166.

[17]Adler, *The Science of Living,* ed. H.L. Ansbacher (New York: Doubleday and Company, Inc., 1969), p. 2.

[18]Adler, *Individual Psychology,* p. 180; Alfred Adler, *What Life Should Mean To You,* ed. Alan Porter (New York: Perigee Books, 1980), pp. 57-59.

[19]Alfred Adler, *The Neurotic Constitution,* trans. H. Ansbacher (New York: Dodd and Company, 1930), p. 18.

[20]Adler, *Social Interest,* p. 39.

[21]Adler, *Science of Living,* p. 8.

[22]Adler, *Individual Psychology,* p. 372.

[23]Adler, *Individual Psychology,* p. 374.

[24]Adler, *Superiority and Social Interest,* p. 54.

[25]Adler, *Individual Psychology,* p. 131.

[26]Adler, *Superiority and Social Interest,* pp. 66-67.

[27]Adler, *Superiority and Social Interest,* p. 72.

[28]Adler, *Individual Psychology,* p. 258; the individual is aware of his inferiority, if aware of it at all, in an effective, not cognitive manner.

[29]Adler, *Individual Psychology,* p. 259.

[30]Adler, *Individual Psychology,* p. 260.

[31]Adler, *Social Interest,* p. 226.

[32]Adler, *Individual Psychology,* p. 373.

[33]Adler, *Social Interest,* p. 29.

[34]Adler, *Social Interest,* p. 224.

[35]Adler, *Individual Psychology*, p. 373-74.

[36]Adler, *Social Interest*, p. 30.

[37]Adler, *Individual Psychology*, p. 378.

[38]Adler, *Superiority and Social Interest*, pp. 76-77.

[39]Adler, *Science of Living*, p. 10.

[40]Adler, *Individual Psychology*, p. 118.

[41]Adler, *Individual Psychology*, p. 59.

[42]Lev Bezymenski, *The Death of Adolf Hitler* (New York: Harcourt Brace Jovanovich, Inc., 1968), p. 67.

[43]Adler, *What Life Should Mean*, p. 245.

[44]Hitler, *Mein Kampf*, p. 6.

[45]Adler, *Science of Living*, pp. 24-25.

[46]Adler, *Understanding Human Nature*, p. 92.

[47] Adler, *Superiority and Social Interest*, p. 78.

[48]Adler, *Individual Psychology*, p. 153.

[49]Adler, *Individual Psychology*, p. 212.

[50]Hitler, *Mein Kampf*, p. 13.

[51]Adler, *Social Interest*, p. 105.

[52]Adler, *Superiority and Social Interest*, p. 65.

[53]Adler, *Individual Psychology*, p. 243.

[54]Adler, *Individual Psychology*, pp. 277-78.

[55]Adler, *Superiority and Social Interest*, p. 75.

[56]Adler, *Individual Psychology*, pp.455-56.

[57]Adler, *Individual Psychology*, p. 456.

[58]Adler, *Individual Psychology*, p. 456.

[59]Adler, *Individual Psychology*, p. 458.

[60]Adler, *Individual Psychology*, p. 459.

[61]Adler, *Superiority and Social Interest*, pp. 74-75.

[62]Adler, *Superiority and Social Interest*, p. 77; Cyclothymia is a depressive state or condition.

[63]Adler, *Superiority and Social Interest*, p. 350.

[64]Adler, *Superiority and Social Interest*, p. 251.

[65]Adler, *Superiority and Social Interest*, p. 252.

Index